May

Dirt Farmer's Son

A True Story: 1942–2020

Terry A. Maurer

Terry A. Maurer

Dirt Farmer's Son

Fulton Books, Inc.
Meadville, PA

Published by Fulton Books 2020

ISBN 978-1-64654-190-4 (paperback)
ISBN 978-1-64654-907-8 (digital)

Printed in the United States of America

Repeating the Dedication from a 1985 fair program
for the Crawford County Fair in Grayling, Michigan,
I dedicate *Dirt Farmer's Son* to my dad,
Bernard Leo Maurer.

Bernard Maurer and his grandmother Lennon, in 1937
on the farm in Crawford County, Michigan.

Terry A. Maurer's New Book "Dirt Farmer's Son" Shares A Beautiful Account Of A Life Across Adversities And Seemingly Insurmountable Challenges.

Terry A. Maurer, a brilliant writer, has completed "Dirt Farmer's Son": a gripping and potent true story about living on the farm during the 40s and 50s and pursuing education, business, and family life whilst battling health complications.

Terry writes, "It's a story of life: covering seventy-eight years (1942–2020). Dirt Farmer's Son is written for a broad audience who have witnessed these times and for those who want to know what happened.

It shares stories of farm life during the '40s and '50s, Catholic military boarding-school, seminary, his wife's two kidney transplants, and the adoption of a Korean child. It also includes chapters on his chemical career and his bottled-water business.

Each chapter can stand alone, but the story flows along easily.

Be sure to see The Secrets of Achievers by Howard Westphal in the front of this book, as well as The Ten Secrets to Success by Investors Business Daily in the back of the book.

Napa Valley and CAMi Wines are in chapter XIV.

This book is available on Amazon."

Published by Fulton Books, Terry A. Maurer's book is a moving journal that chronicles a life journey throughout the years 1942 to 2020 where readers will find an inspiring trek of a life well lived despite the endless adversities and challenges that storm over.

Readers who wish to experience this wonderful work can purchase "Dirt Farmer's Son" at bookstores everywhere, or online at the Apple iTunes store, Amazon, Google Play or Barnes and Noble.

Please direct all media inquiries to Gregory Reeves via email at gregory@fultonbooks.com or via telephone at 877-210-0816.

OnLine review with Dirt Farmer's Son 11 Nov 2020

Official Review: Dirt Farmer's Son by Terry A. Maurer
11 Nov 2020, 06:20
[Following is an official OnlineBookClub.org review
of 'Dirt Farmer's Son' by Terry A. Maurer]

Dirt Farmer's Son is Terry A. Maurer's life story, covering everything from his childhood to his retirement at age 70. Divided according to each American president's term from Maurer's birth to 2020, the book follows Maurer from his time in a military academy to his career in chemicals and bottled water.

One of the things I really liked about this was that Maurer included both personal communications with his friends and articles that he found interesting and relevant. In doing so, he gave the book more of a feeling of a life lived, something that I deeply appreciated. It felt like I was inside of his head, with a clearer picture of where he was mentally during each period he covered.

The pictures were pretty helpful too. They gave a sense of who each person was, illustrating the relationships Maurer talked about in the book. They also provided a sense of the passage of time, as you could see his family growing older visually. This added to the feeling of being with Maurer during the book, making it seem more personal.

I didn't really expect the book to end the way it did. The author made note of how unfulfilled he seemed to feel without work and how much Avita Water meant to him, so I thought he would take it to the very end. That he sold it was surprising, though I don't think it should have been, given that he had always been busier with the chemical side of his business ventures. However, it made sense that he'd always be surrounded by friends and family, given that they figure prominently throughout the book.

Dedication from the 1985 Fair Program

The Crawford County Fair Association
dedicate this premium Fair Program
to Bernard L. Maurer, who passed away April 24, 1985,
at the age of seventy.

We knew him as a judge of livestock at our first fair in 1983.
We knew him as a resident of Crawford County since 1935.

We knew him as a farmer who had interest in agriculture,
horticulture, and animal husbandry.

We knew him as a member of Mercy
Hospital's maintenance staff.

We knew him as a county commissioner for six years.
We knew him as a member of St. Mary's Catholic Church.

We knew him as an outspoken man who lived
and promoted the family, the work ethic, and
the proper role of government as well as other
so-called old-fashioned ideas.

We knew him best as a friend with a sense
of humor and a knowing twinkle in his eye.

These following fourteen attitude patterns were given to me by my father's example. I list them here in order to pass them on to all my grandchildren and their children.

The Secret of Achievers

Why is it that some people perform consistently well while others of equal talent and dedication never realize their full potential? The difference, declares Howard A. Westphall (*Industry Week*, January 1974), is attitude and how you feel about yourself and your environment. Attitude, Mr. Westphall points out, is the key to the full release of human potential, and he identifies fourteen attitude patterns which are exhibited by the high performers:

Self-Esteem

This is the foundation. You review yourself and your abilities in a positive way. You are an important, capable person who can accomplish what you set out to do. You deserve success and are not afraid to confront new situations, feeling that you control your own destiny.

Responsibility

You are accountable for your own actions. As a self-made person, you acknowledge your mistakes and take credit for your successes.

Optimism

You look forward to the next day and confident in your ability and judgment, feel that your efforts will be rewarded and that the future is promising.

Goal Orientation

If you are an achiever, you don't just set goals and forget them. You have your goals, both immediate and long-term, in front of you continually to motivate you daily.

Imaginativeness

You are not limited and bound by the past but project a new experience for yourself. You actively seek and make change.

Awareness

You are sensitive to what is going on around you and absorb information which will be of benefit to you and help you achieve your goals.

Creativeness

The status quo does not satisfy you, and you believe that things can always be improved. You innovate and search for new approaches.

Communicativeness

You recognize the value of communication and ensure that your message is clear and that you understand what people are trying to convey to you. You develop empathy and relate to others.

Growth Orientation

Realizing that you cannot stand still in a world of change, you have chosen to grow and develop. You are concerned with developing your potential and making the most of your talents.

Positive Response to Pressure

When you are faced with crises, deadlines, and decisions, you actually function better. You have learned to take pressure and use it as a positive force to get the adrenalin flowing in your body and motivate you to act decisively.

Trust

You believe that people are basically honest, sincere, and responsible, and you act accordingly. This feeling of trust gives you relationships with others openness and credibility, which makes genuine cooperation possible.

Joyfulness

Life fascinates you, and you feel real enjoyment in whatever you are doing. You are happy with who you are and what you are, and your enthusiasm is passed on to those around you.

Risk-Taking

Recognizing that life never offers complete security, you welcome new ventures and are not afraid of reasonable risks. All activity involves some degree of chance, and you balance the probable gains against the probable losses.

Decision-Making

You relish the moment, and there is a real sense of intensity and urgency about you. You make decisions now, you act now, and you convey a feeling of vitality, motion, and accomplishment.

Portrait of Terry A. Maurer, painted in 2020 from a photograph.
Painting by renowned artist, Catherine McClung

ACKNOWLEDGMENTS

I must thank the following:

Fulton Books

Scott Parker, My PA

Laurie Maurer Shelton, my daughter,
for the suggestion that I write my story

Mary Ann Horning Maurer, my wife of fifty-five years,
for her encouragement and patience

Stephen Andrew Maurer, my son, and my daughter-in-law,
Nicole, for their excitement about the project

Karin Mee-Lyn Maurer, my daughter, for
her contributions to my memoirs

Zaza Urbanek Fetterly, my friend and an artist and
writer (zazafetterly.com) for her invaluable support,
expertise, and diligence, as she orchestrated my
thoughts and my stories into a real book

CONTENTS

Terry Maurer with Napa Valley CAMi Cabernet vines.

INTRODUCTION

Today, December 15, 2010, I am starting to write my life's story so that my grandchildren and great-grandchildren will have a jump on ancestry.com. Everyone has their own story. This is mine. You should write yours as well. I am not sure what the title of my book will ultimately be. It might be *Son of a Poor Michigan Dirt Farmer* or *Autobiography of Wolfgang Savage* (one of my favorite aliases); it could be *Oil and Water: My First Seventy Years or Never Quit*; maybe I'll call it *The Story of Avita Water*, *From Chemicals to Water*, or *Daylight in the Swamp*. Those of you who know me best will understand what's behind my musings here. The rest will get the drift as you read on.

Whatever the title ultimately becomes, this will be the life story of me, Terry A. Maurer, and the times and my reflections beginning with my birth in Grayling, Michigan, USA, on October 1, 1942.

I was born during the early days of World War II when either Roosevelt or Truman was president. It was Roosevelt. I am not going to try and make every date in my book precise, but it will be very close. If you must know exact dates you may Google it or maybe find it on Facebook. I expect to end this book in my seventieth year.

Why am I writing my story? Well, it's not just my story. It's written for a broad audience who have witnessed these times and for those who want to know what happened. It's also a reference for my children, Laurie M. Shelton, Stephen A. Maurer, and Karin M. Maurer, and their children, grandchildren, great-grandchildren, etc. yet to be born. There will be stories they've heard and some they have not heard. It will also be entertaining, I hope, for my grandchildren, Trevor Scott Mansfield, Camille Elizabeth Shelton, Brianna Rose Maurer, Alison Amanda Maurer, and Colette Marie Maurer, and their children and grandchildren to be adults I would imagine in 2050 and 2080. I also have six step-grandchildren, Bryan, Jonathan, and Jessica Shelton and Kim, Mike, and Alec Schisler, who may enjoy parts of my odyssey. Now there are step great grandchildren Dylan and Elliot Riggs and to be born in 2020, a son (to be named Andrew) to Bryan and Sarah Shelton who will likely read this odyssey.

My story will have fourteen chapters and will cover the major events of my life as it unfolded. Interspersed throughout are my views on the events of the day and presidential politics. Obviously it will cover my early days on the farm in Northern Michigan.

My dad, Bernard Maurer, was the oldest son of twelve children of Laurence and Gertrude Lennon Maurer from Nashville, Michigan. He taught Tony, Louie, and me how to earn spending money by selling worms, minnows, strawberries, green onions, and sweet corn and also taught us how to milk cows by hand, raise chickens, and skin cedar rafters.

My mother, Pauline Cherven was from Roscommon. My Mother was always proud of the fact that the actor, Charlton Heston spent his childhood years in St. Helen, Michigan. St. Helen is a village just East of the small town of Roscommon, but still in Roscommon county. Charlton Heston was Moses in the epic film 'The Ten Commandments'. My Mother taught us how to make ice cream, clean chickens, make the best fudge (better than what you get on Mackinaw Island), and how to pray.

My godfather, Dr. Bernard Godfroy originally from Monroe, Michigan, taught us how to fish, make soap from venison tallow, take honey from bees, make wine from apples and chokecherries, *(if someone had told me in 1950 that a person could make a living formulating wine from grapes, I might have moved to Napa Valley instead of Detroit formulating chemicals for fasteners),* load rifle shells, hatch baby chicks, shoot the crossbow, and how to monitor the artesian wells.

When the movie of *Dirt Farmer's Son* is made, Renée Zellweger should play Mary Ann or if it were possible her look-alike, Kim Novak. Brad Pitt or Jeff Daniels could play Terry.

The story ends in Napa Valley, California, with me helping market my daughter Laurie M. Shelton's Cami Wines.

Other chapters will cover events and stories from my days at a Catholic military boarding school in Monroe, Michigan, a grade school for the rich and, in my case, the privileged poor (kind of like Jack Dawson on *Titanic,* the stowaway, who gets the rich girl). Also there are chapters about my time at the seminary in Holy Trinity, Alabama, and my education in four colleges as well as my continued ongoing business career as a chemist and founder of Maurer-Shumaker Industrial Coatings, a chemical manufacturer in Detroit.

This book will also cover my Avita Artesian Water company in Northern Michigan. At this time, Avita markets five major brands: Avita, Ecoviva, Aagwatt, Mr. Waterman, and 1-Litre. There are stories about my marriage to Ann Arbor's cutest redhead, Mary Ann Horning, on July 10, 1965.

Tony Maurer as a child, far left, with the two well drillers, right, on Avita Artesian Water discovery day in 1946.

Terry and his rooster on the farm.

CHAPTER I

Two Cases of Eggs
(1942–1950)

Franklin D. Roosevelt
(1933–1945)

I, Terry A. Maurer, was born in Grayling, Michigan, on October 1, 1942, because that's what my parents, Bernard and Pauline (Cherven) Maurer told me and also what it says in the archives at the Crawford County Courthouse. Jimmy Carter was also born on October 1, so also were my Grayling friend Sammie Williams and HDC friend Emery Rebresh. Grayling is a town put on the map by its Hanson Logging history at the turn of the last century, it is famous for the Au Sable River, once home to many Grayling trout, now extinct like its prairie pike.

Prairie pike
(*Piscatorious terra*)

This unusual specimen was the only true fur-bearing fish known in Michigan. Although its natural habitat was the Au Sable River, it would not hesitate to sneak ashore in order to avoid fishermen. Once on land, it was difficult to track down for its feet faced in opposite directions; thus, one could not tell if it were coming or going. This one was caught by Harold "Spike" MacNeven, who had it mounted for display in Spike's Keg of Nails, Grayling's famous liquid refreshment emporium.

Then came the great fire of '48, which destroyed the Tavern, but Spike at great risk to life and limb rescued the mount from the holocaust and gave it to Fred Bear for safekeeping.

The prairie pike is now completely extinct. This being the only know preserved mount is extremely rare and valuable.

Grayling is also the birthplace of the famous Bear Archery Company. In 1961, I sat with Fred Bear watching his grandson Chris Kroll play basketball for Grayling High School. Going forward, Spike's Keg of Nails bar, Old Au Sable Fly Shop, and the new Ray's Grill, Lake Margrethe, Camp Grayling, Avita Water Black Bear Bike Tour (organized and managed by my good friends, Wayne Koppa and John Alef), fly fishing, hunting, snowmobiling, the Au Sable River Canoe Marathon, Hartwick Pines State Park, Wellington Farms Historic Theme Park, Fox Run Country Club, Forest Dunes premium golf resort featuring one of the first reversible courses in the country, the Loop, and the Kirtland Warbler and the new Kirtland College and Deerfield Estates and now the Arauco plant on four mile road draw folks to Grayling.

ARAUCO's Grayling Particleboard operation officially opened its doors on April 16, 2019. Gathered for the grand opening and ribbon cutting were board members and executives from Chile and North America, state and local officials; ARAUCO employees, and project suppliers including Dieffenbacher. The Grayling facility is the most modern and productive mill of its kind—and marks the renewal of the composite panel industry in North America.

Dr. Martzowka delivered me. I met the doctor's son who was treasurer for the NBD Bank in 1977 when I needed a loan to start my second company Maurer-Shumaker. My dad told me that he'd read something about a Mr. Martz in the *Detroit Free Press* and that his father had delivered me in 1942, and maybe the son would give me a loan. I did meet the doctor's son in the bank's headquarters at the top of the Renaissance Building, now the G. M. Building on the Detroit River downtown. I learned that Mr. Martz was the chief financial officer for the National Bank of Detroit, and he told me that he loans billions to foreign governments over the weekend. He was very considerate and bought my lunch at the NBD executive lunchroom on the top floor. He put me in touch with a branch manager in Livonia who would consider my request for $25,000. I think I did get the loan from his bank, or maybe it was a different bank.

About five years before my dad died in 1985. He told me that when it came time to take me (the newborn) and my mother home from the hospital, he was told by the administrative clerk that he had to pay $35 for the delivery fee. Well, my dad did not have $35, but he knew the hospital still owed him for the last two cases of eggs he had sold them. So my dad told the clerk, "Just keep the egg money and call it a day."

The clerk must have been new to the job because she could not figure out how to make such a transfer. She said, "Mr. Maurer, I can't do that, and you can't take your wife and baby home until you pay the hospital. The delivery department and kitchen department are two different units of the hospital."

So my dad, getting hot under the collar, said, "Okay then, you feed her and the baby all winter, I'm going home."

The next day Bernard Maurer, my dad, was out in the field on the farm in Beaver Creek Township, starting his fall plowing. Sheriff Bill Golnick pulled up in the barnyard with lights flashing. My dad told me he knew the hospital had called the sheriff. Walking down the field where Dad had stopped the Allis-Chalmers with its single bottom plow, Sheriff Golnick was smiling. "The hospital called," Mr. Golnick told my dad. "They figured out how to transfer the egg money they owe you over to the delivery department. So the bill is covered. The hospital wants you to come in and pick up your wife and kid." So I know I was worth at least two cases of eggs.

I don't remember much about that first winter of my life in 1942. I know now that I was born in the middle of World War II. The winters were long and cold in Crawford County, Michigan. More snow then than now (global warming, you know). So cold that our mother frequently heated flat rocks in the kitchen oven and placed them in our bed prior to Tony and me getting in. Mom gave us baths in front of the wood-fired kitchen oven in a metal tub. The outhouse and outdoor clothesline was accepted as normal, more challenging for sure in the winter.

A typical day in 1942 on the farm was sort of like this. My dad would be up around 6:00 a.m. to milk the four to five cows by hand, then carry the milk to the house basement from the barn about seventy-five yards away. He would run it through the hand-turned milk separator. We sold the cream to a butter maker in West Branch, the second town east of Roscommon on the New York Central Railway. Once a week, the seven-gallon cream can would be taken to the station and then shipped to West Branch. A week or so later, the five- to six-dollar check would be delivered to our house by my uncle Frank Cherven, our rural mailman. My uncle would also deliver the day-old *Bay City Times*, his own paper. I looked forward to the comics, especially *Alley Oop* and *Joe Palooka*.

We did not have electricity in 1942. I believe we got the Delco-Light Plant going around 1945; we could run low voltage appliances off that unit.

I always was aware, even as a little child, of the danger of taking a kerosene lantern into the hayloft when Dad threw the hay down for the cows. The salt we threw on the warm hay in the summer was to prevent spontaneous combustion at haying time. It would do nothing to stop a fire if the lantern fell off the nail hook in the rafters. The lantern hanging in the kitchen didn't concern me. Normal electricity arrived at our farm sometime in the very early fifties when Tony and I were already going to the military school in Monroe.

In those days prior to my older brother, Tony, and I being sent to the Catholic military boarding school Hall of the Divine Child, I started first grade in Frederick, Michigan. Frederick was and still is a small village located nearly twenty-five miles north of our farm yet still in Crawford County. We were bused there because the closest town, Grayling, did not have room for the Beaver Creek kids when the one-room schoolhouses in the townships were closed down, probably in 1945 or 1946. I believe I rode the bus about seventy-five miles per day. Sometimes, with either Andy Nielson or Roy Millikin as our bus drivers, on the way home from school, I'd fall asleep on the shoulder of a cute fourth-grade girl from Harry Fiyan's junkyard.

Once the cows were milked in the morning by my dad, he would then take care of the chickens. We had cows and chickens, probably three hundred chickens in two different coops: one coop for the laying hens and the second coop for the pullets. Both groups of chickens required feed and water. Dad would carry in five-gallon pails of water from the house during the winter. He would need to break through a thin layer of ice before adding more water. The next chore would likely be tending to the wood furnace. The wood we threw down the basement always seemed to be coated with ice and snow. The next morning the whole chore routine would be repeated again. What happened between morning and evening chores depended upon the time of the year.

In the late fall, there was wood to cut up using the tractor, and a long fast-moving belt hooked to an open buzz saw—not to OSHA standards, that's for sure. Holding my end of the log two feet from the buzz saw while standing on uneven ground covered with ice and snow always got my attention. Remember Johnny Cash's brother in *Walk the Line*. During the winter there was less to do between chore time.

In the spring, it was all about cleaning the barns and chicken coops (ahh, the sweet smell of fresh manure in May; chicken manure was the worst) and getting ready to plant. We enjoyed watching the new Holstein calves jumping and kicking their heels in the fresh spring air as they were let out for the first time. We were basically subsistent farmers living off venison and eggs, and all the vegetables we stored in our root cellar, and the berries we picked and canned during the summer. We did make some cash by planting extra potatoes, squash, cabbage (unfortunately, my dad did not know brussels sprouts, later my favorite vegetable), strawberries, tomatoes, green onions, and sweet corn to the local wholesaler, Mr. Warren Gill in Grayling. Planting all these vegetables (that's what dirt farmers do) led to drilling for more water at the springs near the swamp. The wells turned out to be flowing wells, wells which we much later, in 1987, started bottling first under the franchised name de Maurier. Later we called this water Avita and Ecoviva.

Summertime was a fun time on the farm for Tony and me. It was finally warm enough to swim in the fish ponds, both the two "little ponds," and then our favorite one, the "big pond." Creative names, but what do you expect from four- and five-year-olds. Our cousins Sue and Sally would spend much of the summer at what we called Mose's Cabin. Our uncle, their dad, was the famous Al "Mose" Leonard, who built his cabin on the northeast corner of our two-hundred-acre farm. The cabin was close enough for Sue and Sally and later Beezer, Mary Margaret, Joey, Tommy, and Jimmy, their younger siblings, to walk over to the farm. Mose was famous in my eyes because he could shoot straighter and faster than anyone I ever knew. He could drive faster than most people too. He always scared the devil out of my mother when he would take us to mass during those summer Sundays. Mom would scream "Slow down" most of the way to church.

Mose liked all things fast, motorcycles and ice planes. The ice plane took his life on Saginaw Bay later in 1971 or 1972 when he hit open water at seventy miles per hour in early spring. Uncle Mose was my confirmation sponsor in 1954 and always was fun to be around. He took us boating on Higgins Lake and rabbit hunting in the swamps with my dad and our best rabbit and deer dog Poochy, also known as Caesar by the adults. Mose always carried hard Christmas candy for the rabbit hunts, usually passing it out after we started a big fire amid the snow-covered cedars in the middle of the mud lake swamps just west of the New York Center railroad tracks.

Louis and Poochy the dog

Sue and Sally
Leonard in 1945

Summertime was still the most fun, especially when our Leonard cousins could walk to the farm across the Sixty—that's what we called the big area between Mose's cabin and the farm. We never really had a name for the farm; it was just our home. Other people called it the old Barber Place or the Godfroy Farm. Dr. Godfroy was my godfather and my dad's cousin and business partner. It eventually became the Maurer Place by the neighbors. The closest neighbors were the Millikins, nearly three miles away. We were in a very remote part of Beaver Creek Township, on a dead-end road. This is definitely an advantage for Avita Water now. The old farm, now in 2011, is owned by my aunt and uncle, Andy and Margaret Cherven, left to them through Doc Godfroy's will in 1980.

When Sue and Sally would make the walk over to the farm, we would usually end up down at the fish pond, swimming. Always we would get a drink at the flowing wells. Sometimes we could get the girls to help weed the carrots or pick strawberries before the swim. Prior to 1950, when we were all under eight years old, my dad did not work us too hard. Picking up the eggs was something Sue and

Sally always wanted to do, being city girls from Saginaw. They also preferred city milk to cow's milk, as they called what we drank, and sometimes squirted them when Tony and I would do the milking.

In the fall, it was time for school at Frederick. I went to first and second grade there. The time before first grade is not very memorable, and even first grade is difficult to remember since I was four years and eleven months old in 1947 when I started school. My parents wanted me to be in the next grade to Tony, so I started early. Tony was five years and seven months old when he started first grade. I think my math is correct.

At any rate, I don't remember too much about first grade. Mrs. Odell was my first-grade teacher, and she gave me a set of cookie jars which looked like strawberries to give to my mother, who loved anything strawberry. I disliked phonics and still don't understand it. Floyd Millikin was my buddy and neighbor from Beaver Creek and was in kindergarten when I started first grade. I skipped kindergarten. Floyd was the third born of this close Millikin family; Marian, Connie, Floyd, Pauline, Bob, Luella, and finally Marci is the birth order. Our families always enjoyed getting together. Floyd and I were friends until he died of a heart attack while presiding over a Road Commission meeting in Crawford County in 1994 or 1995. Floyd helped me set up the first water bottling plant for de Maurier in 1987, my brother and sister-in-law, Dale and Gaelene Horning, were the ones who built the first water bottling installation inside of a 53 foot semi-trailer which Floyd Millikin set up. Floyd also told me about a week before his death (he already had a heart attack about six weeks earlier) that he had eaten too many doughnuts at his job with the Michigan State Police and that he also smoked too many cigarettes. Floyd was fifty-one and is buried in Grayling.

Roscommon was six miles from the farm, and Grayling was ten miles. We went to church at St. Michael's in Roscommon. I remember the first time I saved somebody's life from drowning. I actually saved friends from drowning three times. The first time was during recess from catechism at St. Michael's in Roscommon. It was probably in December 1947; the ice under the bridge on Main Street was frozen but not too thick when Tom and Jerry (the McCutchison twins) and my brother Tony got on the ice. I was still standing on the shore when they, all three, went through the ice with their winter coats and boots.

The water was just over their heads, not really very deep but deep for five- to six-year-olds. Tony immediately started hollering to me, "Help, help!"

I said, "I'll go to town and get somebody. I'll be right back."

He said, "No, we'll drown, you've got to crawl out on the ice and pull us in."

I lay on the thin ice and stretched my arms out to grab my brother. I got Tony's hand and started to pull while Tom and Jerry clung to the ice, treading water in the frigid hole. I got Tony nearly up on the ice when it broke beneath me landing. Now all four of us in the icy water. The good news, we learned that the ice would break all the way back to the shore, probably ten feet. We all managed to get to the bank. The twins, who lived in town, ran home. Tony and I went to the nearby rectory where Father Grill's housekeeper stripped us down, got the priest's bathrobes, and sat us on the floor radiator until our mother came to pick us up. I never heard nor do I remember what she said about the situation. I am sure it wasn't good. She was always worried, maybe from that time on that Tony and I would fall into mud lake and drown on our many hikes to the fish ponds with the flowing wells.

Frequently after church in Roscommon, our family would stop at Grandma Cherven's little farm for a visit. She always seemed to have Glenn Miller on her big old radio. My mother was the third of ten. She had three sisters, Ann, Teen (married to Mose), and Fran. She had six brothers, Frank, John, Al, Mike, Ed, and Andy. All but Frank served in World War II and all returned in one piece. Here is an article published in the newspaper *The Roscommon Herald* in 1942:

Five sons in U.S. Army

This week we pay tribute to Mrs. Justine Cherven, the mother of five sons in the US service. Mrs. Cherven, the mother of 10 children, was born in 1886 in what was once Slovakia and then Poland after the First World War.

Mrs. Cherven came to the U.S. and Chicago when she was 16. She was married there in 1907 to Andrew Cherven who was also a native of the same country. The Chervens then moved to a farm 4 miles North of Roscommon in 1910 and moving in 1923 to their present home one mile Northwest of Roscommon. Mr. Cherven passed away three years ago.

Mrs. Cherven has worked hard through the years to raise her fine large family and the esteem with which the community looks on them shows how well she has done her job.

One by one Mrs. Cherven has given her sons to fight for America, her adopted country. Alois, 27, left first and is now Sargent at Camp Murphy, FL; Edward, 25, left 14 months ago and is stationed in Orlando, FL; Andrew, 21, enlisted and is in Colorado Springs, CO; Pfc. John, 29, now en route to a California camp; and Michael, 18, the youngest son, left Tuesday evening for Camp Custer.

Mrs. Cherven's other children are Frank, Mrs. Bernard Maurer, and Frances, all of Roscommon, the latter daughter, living at home, Mrs. Henry Friday, Jr. of Cheboygan and Mrs. A. L. Leonard of Texas, whose husband is in the army.

To Mrs. Cherven, a quiet, pleasant woman, and wonderful mother we pay her tribute, in giving her five sons to fight so that this land of ours may remain forever the home of the free and the brave. She is more than giving her share.

To our knowledge, Mrs. Cherven is the only mother in Roscommon County with five sons in the armed services.

Roscommon, Michigan

Terry's Cherven uncles—Michael, Edward, John, Andrew,
and Albert—with their mother, my grandmother,
Justine Cherven in 1943, all WWII veterans.

Terry's Maurer uncles, Lenny, Bug, Dale, and
Edward, in 1943, all WWII veterans.

On those visits, I would go upstairs and find khaki uniforms hanging everywhere. It was from 1944 to 1947 I'd see this. It looked like a military barrack, something I saw a lot of in the early '60s when I worked summer jobs at Camp Grayling, the Michigan National Guard Camp near the four-mile road farm. I personally spent six years in uniform from 1950 to 1956 at the military school. I always say that my dad was too old for World War II, I was too old for Vietnam, and my son, Stephen, was too old for Iraq. The US would have a war every twenty-five years, whether they needed one or not. My family was just born at the right time. I think it was Will Rogers who said there should be a law saying, "You can't start another war until you've paid for the previous one."

My grandma Cherven would always have a bag of wax bread wrappers for my mother to take home to use for cleaning the top of the woodstove in our kitchen. Sometimes my grandma's brother, Uncle Emil Glusak, would be there. Once, he asked Tony and me to help find his eyes. We really thought he lost his eyeballs. I thought, *How can* he *look for anything?* "None are so blind as those who can't see," according to Yogi. Then he told us that he lost his glasses. I don't remember if we found them.

There was another great uncle in my life in those early days. Uncle Mac was Doc Godfroy's (Uncle Doc is what we called Dr. Godfroy) father. I am sure he was in his late eighties when he lived with us on the farm. He had his own room downstairs in the big house and even had furniture (fancy stuff) made of horsehair, I was told. Besides remembering his funeral at the house, he was laid out in the front room for everyone to see. Probably a year or so before he died, Uncle Mac gave me a dime once and said, "Split this with Tony." I knew I had a big job to do, so I got a hammer, placed the dime on the metal piece cemented to the back steps (the piece of metal used to scrape manure off your shoes), and proceeded to pound on the dime. I thought the thin piece of metal and the hammering would allow me to cut the dime in half. My mother saw me and asked what I was doing. I told her, "Uncle Mac said to split the dime with Tony, and I'm splitting it."

Uncle Mac and Uncle Doc came to Roscommon from Monroe, Michigan, at the start of the Depression (1930 or so). I learned that Uncle Mac worked for the railroad which traveled from Detroit to Mackinaw City, traveling through Roscommon. Somehow, he learned about the (Fred) Barber Farm and decided to move north from Monroe with his son and only child, my uncle Doc, and a bunch of chickens. Sometime in 1985 (some fifty-five years later) I met the man who drove the moving van from Monroe to Roscommon loaded with Mac Godfroy and his son, Bernard Godfroy. We were visiting Dick and Marie Powers, longtime friends of my wife, Mary Ann Horning Maurer, on their son's (Earl's) farm near Battle Creek, Michigan.

It wasn't until 2011 in Redwood City, California, when Mary Ann and I were visiting the Powers' daughter, Barb Kirkpatrick, when I asked her who it was I met in Battle Creek, Michigan, twenty-five years earlier at her parents' farm. It didn't take long to figure out that it was her great uncle, Lauren Munson—wife was Mae from Monroe, Michigan, who moved my uncle Doc and his father to Roscommon in 1930. Munson owned a general store in Monroe and had no children. Uncle Doc's mother had died earlier of what I don't know, maybe from the flu of 1918. They are all now buried in the big cemetery on Front Street in Monroe, Michigan. It is the same cemetery where the IHM nuns are buried. There is a very large marker near their site for a Maurer. Must be a distant Maurer to my dad's family, which was from the Nashville and Hastings, Michigan, area.

Actually, my grandpa Laurence Maurer and his father, I think Jacob, are both buried in Hastings. There is a Godfroy Street in Monroe, just south and adjacent to the IHM motherhouse and St. Mary's Academy, and the old military school where I spent six years of my life. That academy was called the Hall of the Divine Child (HDC), and in 1985 it became Norman Towers retirement home. The Hall was closed due to declining enrollment and the high cost of lay teachers after the Second Vatican Council.

Actually Uncle Mac or maybe it was his father who lived in Monroe, in the very early days of the state, was friendly with the local Native Americans. Michigan became a state in 1837. At any rate my dad told me that my Uncle Doc's father or grandfather smoked the pipe with the Native Americans who lived along the Raison River. Sometimes Mr. Godfroy would wake up in his house to find six or eight Native Americans asleep on the floor in front of the big fireplace. They frequented the warm house, especially in winter. His house was always open for the Indians.

Monroe is the birthplace of General Custer, and there is a large beautiful statue of the general on his steed. The statue is directly across from the Catholic church on the corner of Elm and Main Streets, next to the river. Well, the reason for mentioning Mr. Godfroy and the Indians is that one night, the chief had a dream about Mr. Godfroy riding into the Indian campgrounds on a great white stallion. The chief interpreted the dream, believing it was a sign that he should give the property along the east side of the Raison River from Dundee to Monroe to Mr. Godfroy. That would be about thirty miles of river frontage valuable then but a fortune in 2010. My dad says I could go to the Monroe abstracts and verify the claim. I never took the time, but you can only claim what you can defend I always say.

Just a note about the relationship of my dad, Bernard L. Maurer, to Dr. Bernard Godfroy. My dad's maternal grandmother was a sister to Doc Bernard Godfroy's mother. I think that made them second cousins. So now, here is how I came to be born in Grayling and raised in Roscommon.

In 1935, my dad went to visit his cousin Bernard Godfroy for deer season at the Roscommon farm. He never returned to live in Nashville again. Godfroy wanted to be a doctor, but he had to finish high school first. So he made a deal with my dad to milk the cows and take care of the farm while he finished high school at night. He then went to Olivet College and got his medical degree from St. Louis University in the mid-1940s. He was a dermatologist. My dad met my mother, Pauline Elizabeth Cherven, at church in Roscommon, and they were married in 1939.

Here now is a letter from my dad, Bernard Maurer, soon after his marriage to my mother, Pauline Cherven, in 1939, to Bernard Godfroy, who was in med school at St. Louis University. This letter really lays out what a dirt farmer was doing on the farm as the country is coming out of the Great Depression.

November 9, 1939

Dear Bernard,

Winter is here, for the ground is covered with snow and looks as if it would stay, it came yesterday, plenty, wild and woolly.

Been busy every day, thought that my work would be all caught up by this time. Am after the wood, just seemed as though I couldn't get to it before. Have just one load of ashes to put on the potato ground, then that is all done. About three loads left so I'll put that on the corn field. The wheat looks good, have but two loads to finish covering the whole field on the hill. The quack grass should be sick for spring. Dragged it four times and disked it once, of course each time I went over it twice. Annabell had a heifer calf the other day and it was a nice one, about time, luck was coming our way, don't you think?

The pullets are coming right along and the old hens are taking their own sweet time. Most I get from them is 15, am putting the lights out at 2:30, going to put them out at 2:00 next week. Wish they would get going so I could get some money for us.

It is giving just about enough for feed, cost an average $17.00 every 10 to 12 days. But in ten days I expect them to get over the 100 mark if they keep on the way they have. The pullets sure are laying big eggs, you wouldn't know they were pullet eggs, no small at all so far, mix them up with the eggs from the old hens and you can hardly tell the difference.

I am going to try cooking up the scraps from the table along with a little mash and give it to them about four o'clock, what do you think about it? If it works it would pay to buy some cull potatoes at Gaylord for 20 to 25 cents to cook up.

Am feeding them 100 lbs. of whole corn a night. By this I mean a 100 lbs. lasts as long as a batch of mash so they are getting with the ground corn 250 lbs. Most of the corn goes to the pullets.

Pauline is still cleaning house and getting things the way she wants them. You won't know the old shack when you come home. I tell her not to work so hard but it does no good, she is going from the time she gets up until 8:00 or 9:00 o'clock at night.

About the wedding I'll send you what was in the paper and that will tell you better than I can. Everybody gave us a good time. All the presents I'll leave that up to Pauline to write and tell you.

Oh yes the shamrock is blossoming. The rose is growing ail the old leaves died but is starting up again. Was real green until I brought it in the house but guess it'll make the grade. Here is one of Pauline's flowers she wore at the wedding. Not much else to say for this time. Save the piece about the wedding for Pauline wants to keep it.

Will sign off.

As ever,
Bernard

I remember my mother crying in the old farm kitchen in 1948. My dad had just told her he'd been charged by the State of Michigan for shooting deer out of season, something Doc Godfroy and Uncle Mose did a lot of. He said he had to either pay $5,000 in fines or go to jail for six months. My dad said, "I don't have $5,000, so I guess it's jail."

My mother was pleading, "Who's going to feed the chickens and milk the cows?"

Just then, Doc Godfroy walked in. He said, "Don't worry, Bernard, we'll get you a good Jewish attorney."

My dad said, "Where are we going to find a Jewish attorney up here in Crawford County, Northern Michigan?"

Doc said, "Well, you have a cousin who is a monsignor and lives in Mt. Clemens near Detroit. He must know a rabbi and the rabbi would surely know a Jewish attorney."

The call was made to the cousin in Mt. Clemens, and the rest is history. My dad did not serve time nor pay the $5,000. Dad's attorney countersued the State of Michigan for crop damages, suing for the same $5,000, saying that "if the deer belong to the state, then it was the state's responsibility to keep their deer out of Mr. Maurer's crops." The trial took three years, ending essentially in a draw. My dad and Doc Godfroy were ultimately fined six cents. I was in the courtroom when the judge pronounced "guilty" and "The fine is six cents."

Uncle Doc said, "We are not going to pay it."

I then said, "I can pay it. I've got six cents in my pocket left over from my school milk allowance."

My uncle slapped my hand with the nickel and penny, saying, "I said we're not paying it." The change flew across the floor. Somebody must have paid, maybe the attorney, because no one went to jail. I was five years old.

In preparation for the final days of the trial, the conservation department, under the direction of Officer Clarence Roberts and Mr. Wright of the Crawford County field office, staged a twenty-man raid on the Godfroy farm, where we lived. My mother told me later that the "bad" conservation officers searched every inch of the farmhouse, including under the bed where Tony and I were sleeping, looking for canned venison. All the canned venison had already been buried in wooden wine barrels under the apple trees in the orchard. The officers did collect as evidence many horns nailed to the rafters in the new tractor barn.

Here now is a portion of the write-up in the Bay City paper, first laying out the pending case against my dad for shooting deer and then the article on the six-cent judgment.

Two Pending Cases
The Bay City paper
October 1947

The pending cases involve the alleged killing of a vast number of fish in the Kalamazoo river by the spot dumping therein, a deadly poison in the form of industrial waste (filed weeks ago at Albion but not yet tried) and last week's filing of a $5,000 damage suit in the Crawford county immediately followed the sentencing of Bernard Maurer, a farmer, in justice court, on a jury finding of guilty on two counts of illegal possession of venison. The suit is directed at Maurer and at Dr. Bernard M. Godfroy of Traverse City, owner of the farm where conservation officers, during the recent deer season, searched a barn and said they found portions of the remains of 55 animals both does and bucks. The penalty imposed of Maurer for the purported game law violation itself was 60 days in jail plus $19.85.

Scalps Put in Evidence

Specifically involved in the trial were scalps and other remnants of 49 animals which officers said they found tacked up on inside walls of a barn at the Godfroy-Maurer place. They were exhibited in court.

The defense contended all the deer were killed from May 20 to Sept. 30, a period covered by a permit, which required Dr. Godfroy and Maurer to turn the slaughtered deer over to proper authorities within the meaning of the permit provision. At one point Attorney Nicholas V. Olds for the state told the court the purpose of certain testimony was to show a studied intent on the part of these defendants not to comply with the provisions of the permits issued in 1947 and subsequent years. Crux of the defense case as presented by Attorney Fred Van Fleteren was that the deer were doing tremendous damage at the Godfroy-Maurer place, that Dr. Godfroy had to fight through two months of delay and red tape to get a permit, that the deer were "turned over" even though not immediately and that wording of the permit did not specify immediate notification or any obligation whatever to deliver the slaughtered deer to Conservation Officer Clarence Roberts. Over objections of the state, the defense was permitted to enter as evidence copies of deer killing permits for years after 1947, showing a change in terminology that put more definite obligation on permittees.

Used for Fertilizer

Meat value of the animals was the basis for damages claimed. The state sought to impress the court with the point that deer meat is edible at all times of year and that, had terms of the permit been complied with, the meat could have been put to good use. The defense clung to the point that most of the deer were killed in early June, that they were not in good condition and that the meat had spoiled in the time it would have taken officers to pick it up. Maurer testified deer were plowed under for fertilizer. He was then confronted with testimony he had given at the criminal trial in which he was acquitted of illegal possession of deer after Dr. Godfroy took full responsibility for the killings. He and Maurer denied any of the deer being utilized as food, and both insisted throughout long questioning that the bulk of the deer involved had been killed in June. The state displayed numerous scalps from its exhibit, and expert witnesses said that deer with antlers and hair like these were not June condition deer.

Admitted slaughter

Supporting his contentions of "studied intent" not to comply, Olds presented testimony that Dr. Godfroy and Maurer had gone to conservation headquarters in June 1947, after several nights in which many deer were killed, and that Godfroy there told a conservation official not to bother about the deer at his place because "I have killed them all off." What happened under a permit issued in 1949 also went into the trial record. The plaintiff presented a series of handwritten demands for damages from the conservation department, each stating that a certain deer which had been killed under the permit would be held until settlement had been made of $100 damages, and in one case $200. Each such notice, some signed by Maurer and by Dr. Godfroy, specified that no physical resistance would be offered an officer removing the deer, but that if the deer was removed it was done under protest. The defense introduced a witness, Elroy Milliken, Crawford County farmer, who also has killed deer under permit. He testified he did not believe deer killed by him left in the field overnight would be fit for human use next day.

State Wins 6-cent damages
in Crawford Deer-Kill trial
by Jim McKenna

Grayling—A six cent judgment was awarded to the conservation against Dr. Bernard M. Godfroy of Traverse City in the deer-killing civil trial which ended Friday. Judge John C. Shaffer excluded the codefendant, Bernard Maurer. It is the first case in which the state has ever sued for recovery of damages on game animals. Two full days of testimony had been taken in the department's suit against Dr. Godfroy and Maurer, tenant of Godfroy's Crawford county farm where, in the spring of 1947, Dr. Godfroy admittedly made a mass killing of deer which he contended were ruining the crops.

Tony Maurer with ten-point mount in 1999.

The Laurence Maurer family in 1946, Bernard
Maurer, center fifth from right, and Pauline
Maurer holding Terry Maurer, front far left.

Bernard Maurer, Dr. Bernard Godfroy and Mac Godfroy: 1942

Mary Ann with her parents and grandparents: 1942

A LITTLE different view of the band provides an unusual photo of Terry Maurer deep in his music.

Me with Saxophone

CHAPTER II

Military School (1950–1956)
Harry S. Truman
(1945–1953)

One day in early September 1949, I heard Dad telling Mom that the boys (my brother and I) would be going to a Catholic military boarding school in Monroe (Tony was eight and l was six). My mom cried and replied, "No, they can't go." My dad said that the decision had already been made and that we would be leaving in seven days. He told my mom that Uncle Doc would be paying the tuition ($500 per year for nine months room and board—a lot of money in 1950), and the boys would get a good education, better than at the public school in Frederick. Also we would not need to ride the school bus seventy-five miles per day anymore. He then called Tony and me to tell us the news. I remember Dad saying, "There will even be kids from Detroit at this school," as if that would impress a six-year-old like me. But I could tell by the way he said Detroit that it meant something to him.

Pauline, Louis, Tony, Bernard, and Terry in 1954.

We drove to Monroe, probably in Uncle Doc's Buick. We only drove that two hundred miles two or three more times in the next thirty-one round trips, which I made over the next six years. It was always the midnight train from Roscommon with a four-hour layover in Detroit's Grand Central Station and the same in reverse when coming back to Roscommon for the Thanksgiving, Christmas, and Easter furloughs. We got to know every inch of Grand Central Station's ground floor. We saw the trains go from the transportation of choice with its fancy conductors in uniform and clean seats with fresh white paper-covered headrests on every seat to something less by 1956.

I continued to ride the trains from 1956 to 1961 when I went to high school in Holy Trinity, Alabama, and then first year of college in Monroe, Virginia. For sure, by 1957, one could observe the decline in service and less attention to detail in all areas of train travel. The era of air travel was getting started for not just the rich but even for some of the privileged poor. That's what I thought of myself. I didn't get on a commercial plane until I flew to Mexico City in 1962, but one could see that the passenger trains were not the future.

The first night at military school was memorable. I was assigned to one of the special tower rooms with its one-foot window ledges and eerie tall ceilings. It held four students. There was a big thunderstorm passing through as we heard "taps" for the first time, and then I could hear my bunkmates crying. I am not sure if they were scared of the storm or scared of being alone away from their parents for the first time. I don't think I cried. I would always cry when I saw my parents. Tony would always cry when he left them. Neither of us cried at the same time. My parents told me they were going to be spending the night with Uncle Doc's aunt in the city, so I knew they were not too far away that first night. School got started the next day, and I did not see any parents again until Thanksgiving vacation nearly three months later.

Third grade was the year that most of my classmates started classes at HDC. Mike Sweeney started in first grade, but my best friends, Cadets Paul Ewing, Dennis McIntyre, Eugene Willis, Paul Hebert, Tim Gillet, and John Vandegrift, started with me in third grade. Gordon Rebresh started military school in the fifth grade. Sweeney was also one of my best friends. He and I were altar boys together, and in sixth, seventh, eighth grades, we were always paired up to do the serving for the annual first communion mass, usually for the second graders.

I remember thinking I was too old to play in the sandbox with some of my classmates who thought it was really cool. We never had a sandbox on the farm—who needed a sandbox? There was dirt everywhere—but I did fall asleep in the chicken yard once and woke up when a rooster pecked at my bare feet.

In 1950, we learned to play soccer. Our fourth-grade nun, Sister Thomas Ellen, had a brother who was a professional soccer player, and she knew all the rules. I also saw the movie *The Pride of St. Louis* about Jerome "Dizzy" Dean, the St. Louis Cardinal player who won thirty games pitching. I started pitching then and didn't stop until 1960. I even got Denny McClain's autograph with my son, Stephen, when Denny won his twenty-eighth game for Detroit in

1968. Denny finally beat Dizzy Dean's record by winning thirty-one games that year. I thought I was so good that I even took my confirmation name in 1954 after Mr. Dean. The name was Jerome. My first grading period in third grade was not pretty. I was a straight-A student in Frederick, but at HDC, the nun said I was so far behind they wouldn't embarrass me with a grade for any of my classes.

I don't remember much about that first summer back home. However, I was ready to go back to Monroe for fourth grade. I did and I improved in my classes, and I was made a corporal that year. Maybe it was even sergeant. Sister Thomas Ellen was our fourth-grade nun. She was probably not yet thirty and not bad looking (even covered head to toe in the traditional religious habit), in my opinion, as a mature eight-year-old.

One day, as our fourth-grade class was getting into outdoor play clothes in the basement locker area, I said to Eugene Willis, "Sister Thomas Ellen gets to watch us boys take our pants off every day. I would like to see her take her pants off just once."

Well, Willis immediately ran up to Sister, and I saw him whisper something in her ear. I presumed it was verbatim what I had just said, but nothing happened until later. After play period, Sister came up to me and said, "What did you say earlier?"

I said, "I can't tell you."

So we went to the refectory, and again after supper, she continued, "What did you say earlier?"

I said again, "I can't tell you, Sister," getting a little worried now.

Eugene Willis, Terry A. Maurer 1955
Hall of the Devine Child, Monroe, Mich.

As study hall was ending, Sister Thomas Ellen came to my desk, tapped me on the shoulder, and said for the third time, "Tell me what you said earlier," and she added, "If you don't, you will have to go see Sister Hermann Joseph, the mother superior."

Well, I knew what that meant, probably expulsion and a trip back to Roscommon on the next train. So I figured she already knew what I said and just wanted me to repeat it. So I started to cry and through my tears told her exactly what I said expecting the worst. I said, "Sister, I told Eugene Willis that you get to watch us take our pants off every day, and I would like to see you take yours off just once."

She stood up straight (she had been leaning over my shoulder) and said, "Okay then."

Nothing more was ever said about it, either that night nor that school year, nor the next four and one half more years at HDC. My guess is that at the evening gathering of the nuns, Sister probably told the other nuns, "You'll never believe just what one of my students said."

In the fifth grade I started playing the tenor saxophone and was good enough to play in the school marching band. Our band was invited to play in Briggs Stadium (later called Tiger Stadium). We also played in the Marion year parade in Windsor, Ontario, in 1954. I have included a picture of myself playing the tenor sax, which appeared in the parade section of the *Detroit Free Press*. Tony played the trombone and traveled to the same events.

We didn't see each other every day, at least not to talk. His class of about forty to forty-five students were moving through the halls of the Hall independent of my class. We marched everywhere in two files. We would bump into each other for band practice, later for football practice and games. We also both played on the school team. Of course, when it was time for vacations back up north in Roscommon, we would either take the taxi together or our military drill instructor, Lieutenant Hyland, might drive us to the Monroe Depot. We both seemed to like our independence. I wasn't leaning on Tony, and he didn't feel like the needed big brother.

A typical day at the Hall of the Divine Child was to be up at 7:00 a.m., awakened by reveille, always reveille. Head to the bathroom and sink areas. Each class had its own sink area with probably forty sinks. Every other day, it was to the chapel for mass; Fr. Stanley Bowers was our chaplain for all of my six years at HDC. He was an ex-boxer, either college, military, or pro, I never found out. We knew we didn't want to be on the wrong side of Father Bowers. He was the ultimate disciplinarian. Much later, sometime in the mid-'60s through the eighties, Father Bowers was the pastor at a church in Dundee, Michigan, and became friends with my future wife's cousin, Bob Miller, pastor for the local Lutheran church in the same town. Pastor Robert J. Miller wrote a book about his time as a missionary in Ethiopia, *Tales of Tchinia: Two Families in Ethiopia*.

One time when our seventh-grade class was in chapel for our biweekly mandatory confessions, the entire class (forty students) were on our knees examining our conscience in preparation for our turns in the confessional box with Father Bowers. We heard Father Bowers exclaim from the dark confessional box "You did what!" as he slammed the privacy door. Immediately all forty heads turned to the right to see who it was that could provoke such a response. Then Regelski came out and with head down, trying to look invisible as he made his way up the side aisle toward the front of the chapel where we'd normally say our penance. I'm sure we all saw who it was and prayed that our sins would not get the same response from Father Bowers.

There was a book, at least a manuscript written about Father Bowers and the Hall of the Divine Child by my classmate, Dennis McIntyre. I know that because Dennis let me read the manuscript when I met him, Mike Sweeney, and Paul Ewing at the University of Michigan in 1964. McIntyre won the prestigious Hopwood Award for Literature that year at the University of Michigan. Dennis later went to New York and had a very successful career as a playwright. Probably his most successful play was *Split Second*, which appeared in a theater just off-Broadway. I was in New York when it was playing, but I am sorry to say that I couldn't get a ticket. *National Anthems*, *Modigliani*, *Children in the Rain*, and *Established Price* are other plays by Dennis McIntyre.

McIntyre died of stomach cancer in 1990, I spoke to him on the phone a few weeks before the end. Dennis told me that he had a new play for which Al Pacino was considering taking the lead role. McIntyre said to me, "If Pacino takes it, I could make a million dollars, but Terry I won't live long enough to know." Paul Ewing has his manuscript about the Hall of the Divine Child, entitled "The Divine Child," and it remains unpublished to this day.

Following chapel, it was to the refectory for breakfast. We always had plenty to eat and usually a good choice. Then it was morning classes, lunch, and afternoon classes followed by probably two hours of free outdoor recreation. We could play any type of ball. I usually played whatever was in season. It seemed that most of the students played ball. We would have baseball, soccer, and basketball, and even handball courts were available. I didn't play much handball. In the spring it was marbles and kites. I was definitely the "king" of marbles in my seventh- and eighth-grade years. Some students and I were few of those who would be a merchant or vendor. Here's the deal: The vendors would make a hole in the ground, say six to ten inches deep and wide, then place a boulder or several "desirable" marbles in front of the hole, just close enough to the hole, so that when the players (the richer kids whose parents could buy them lots of shooter marbles) started throwing their marbles at my prize marbles from behind a line in the sand, they would win the big marble when they knocked it in the hole. The vendor (myself) got to keep all the marbles being thrown. Sometimes you'd have three or four boys firing their marbles at the same time. You could win lots of marbles. I still have many of my winnings some sixty years later.

My little brother, Louie, played with my winnings with our Leonard cousins back on the farm in Roscommon. Naturally, some marbles were lost. I found some in the chicken yard. Louie, who was born in 1951, was not sent to the boarding school. He was conceived on the recommendation of my grandma Cherven. I heard my mom complaining to her about Tony and me being sent to Monroe. I heard my grandmom tell my mom, "Well, just make another baby!"

I think I was present at my little brother's conception. It happened one night when I decided to scare my parents by holding up my glow in the dark coonskin cap from under their bed. Our parents had gotten Tony and I both Daniel Boon–style coonskin caps for Christmas in 1950, the ones with glow in the dark eyes in the front. If you held them near a lightbulb for a while, the glowing would become quite bright and last for twenty to thirty minutes. So after charging up my cap, I crawled from my bedroom to Mom and Dad's room, hiding under their bed, waiting for them to come upstairs. Well, I didn't wait long before they were in bed, and I could tell by the commotion that Dad was getting frisky. I didn't expect anything like that, but I had invested considerable time getting ready to scare them with the glowing eyes, so I made my move before I thought the old swayed bed would come down on me.

When I raised the coonskin cap up over the side of the bed, right over as it turned out, my mom's head, my mom shrieked, "Bernie, I'm seeing stars!"

My dad said, thinking he was doing a good job, "That's all right, Pauline."

She continued, "No, I really am seeing stars."

I figured my job was done and quickly crawled back to my room before being discovered. I never had the courage to ask either Mom or Dad about that night. Louie was born on October 14, 1951.

Back to the schedule, following the recreation period, it was time to clean up for dinner (supper in those days). I learned that farm people like me had dinner and supper and city people had lunch and dinner. Then another ninety minutes of study before taps, and the cycle started again. Saturdays and Sundays were different. Most of Saturday was free recreation time. In winter we could ice skate at the pond. There was always a hockey game going on at the far end. James Benso was the best goalie. He had all the equipment, and Paul Ewing was the best center. He could score at will, stick-handling the puck all the way down the ice. I am sure the great Wayne Gretzky was no better than Ewing at thirteen to fourteen years old.

When I was in third grade, I must have been cute because one of my classmates' sister from St. Mary's, the adjacent girls' academy, chased me down on the ice, knocked me down, jumped on top of me and proceeded to kiss me repeatedly while our third-grade nun stood nearby, watching with a smile on her face. I was helpless because my classmates held me down for the duration. The girl, maybe it was Linda Wells, broke a serious rule on the pond: boys on one side and girls on the other and rarely was that rule ever broken. The nuns usually strictly enforced it.

Sundays were always special days. For one thing, we had a full-length current movie every Sunday evening. One movie I do remember was *The Long Gray Line* about a boy in military school who got into trouble for contacting a girl at the nearby girls' academy, reported on himself, and was expelled. After seeing the movie, my good friend, Eugene Willis, reported on himself for doing the exact same thing and was expelled from the Hall just before eighth-grade graduation. There is a picture of me and Willis in our football uniforms in this chapter.

Also, in late morning, it was a full military review in our dress uniforms. There was usually a white-glove inspection of our lockers by the military commandant. He would usually reach into the highest shelf, running his gloved finger across the full length of the shelf. Any sign of dust would be serious demerits, maybe enough to cause a student to lose movie privileges that night. After inspections and full-dress review came visiting hours from 1:00 p.m. to usually 6:00 p.m.

My parents came to visit Tony and me just once per year; that was on Mother's Day. Mother's Day came on the second Sunday in May and was the school's biggest day of the year, the military review (like the annual tattoo in Edinburgh). Every class, first through the eighth participated in full dress review and marching competition. It took two to three hours of marching and standing at attention before it was over. It was the day for the entire school to show off what we learned about marching. The band was front and center as well as the special drill team with maneuvers with fake rifles. It was in 1954 on Mother's Day that I was recognized as honor corporal for the entire school. I was chosen as the best corporal out of more than thirty corporals schoolwide. That is the picture of me receiving the medal from Lieutenant Hyland, the commandant, on the cover of this book.

Since Mother's Day was the only time my parents came to visit and there was visiting every Sunday, that is if the students' parents could get to Monroe. Most students were from a reasonable driving distance; that's from Detroit, Toledo, and other towns within sixty to seventy miles of Monroe. Paul Hebert and Tim Gillett were from Mt. Clemens. Michael Day was from Cleveland, Mike Sweeney, and the Saab twins, Arthur and Allen, were from Toledo. Most of the students were from wealthy families. The wealthiest in my class was Everett Fisher from Detroit. His father was one of the "Fisher body" brothers, and his mom was part of the Briggs family. His mom's family-owned Briggs Stadium, later to be called Tiger Stadium. My classmates would invite me to join them and their family for dinner or some other outing nearly every Sunday. The Fishers would come in their Flying Dutchman, a first-class motor coach, the size of a Greyhound bus. It was always a memorable day when I'd get to ride around Monroe in the Flying Dutchman*.

One of the most accomplished graduates from the Hall of the Divine Child who I met in the '80s was Jay Wetzel. Mr. Wetzel was a 1950 graduate who was picked by General Motors' chairman, Roger Smith, to be the first Saturn employee. Jay told me he was allowed to select any seven leaders from sales, manufacturing, finance, market-

---

*   go to page 58

ing, research within GM, to assist him setting up the new Saturn car company in Tennessee.

As it happened, fresh out of Bowling Green University in 1991, my son, Stephen, was one of the first Saturn sales associates for Saturn of Plymouth. Jay Wetzel's Saturn car sold very well. Steve frequently was the lead salesperson, corporate-wide, even outselling Mary Wetzel (Jay's daughter), who was at a different Michigan dealership.

Perhaps the most popular students at HDC during my time were the Schoenith twins, Tom and Jerry. Their father, Joe, owned the Gail Electric Company, which sponsored the Gail hydroplane racing boats on the Detroit River. Later, their Roostertail Restaurant was a very popular spot for the Motown crowd, including the Supremes, Smokey Robinson, and Marvin Gaye.

In the summertime, some of these HDC families would visit our family farm in Roscommon some two hundred miles north of Monroe. My dad always enjoyed showing these rich city folks our flowing wells. One of the parents told my dad in 1955 that the artesian water tasted so good that he should bottle it and sell it to the folks in Detroit. My dad would laugh and go back to the barn and shovel some more manure, knowing that what he was doing was far more important than listening to the crazy city people. It would be another thirty years before Terry Maurer (me) would put the first of this most remarkable artesian water in a glass bottle and offer it for sale as deMaurier and later Avita.

In seventh grade, we were considered upperclassmen and could play on the varsity sports teams, if we were good enough to make the team. My brother and I both played varsity football. However, my most memorable year on the team was in eighth grade when HDC went undefeated again. Our 1955–1956 team was led by Paul Ewing as quarterback. I was first string left half back. I scored three touchdowns in one game against the weakest team in our CYO (Catholic Youth Organization) league, St. Michael's from Monroe. Even so I remember that Joe Turowski called me the hero of the game. Joe's gorgeous older sister had a date with Kirk Douglas on a vacation to Los Angeles in 1955. I don't remember the final score.

In another game that year against our toughest rival, Trenton, I made a game-saving tackle on defense. Here's what happened: we kicked off late in the game, and the biggest guy on Trenton's team received the ball and was speeding through all our defenders. There were two "deep" defenders, me at 4'10" and either 5'8" Gordon Rebresh or Willis between their goal line and a game-winning touchdown. I could see the Trenton fullback turn toward my side of the field at full speed. I knew our coaches, and everybody on the sideline was watching the action. There was no way that I could fake a tackle and lose the game, so I decided not to wait for the Trenton full-back to reach me. I ran full speed directly at him and left my feet and hit him like a torpedo in the midsection. He went down like a sack of potatoes. He couldn't believe that the little defender did not chicken out. Well, when I got to the sidelines, our coach was bragging to his assistant about the great tackle which Tom Kulick just made. Tom Kulick is just about my size, but it was my tackle, not Kulick's. Only my friends knew I saved the game, and I never told the coach it was me.

As an adult, Paul Ewing could play the piano like a concert pianist, and he was a very successful businessman in Detroit, manufacturing automotive and heavy equipment fasteners at his NSS Company. His wife, Mary Sue, sang for the Detroit Opera. They both entertained us at our home, Paul playing and Mary Sue singing. The music was remarkable.

Also, a turning point in my future education was developing for me during seventh grade. Ironically it involved a girl, Linda Wells, from St. Mary's Academy who saw me serving mass at the IHM Convent on Sunday and for all of the Academy girls, all four hundred of them at their chapel. As it happened Linda decided to send me a bracelet with both my and her name engraved on it. Now, it is true we never spoke to each other either before or after the gift. It was all about eye contact as I held the paten under her chin when I was the altar boy for Monsignor Marron at the girls' mass. The bracelet arrived in my hand through one of my classmates who had a sister in Linda's class at the Academy.

It was probably the next week that the new Mother Ursula, head nun, pulled me out of my seventh-grade religion class into the hallway, grabbing my wrist and my bracelet. She said, "You are being expelled from school for making contact with a girl from the Academy. The commandant will take you to the train depot this afternoon." I was shocked! She also said, "The girl has already been sent back to Ann Arbor, expelled, gone for the breaking this unholy rule about no contact between the boys and the girls." The new mother superior was making a statement, letting everyone know how tough she was. Much like Bowie Kuhn, commissioner of baseball, suspending Denny McClain in 1969. Go after the popular kid, and then everyone will fear you. It happens all over the animal kingdom.

Mother Ursula had to inform my brother that I was being sent home. The mother superior told me it would be later in the day before I would be taken to the depot. During that time, my brother Tony was able to convince this new disciplinarian that I should not be kicked out. What happened instead was a formal military court-martial. I got busted. Tony was on the battalion staff as a first lieutenant. The battalion staff was like the joint chiefs of staff in the real military, a big deal. So on the scheduled day, I appeared in front of this four-member group. A fellow named Valmassi was the chief of staff with my brother and two others. I remember Valmassi reading something about the bracelet from Linda Wells. I said something like "I didn't ask for it" and "never really met the girl." No luck, they told me that I broke the rule and my rank would go back to buck private. At least I was not kicked out of school. So although I was not happy that my own brother voted against me, it obviously was the best compromise and did stop the immediate expulsion. At Thanksgiving vacation that year, our friend Floyd Millikin gave Tony the raspberries for busting his own brother. That same day, my friend Paul Ewing also got court-martialed, and I learned later directly from Paul that it also had to do with a girl from the Academy who lived in Monroe.

My days and years at the Hall of the Divine Child Catholic Military School in Monroe, Michigan, were happy days. I had many good friends and got a good elementary education. The opportunity to play all the sports, learn to swim, and have picnics in the big woods and the little woods. I did not mind all the marching and day uniforms and Sunday dress uniforms. We were always told to wear our dress uniforms when we went to mass on Thanksgiving, Christmas, and Easter vacations in our hometowns. Maybe the uniform code was to advertise the school or so that we would not forget how to behave. The uniform has a way of improving one's behavior. My parents always, I am sure, were proud to show us off. Well, you can't blame them for that because we were only home for a short time during the nine months of the school calendar. It seemed we were forever catching the train, coming or going between Roscommon and Monroe.

Last-minute projects sometimes made us late for the midnight train out of Roscommon. On one particular vacation night, the steam engine was already about to pull out of our little village, population of 750 in 1955, when we arrived in a big hurry in Dad's old red GMC pickup. All five of us, Dad, Mom holding Louie, Tony, and I were in the one-seater. As we crossed the tracks in front of the train on Main Street, Dad said, "I think the train is starting to leave the station, you're going to miss the train unless I stop right here on the tracks."

Mom said, "You can't stop on the tracks!"

Dad stopped in the middle of the tracks anyway while the glaring light on the locomotive lit up the pickup. All the while, the steam engine's whistle was warning us to move off the tracks. Mom said, "What are you doing?"

Dad answered, "The train won't leave as long as the pickup is on the tracks. Boys, grab your suitcases and run with me to the depot!"

It was about forty yards away. That's what we did, hollering, all the time, our goodbyes to Mom and Louie, who we presumed would not stay in the truck*.

---

* A second 'Fisher Body' brother (Fred) married a sister to the Briggs sister I've already mentioned. This was told to me by my grand daughter's (Camille) baby sister (Ce-Ce Ramirez) in 2003. "Frequently it takes a large fortune to make a small fortune in the wine business". This is something I heard Thomas Shelton, then president of Joseph Phelps Winery and also my son-in-law say several times over the years. *Fred and his wife started the Fisher Winery in Napa Valley.*

Grandma Cherven, Terry, and Pauline at HDC.

When we finally got to the station, the train was nearly full of passengers. Tony, Pat Jansen's brother Charlie, and I finally boarded the midnight express. Pat Jansen was later to be Tony's first girlfriend when he finished eighth grade at the military school and started his freshman year at Grayling High School in 1956. That same year Elvis Presley made a hit with "Heartbreak Hotel." So Tony told me to take a seat by myself at the end of the first passenger car, and he would sit with the new kid, Jansen, in one of the first seats.

Terry Maurer, front row, second from right.

We were all showered and dressed up in our Sunday uniforms, looking like little soldiers. The shower was necessary because we had just finished helping Mom and Dad cut the heads off thirty to forty chickens and pluck all the feathers. Dad always had last-minute projects for Tony and me so as to get the final free labor out of us before returning to school. Now, back to finding my seat on the train, I proceeded to walk the length of the railroad car by myself, when coming to the end, I bumped into a very attractive young lady, probably eighteen to nineteen years old, talking to three or four of the train conductors who had time and were eager to visit with the young lady as the train was late departing (there was a truck on the track). Ignoring them, except for the enticing perfume, I squeezed by and took my seat alone. Now, I went to sleep almost immediately but woke up when we stopped in West Branch to pick up more passengers and more than likely drop off the cream cans for processing into butter at the local creamery. I thought I was in heaven, twelve-year-old heaven, because I found myself in the fragrant arms of the beautiful nineteen-year-old whom I had noticed as I took my seat.

I said to her, as we were face to face, that was the position I found myself, through no fault of my own, "How did you get into my seat?"

She answered in a low soft voice, "Well, when the train stopped in St. Helen, two nuns got on board, and they wanted to sit together, so I gave them my seat and came back to sit with you."

I said, "I'm thirsty."

The mirage beauty said, "I'll get you a drink."

So she got up, walked to the front of the train, got a paper cup of artesian water (at least it tasted like artesian water on that night), and brought it back to me. I asked her where she was going. She told me that she was a sophomore at Mary Grove College in Detroit and was returning back to school like me after the Christmas break.

She said, "Why don't we get back into our position?"

I never wanted to go to sleep, but I did. And I didn't want the train ride to end. But it did. Obviously, one remembers a train ride like that. I do remember the first popular song, which I really liked: It was "Why Do Fools Fall in Love?" by Frankie Lyman.

Toward the end of my eighth-grade year at HDC, I began to think of my future. Most of my classmates were talking about where they would go to high school, places like Marmion, the military high school where Eugene Willis actually did go and did exceedingly well,

Divine Child in Detroit, Assumption in Windsor, Canada, and of course Cooley and Denby. I am not sure when I thought about Holy Trinity for myself, but I do remember a missionary priest with a dramatic priestly habit, a wide cincture holding a large crucifix on the side, visiting our school in 1954, two years before my graduation. So I asked Father Bowers if he remembered the visit from the missionary priest from Alabama. He did and put me in touch with the religious order headquartered in Silver Springs, Maryland. It wasn't long before I got a visit from Father Doherty, the vocation director for the order. I was accepted to the minor seminary in Alabama and would start as a freshman in the 1956 class in the fall.

The summer of 1956, before beginning seminary in Alabama, is when I saved someone from drowning for the second time. This time it was my best friend Floyd Millikin, who we all knew could not swim. Floyd's neighbors, or rather his parents', Roy and Virginia's, neighbors, owned this little gas station with attached coffee and sandwich shop. A very common arrangement throughout Northern Michigan, and I believe throughout the country before the interstate highway system replaced those family businesses with McDonald's, Burger King, and others along the expressways. It was I-75 that changed our part of the country and not for the better, according to my dad. Well, the fellow who owned the station had a cute, thirteen-old-year daughter named Holly who lived down Fletcher Road. Holly had a friend named Bridgette. Both girls would go waterskiing while their dad piloted his speed boat on Higgins Lake.

On this particular summer day, the girls invited Floyd, Tony, and me to go skiing with them. Off we went, putting in near the B&B Marina on Higgins Lake's North Shore. Tony skied first, then I skied; all the while the two girls watched from the safety of the boat. Finally, Mr. Potts asked Floyd if he wanted to give it a try. I remember the last thing Floyd's mom, Virginia, said as we left her doorway, "Remember, Floyd can't swim, so he can't ski." Well, Floyd said he'd like a turn on the skis, and he did quite well getting up on the first attempt.

Now, I'm in the boat telling Mr. Potts, "Floyd can't swim, so just go straight so that he won't fall on the turn." He went straight all right, straight out into the dark-blue water and past the drop-off. When I noticed the color of the water, I said to Mr. Potts, "Holy cow, you better get back to shallow water, but make a slow turn, because Floyd might fall, and he can't swim and he doesn't have a life jacket." Just as soon as the turn started, Floyd fell off into Higgins Lake, past the drop-off where the water was easily one hundred feet deep.

Floyd and Tony in 1958.

Knowing Floyd couldn't swim, I immediately jumped off the boat, swimming toward Floyd as fast as I could. He was kicking himself back to the surface for the second or third time when I got to him. Immediately he grabbed on to me like I was a sturdy red pine. Down we both went with Floyd grabbing my arms, making it impossible for me to swim or help keep Floyd's head above water. Finally, I was ready to punch him in the mouth, hoping I'd knock him out (I heard once that this should be done). Then I heard Tony howling from the shallow waters to the screaming girls, "Throw them some seat cushions!" Mr. Potts had stalled his boat at least thirty yards from Floyd and me. He was pulling the starting rope repeatedly with no luck. It was the cushions and me dragging and talking to Floyd, "Hang on, hold on, we're almost to the boat" that kept him from going down for good. I am sure Floyd coughed up at least two liters of Higgins Lake. I think he learned to swim when he became a Michigan state trooper.

Hall of the Divine Child, Catholic Military boarding school.

The last graduating class of Holy Trinity, Alabama 1960. Back row: left to right, Carl Seeba, David Lopata, Wayne Putnam, Bruce Cummings, Rich Schoessow, Marty Hendricson. Front row: Pete Krebs, Clif Marquis, Roland Haag, Terry Maurer, Roger Skifton.

CHAPTER III

Holy Trinity, Alabama (1956–1961)

Dwight D. Eisenhower
(1953–1961)

Before the summer of 1956 was over, I was on the train heading south to Alabama. My mother, Pauline, went with me on the train as far as Chicago in late August that year. I was to be fourteen years old in another month on October 1. My mother had cousins in Chicago who invited her and me to stay the weekend with them as I waited to catch the midnight train to Georgia, (Columbus, Georgia). We had a great time in Chicago with my mother's cousins, Jack and Peppy Cerven, who had a beautiful brick house near Midway Airport on Wheeler Street. Their youngest daughter, Linda, was nine or ten years old and took me golfing for the first time in the playfield behind their home. We used a nine iron, which belonged to her middle sister, Cynthia's boyfriend. All three sisters, the oldest I think was away in college, were very pretty. They took after their mother, Peppy, I am quite sure. Jack was famous in the family for his musical ability. He played the banjo on a pogo stick with cymbals and bells on the top, a real one-man band. We visited Buckingham fountain on the shore of Lake Michigan in downtown Chicago. I remember there was a lady walking around the fountain with a pet skunk on a leash. The skunk drew a lot of attention especially from my mother, a northern woods lady, probably on her first visit to the big city of Chicago.

Actually, my mother's parents had once lived in Chicago, moving to Roscommon, Michigan, in 1902 for my grandfather Andrew Cherven's health. Andrew worked in the Chicago stockyards, and the doctors thought he should go north to get some fresh air to breathe. I never met him. I did meet my other grandparents. He died in 1940 from some breathing disorder. Uncle Frank was the only baby when they moved, but the fresh air must have been good for my maternal grandfather because nine more children were born in Roscommon.

The weekend came to an end, and my mother told me goodbye at Grand Central Station in Chicago. There were at least forty of us young seminarians boarding the train that day for the South. We were the boys from the Midwest, and we filled an entire private railcar. I had already said goodbye to my dad and brothers in Roscommon and now goodbye to my mother in Chicago as I boarded the train for the second half of the trip to Holy Trinity, also known as St. Joseph's Preparatory Seminary. There was another train car departing New York, stopping in Newark, Trenton, Philly, Baltimore, and Washington, picking up the seminarians from the eastern part of the country, including Ed Murphy, Jim Gillin, John Cox, Jim Weighorst, and Tom Farrell. There would be others converging on Holy Trinity from some of the Southern states. Will Booth from Mississippi, Carl Seeba from Dothan, Alabama, the Evans brothers from Birmingham. In my first year, I am sure, there were twenty states represented out of the approximately 120 students.

We all expected to become missionary priests with a mission to assist the rural black people in the Southern half of the US. This was the master plan laid out by the founder of the religious order, Missionary Servants of the Most Holy Trinity, Father Thomas Augustine Judge.

I read the book *The Flight of the Enola Gay* by Paul W. Tibbets, written in 1989. Colonel Tibbets, on the morning of August 6, 1945, flew the Enola Gay (a B-29 bomber), dropping the world's first atomic bomb on Hiroshima. This ended World War II. What amazed me is that Colonel Tibbets was married in 1938 at my seminary in Holy Trinity.

Quoting directly from his book, "The ceremony took place on the evening of June 19 at a Catholic seminary in the village of Holy Trinity, Alabama, a short distance southwest of the Fort Benning reservation on the opposite side of the Chattahoochee River. Although nominally a protestant, I was not a practicing churchgoer. Lucy was a Catholic (from Columbus, Georgia)." It's very likely that Colonel Tibbets was married by Father Judge himself.

Sometime after Vatican II (1963) and the worldwide convocation of bishops and cardinals, most of the minor seminaries were closed. This minor seminary was no exception, closing its doors I believe in the mid-'70s. I myself was one of thirty-two boys beginning this religious experience in 1956 and finally leaving the seminary after my first year of college in 1961. I am not sure exactly why I started the journey toward priesthood. We were recruited, much like young people were recruited to the Peace Corps by John Kennedy. It was a higher calling, we were told. The short film *Going My Way*, shown at the military school depicting Frank Walsh, a young seminarian, going through a typical day in Holy Trinity, did have an influence on me, and I suppose many of the other recruits.

We were a little young to consider fully the choice we were making. It gave us all a purpose, a noble career which most of our parents took pride in during the mid-'50s. Once admitted we were told, "Many are called, but few are chosen." So we all worked hard to be chosen. We did not want to leave nor to be asked to leave. Even now for me some fifty years after leaving, I tell people when the subject comes up, that I was one of the six originals still there at the time of my departure. Those from my class still in the seminary when I left were Pete Krebs, John Marquis, Bruce Cummings, David Lopata, and Roland Haag.

Holy Trinity, Alabama: chapel, library, dorms.

Twenty-six of my classmates were either asked to leave or left on their own before me. It was not a stigma to leave, at least not for long; it was also about bragging rights that you hung on longer than someone else. Pete Krebs and John Marquis were ordained in 1969. Two out of thirty-two is probably more than the average, completing the grueling thirteen years of training required. It was four years of high school, two years of college, one year of novitiate (where first vows are taken), two years of philosophy, and finally four years of theology.

Late August 1956 was just the beginning of what was to be the first of five years in the seminary for me. We arrived in Columbus, Georgia, early afternoon and boarded either an old school bus or open state truck for the trip to Holy Trinity crossing the Chattahoochee River into Phenix City then South on the Gerry Pruitt Highway through cotton fields and peanut fields some twenty miles to the entrance drive on the west side of the road up to the seminary campus. Most of the students knew each other from last year; we were the new guys and just soaked in the whole experience. The hot, humid summer weather felt strange to boys who had never seen cotton fields ready for the harvest or scrawny cattle scattered on sparse pasture fields with more red clay visible than green grass. We learned quickly that Attorney General Patterson of Alabama was murdered a year or two earlier for trying to clean up the red-light and gambling city of Phenix City. Phenix City was the sin city patronized by the regular army troops at nearby Fort Benning. There is a movie entitled *Phenix City* about the Paterson murder. We students did not have to worry much about any of that because we only got to town a couple times a year. We were isolated in the Alabama pines on about three hundred acres that had its own farm with milk, chickens, eggs, and beef.

Back in Michigan, Doc Godfroy and my dad had 640 acres to watch over. It wasn't all in one place. In fact, three different plots, much of it wooded, which my dad was always trying to clear. The smaller plot of sixty acres on the west side of military road (now Wellington Farms) was mostly wooded. Dad was determined to clear it, and all that remained in the summer of 1956 were about six large stump piles waiting to be torched. I was there with Dad going from one pile to the next, dozing them with the mixture of gasoline and oil from a five-gallon can. After all were lit and burning, we were returning to each pile, hitting them with a little extra petrol. Well, we got too close to the fire, and the gas and oil can caught fire in my dad's hands.

As I saw it now burning like a blowtorch, I began to run for my life, expecting an explosion. I stumbled and fell in the dirt, looking back while trying to put distance between me and the burning can still in my dad's hands. Then I saw Dad calmly remove his hat and placed it over the fiery spout, suffocating the fire. Now, I felt foolish and embarrassed at my rapid departure. As I sheepishly walked back, I asked Dad, "Weren't you afraid that the gas can would explode?"

Dad said, "Yes. I thought it might, but I couldn't take a chance, it was my last can of gas."

Although the seminary farms reminded me of our family farms in the Roscommon-Grayling area, there was one major difference: In Michigan, my dad had us picking acres of sweet corn. Here in Alabama, the seminary had us all picking peanuts. The school had at least fifty acres of peanuts, and we were all (120 of us) required to work the peanut fields for a full week. We pulled the loosened peanuts clinging on vines like potatoes, shook off the red-dry clay, and wrapped the vines, peanuts to the outside, around ten-foot pea-nut polls: These days combining driers and shakers do it all. All the while Father Norbert would jump from row to row barking "Hubba, hubba" to keep us picking in the Alabama heat.

On our first trip back to Columbus, Georgia, for Christmas shopping, Columbus, because Phenix City had no real shopping area, just closed-down bars and brothels. The persistent prejudice toward Southern blacks became clear to me as I was drinking from the foun-tain at the Greyhound bus station when a stranger slapped me on the shoulder and said, "Can't you read, boy?" I had no idea why he said that until I looked up and read the sign above the fountain: "colored only." The guy informing me of my mistake was white, and I guess he wanted to be sure that the "colored" would not see me at the wrong fountain lest they might try the water at the "whites only" fountain. I remember thinking that water from a "colored only" tasted exactly the same as the "whites only" fountain, and both tasted very much like the artesian from our flowing wells at home in Michigan.

Klu Klux Klan burnt cross. Terry and Jim Weighorst in 1956.

One night in 1957, the Klu Klux Klan burned an eight-foot cross on the seminary grounds. The Klan did not like "colored" folks, nor did they like Catholics helping out the impoverished blacks; our mission was to do just that. There is a picture of me holding the burnt cross in this chapter. I was not aware of any other issues like this during my four years in Alabama. However, even now in 2014, one African American writer for *USA Today*, Adrienne Thompson, laments, "Being black in America is like walking through an ice storm. It's cold, isolating and exhausting. You're not sure if you're gonna make it, and you can't see what's coming for you."

Quickly we settled into the seminary routine. It was all about studies and prayer time. The necessities of food, hygiene, and recreation were mixed in. Latin was king at the seminary. It seemed that nothing was more important. Before it was over, those of us who survived for five years had translated Caesar, Cicero, Virgil, and Homer. I spent at least 40–50 percent of my study time in Latin. It didn't come easy for me; only Cummings, Marquis, Haag, Krebs, and Lopata, who had to work harder than the first four seemed to enjoy it. I was sure it nearly caused Wayne Carlson to have a nervous breakdown; at least I did notice a nervous twitch. If I had spent as much time studying math as I did Latin, I might have given Anthony Zuppero a run for his money. Anthony Zuppero was two years behind me and was recognized in 1958 as probably the brightest mind in the seminary.

We all thought he was balancing some kind of equations in his head as he walked from dormitory to chapel to refectory. I learned twenty years later that he got a doctorate in nuclear physics and was working for the jet propulsion labs in New Mexico. This was told to me in 1974 by Bill Saas, my big boss at Lubrizol, then R. O. Hull Company in Cleveland. One day Bill Saas asked me where I went to high school, and I said "Holy Trinity, Alabama." He said that his mentor when he was getting his PhD in chemistry from John Carroll went to a private school in Alabama. He said that although this guy was several years younger than himself, he was the smartest guy he ever knew. I said, "That must have been Tony Zuppero." Bill Sass couldn't believe that I knew Tony Zuppero and further that everyone at Holy Trinity recognized Anthony Zuppero's intellect. Now, fifty-two years later Dr. Zuppero and I have exchanged a few emails. Here is one of them:

To: Avitawater
Subject: Hydrogenics Corp Splitting Water Date: Friday, November 12, 2010,

Hi Terry Maurer; Anthony Zuppero here, one time Holy Trinity, Alabama, part time resident, back during the late 1950's. Much older now. Yes, Brother Carlos on occasion communicates with me. When I picture either him or you, I see those young boys in Alabama, not us old codgers.

Thank you for thinking of me. No, the NASA project was not mine. The fuel cell project was not mine. But I still keep things in the fire that give me a 0.1% chance of being a trillionaire someday. I thought I was "retired," but just today someone else gave me money to do another patent. When we opened the account at a bank the lady asked me if I were employed. I said, "yes," for the first time in a long time, it sure felt different. The venture I co-founded back in 1999 "employed" me as our own CTO. But I never thought of it as "employment." During 20071 "retired." I had to abandon the "fuel cell" work because the required technology elements just would not work out. Then I took the bar exam to prosecute patents. See http:// neofuel. com/space for visions of sugar plums and trillion-naires, and http://neofuel. com/patents for free patent advice.

The "hydrogen water splitting energy" game seems to be quite limited by a simple tech-nical obstacle: hydrogen storage capacity per pound hydrogen or per cubic meter is simply inadequate for transportation purposes. I could not help perusing the titles of the other articles. What do you think about gold or about Obama's "one world economy"? If you need a patent, I can do it. I am picky about what I choose to do.

Students at Holy Trinity got to go home for summer vaca-tions only. We were nine months away at a time. We celebrated Thanksgiving, Christmas, and Easter at the school. We always got fed well; the head cooks were old-maid sisters from Minnesota. They had plenty of help from the local black ladies from the area. I still believe that if I had gotten the recipe for their pineapple cheesecake, I could have given Marie Callender a real run for her money. Those pies were so good, students would trade three or four future desserts for a second piece of the pineapple cheesecake.

One of our favorite priest teachers was Father Brendan. I remember Father Brendan from 1956 to 1960 as our assistant prefect at Holy Trinity. Father could always be seen carrying stacks of ungraded English papers all awry. I saw him many times working late into the night on his hands and knees, painting the finishing touches on the large backdrops for the play he was directing whether it be *My Fair Lady* or *The Cain Mutiny*. On February 3, 1959 (my junior year), Father Brendan came to our evening study period with alarming news. He told Jim Weighorst and me that Buddy Holly, the Big Bopper, and Richie Valens had all died together in a single-engine plane crash in an Iowa snowstorm. Father Brendan knew that even in the seminary. Jim was a dedicated fan of all three young singing stars. I knew of Peggy Sue, Chantilly Lace, and Donna, but Father Brendan knew this news would be hard for Jim to swallow and made a special effort to tell him immediately. Don McLean's "The Day the Music Died" in 1971 (*American Pie*) immortalized these three music legends.

It was in the second summer of my seminary years (1958) that my dad ran over me with the combine. He wasn't trying to do it. It was an accident. I was helping combine the oats on the field next to the flowing wells. We had a John Deere model B tractor with a new John Deere pull-behind combine. I was riding on the tractor, standing on the right side of the driver's seat. Dad asked me to jump off and see if we had enough room in the hopper to make another trip around the field. He was making a slow turn to the left when I got off the moving tractor, stepping to the ground, and stepped up on the rail of the combine hooked to the tractor. I was fifteen, almost sixteen, and athletic. It did not require much skill to do what I was about to do. As I reached up to grab onto a steel rod near the hopper while at the same time stepping onto the rail pulling the combine, my foot slipped off the rail and right in front of the moving tire. The ground was wet at the edge of the field near the swamp and the springs. I still had a hold of the rod with my right hand and figured that my dad was watching me and would stop the tractor.

He did not stop because he was watching his turn. As I was being stretched like on a medieval rack, I had to let go with my right hand as the tire was running over my right foot. I immediately fell backward, landing on my back with a good view of the approaching tire moving up my right leg heading for my head. I still thought my dad was going to stop as the tire kept coming. He did not stop. The tire ran the entire length of my right leg as I turned my head in what I believe turned out to be the wrong direction because now the tire was on my chest and finished by crossing over my left shoulder. I thought, *This is the end of me.* Once the tire was off, I immediately jumped to my feet to let my dad know I was okay. I saw him stopping the tractor as I fell back to the ground. I got up for the second time before falling this time into my dad's arms. He carried me to the pickup truck, loaded with bags of grain, threw me on the burlap, and headed for the house some three hundred yards up the lane.

When we got near the house, he jumped out, hollering to my mother inside that he had just run over Terry. I thought I was dying because of the pain. I also heard him say that he was going to get my great uncle Lenus who could drive me to the hospital. Uncle Lenus, who normally only came north from Nashville, Michigan, for deer season, was spending the summer with us working on an addition to our big barn. My mother started to scream and run down the field pulling my little brother Louie as she ran. She thought I was squashed all flat by the combine. I couldn't shout to say that I was on the back of the truck because of the pain in my chest.

When my dad came back to me with Lenus and his old Chevy, which he never drove faster than thirty-five miles per hour, my mother was down the field. Then I heard my dad start to yell at my mother. She was hysterical by now, then I heard my dad slap her to calm her down. More screaming, I felt so sorry for my mother, but I could not move. Finally we all five were into Uncle Lenus's car. Lenus behind the wheel, my mother in the middle holding six-year-old Louie, and my dad riding shotgun, and me laid out in the back seat moaning. Grayling Mercy Hospital was ten miles away. Three miles on bumpy gravel roads and seven miles on old tarmac.

As we drove and hit the bumps, the pain was nearly unbearable, and I was sure I'd be dead before we got there. The more I moaned, the faster Dad wanted Lenus to go, and the faster Lenus drove, and the more my mother thought we were going to crash and all die. I was amazed when we pulled up to the old hospital. With no red emergency entrance like today, somehow I found myself on a stretcher as I heard somebody telling me the priest was on his way. I didn't want a priest; I wanted a doctor to save me. However, Father Grill from Roscommon arrived before the doctor and wanted to hear my last confession and give me last rites. I think Dr. Dosch arrived before the last rites were given. X-rays were taken, and the doctor told me that I had fractured some ribs, but he was quite sure I would live.

I was excited to live and to start my third year in the seminary. I actually didn't get over the broken ribs from the John Deere combine accident until about November of that year. But ribs do heal, and eventually I never thought about it again.

Esau's grandson riding his mule. Esau was the seminary's custodian.

The third year was all about translating Cicero and now our first year of French with Father Sebastian. His nickname was Slush because if you were in the front row you would get spit on as Father Sebastian enunciated the language. We were upperclassmen now, not yet seniors, but we did command quite a bit of respect from the freshmen and sophomores. Marty Hendrickson was our ace basketball player Bouncie-Bouncie as Father Sebastian liked to call the game. Father liked golf and even built his own putting green near the refectory. As more adventurous juniors, our hikes to the Chattahoochee were more frequent and longer. We had more members on the student body softball team when we played the faculty in the annual Turkey Bowl. It was the Cobras versus the Tigers. The students were the Cobras. I myself always made the team usually playing second base or shortstop.

The school day was something like this: Up at 5:30 a.m., rain or shine. In chapel for morning prayers and daily mass at 6:00 a.m. We always had a half hour of meditation before mass. Many of us took this time to catch up on our sleep. Breakfast at 7:30 a.m. Back to the chapel for fifteen minutes of prayers before morning chores. Morning chores could be a variety of things. Everyone had a job: Maybe cleaning the jakes (actually toilets), sweeping the floors, doing the dishes, gardening, moving the laundry (one of my jobs), whatever was needed to be done keeping the place clean. Classes started at 9:00 a.m., then back to the chapel again for fifteen minutes after lunch, then back to classes for the afternoon. Finally two hours of free time at 3:00 p.m. Back to chapel again at 5:30 p.m. for fifteen minutes before dinner. Then chapel again, more prayers, before thirty minutes more free time, ahead of evening study at 7:00 p.m. Study was over at 9:00 p.m., then back to chapel for a final evening prayer before heading for the Spartan dorms for bed. We spent so much time on our knees that we all got "chapel knees" from the hard wooden kneelers. Chapel knee is a callus about two inches square. The basketball team from Phenix City knew the seminarians by our knees.

As I am writing today on January 17, 2011, I realize that today would be my dad's ninety-sixth birthday. My dad, Bernard Maurer, was always proud of what I was doing. I could feel it when in military school, then in seminary, and then later, he followed my business career and my family. Well, happy ninety-sixth, Dad!

Mary Ann and I had a great breakfast brunch at the Brix Restaurant in St. Helena with our new friends from Grace Episcopal Church out here, Chuck and Jan McKinnon. Chuck is the father of our old neighbor, also Chuck McKinnon, from Ann Arbor back in 1971, that is a story in itself. Mr. McKinnon will turn ninety-five years old on March 9 this year. He was chief corporate pilot for IBM from 1964 to 1971. He is credited for keeping the old French airport, Le Bourget, open when the new Charles de Gaulle Airport was built. The French government wanted to close Le Bourget Airport, but Mr. McKinnon told Tom Watson, president of IBM, that he would have to move the IBM planes to Germany or Switzerland if Le Bourget were to be closed. Tom Watson then said he'd have to move the entire seven hundred IBM personnel out of Paris to be near the IBM planes. The end result was that the old airport (Lindbergh landed at Le Bourget) was kept open because the French government did not want to lose seven hundred high-paying IBM jobs in Paris. This year Chuck McKinnon was recognized and given credit by the French government for keeping Le Bourget open. My dad would be the same age as Mr. McKinnon now, and I really enjoy the stories coming from that generation.

Also today, my old seminary friend, Ed Murphy, who now lives in Berkeley, California, not far from the Napa Valley, called to say he will be coming up for a visit and some wine tasting. Murphy and I have been in contact ever since 1956, my first year in Alabama, but this visit he'll be bringing one of his old classmates and former priest, Jim Gillin. I am looking forward to seeing Jim again; the last time was fifty years ago. Jim lives in Portland. Ed Murphy is organizing a get together of more Holy Trinity classmates for the fall of 2015 on the East Coast. Likely to attend are Murphy, Joe Brooks, Father Charlie Gordon, Jim Gillin, the famous New Orleans attorney George Parnam, Bill Daack, Bill Murphy, Degnan, Fr. Pete Krebs, and me. This group may rendezvous with classmates three years behind, including Joe Apollo, Paul Hendrickson (the renowned author), Joe Schaeffer, Bob Rink, and perhaps others who will have their own Holy Trinity reunion on the Jersey shore at the same time.

Back in 1959, the summer of my junior year while still in the seminary, we would finish school the first week in June, and we were always reminded by some faculty member, not to forget our "vocation." They wanted to see us back again in the fall. That meant, don't get to close to any of the girls we might meet while on summer vacation. Well, that's like the baseball coach telling his pitcher,

"Whatever you do, don't throw him a high outside pitch." That's the last thing the pitcher heard, and that's exactly what he threw. The batter knocked it out of the park. So what do you think happened to many of the seminarians? They met a girl and I was no different.

Her name was Pat Thrush, and I met her on the next to the last Saturday before returning to Holy Trinity for my senior year. We met at the famous Music Box hangout in Prudenville, Michigan. There was no more popular place for young people to go for at least a sixty-mile radius of Prudenville in the early '50s through the mid-'60s. On a Labor Day weekend, they could pack at least two thousand hot-blooded teenagers in the complex. All records, no alcohol, just music, music, music, music, and for us guys, just girls, girls, girls. That's where I met her. Two enchanted evenings were enough to fill my head for the next nine months as I wrestled with my studies of Latin, French, English, and advanced algebra, and dreamed of becoming a missionary priest who would take the vows of poverty, chastity, and obedience. The middle one meant no getting married.

I got Pat's "Dear John" letter around Eastertime in 1960. We were able to exchange secret letters hidden in packages. Packages from home were never opened, but letters were always prescreened and read by the prefect. Pat sent me many packages with her letters and pictures of herself. Brother Antone, the seminary shopper, would drop my return letters off on his weekly trips to Columbus, Georgia. He understood my thorn-bird romance. A few of my classmates were also aware: John Marquis and Dave Lopata, and maybe Skifton. Marquis would always make a big deal in French class when the word for bird, namely *oiseau*, would come up.

Thrush is a bird for those who don't know. He'd clear his throat and say "oiseau, oiseau" and look in my direction. Pat's letter didn't surprise me too much. Nonetheless, I can't say that I was happy about it. She said she'd had no dates in her senior year since she'd met me. She was a pretty cheerleader and popular, I knew. In an early letter she said, "I am chairman of the senior class float, so I'll be busy now. We have to start working on it right away. I don't know where I'm going to get the idea, but the theme is "Some Enchanted Evening." She was finally convinced I was not going to leave the seminary for her and obviously threw in the towel. I hadn't crossed that bridge yet myself. Pat made the decision for me. It made it easier for me to mentally prepare for my first year in college. Now only two years from taking temporary vows.

Saint Joseph Preparatory Seminary
of the Most Holy Trinity, Alabama

June 16, 1960

Dear Terry,

May the grace and peace of the
Holy Ghost be with us forever.

Fr. Thomas asked us to write you and let you know that the summer Latin will be given by Father Vincent at Holy Trinity Mission Seminary, Winchester Virginia, beginning on Thursday July 7th. It would be best for you to arrive there on Wednesday, July 6th, and plan on going directly to the new Seminary at Monroe when the classes are over.

I'm sorry for the delay in writing you, but I was away on retreat last week, and now we are in the midst of priest retreat here in Holy Trinity. The weather is quite warm, but all is going well in spite of it.

Hoping you have a very enjoyable vacation, and looking forward to seeing you.

In the Most Holy Trinity
Father Killian

P.S. I'm enclosing the address and telephone number of Holy Trinity Seminary.

The summer of 1960 was a short one. My family had moved from the Godfroy Farm with the artesian wells to the four-mile road farm closer to Grayling and civilization. I struggled with my first year of Greek and was required to go to summer school in late July in Winchester, Virginia, for more Greek and Latin.

My new friend and golfing buddy, W. Larry Richards' textbook entitled *Read Greek in 30 Days* would have made Greek much easier for me. Larry hadn't written his book yet, back in 1960. Larry and I met in St. Helena, California, in 2012. So Father Vincent would be teaching, and a couple of other struggling Latin scholars, Fred Horac and Bob Dunne, would be joining me.

No time to think much about the *oiseau* and for sure not enough time to drive to her famous address at 327 Allen Street in a town to remain anonymous—no need anyway since Pat Thrush had told me in her last letter that she would be getting married soon. My cousins Jerry and John Friday drove me all the way from Grayling, Michigan, to Winchester, Virginia. I was now totally refocused on my vocation and ready to go all the way. Summer school was not so challenging, and I enjoyed the major seminarians who were in Winchester (a civil war town) and no longer got summers off. These were the upper-classmen who were three or four years ahead of me but who I knew quite well from earlier days in Alabama. Guys like Bill Reigh, maybe Dick Ort, Neusil, John Dono, Tex Wiltrakis, and others who would have graduated high school in '55, '56, and '57 from Holy Trinity.

In late August, we were on our way to Monroe, Virginia. Monroe was the brand-new, state-of-the-art minor seminary in the foothills of the famous Blue Ridge Mountains. My graduating class of 1960 from Holy Trinity would be the first seminarians to lay eyes on this dream place with an Olympic-size swimming pool and new everything—new beds, new sheets, new dishes, new chapel, new chemistry labs, new track and ball diamonds.

Switching locations from Holy Trinity, Alabama, to Monroe, Virginia, was like going from my familiar hometown to the other end of the world. In the one year, I was there it was impossible to duplicate the character and history that was Holy Trinity. In fact St. Joseph's in Monroe never stayed open long enough to develop its own mystique. The changes in the Catholic Church brought on by Vatican II called by Pope John XXIII, forced the early closure of St. Joseph's in Monroe, but also probably every other minor seminary and most convents in the US. History will show that these changes in the church undermined the moral compass of the United States and other countries as well. Fewer good priests and nuns meant fewer parochial schools, which resulted in a decline in ethics and morals in the broader population. It's logic. No matter, I chose on my own not to return for my last year in the minor seminary after one year of college in Monroe. Not girls, just a sense that I did not want to continue in the same direction.

When I left the seminary, there were five remaining of my original class of thirty-two, and of those five, only Pete Krebs and Clif Marquis were ordained priests in 1969 and still are active in their vocations in 2011. Pete in Sterling, New Jersey, and Clif (John to me) in Holy Trinity, Alabama.

I recommend the book *Seminary* written by Paul Hendrickson. Paul was my classmate Marty's younger brother, and he is an award-winning author. In *Seminary*, Paul writes about his seminary days at both Holy Trinity, Alabama, and Monroe, Virginia. I know all the players in his book, both the students and the priests who taught us.

Also by Paul Hendrickson: *Looking for the Light: The Hidden Life and Art of Marion Post Wolcott; The Living and the Dead: Robert McNamara and Five Lives of a Lost War; Sons of Mississippi: A Story of Race and Its Legacy; Hemingway's Boat: Everything He Loved in Life, and Lost, 1934–1961.* And now, Paul Hendrickson's latest book: *Plagued by Fire The Dreams and Furies of Frank Lloyd Wright.*

Here is what the Spes Gregis yearbook had to say about me at the end of each of my five years at Holy Trinity. First year was '56–'57.

Holy Trinity, Alabama

In the "Spes Gregis" ("Hope of the Flock") Yearbook, the editors always included a brief write-up of each student. Here is what was said about me each year.

Freshmen 1957

Terry Maurer, from Roscommon, Michigan, came to Holy Trinity from a military school and is forever being kidded about it. The school must have done much for him because Terry is an all-around athlete and has a fine personality along with above-average scholastic abilities.

Sophomores 1958

"Let's take a walk down to the rec rooms, Perry." "Sure. That ought to be fun." Here we are—right in the middle of a ping-pong tournament with Mike King, "Killer King" at the ping-pong table, facing his worthy opponent, Terry Maurer. They seem to be having quite a time of it too. Mike hails from Minneapolis, and is a member of the Craft Club and also a fan of billiards, swimming and volleyball.

Terry Maurer was our representative to the Varsity Baseball Team last year. We hope he will be the second bagger again this year. "I'm sure he will," says Perry Winkle. Terry also is hep when it comes to his studies.

Juniors 1959

So that everything stays "ship shape," the fleet has employed Terry Maurer to take care of the ship's laundry. Terry is such an eager beaver and works so hard that when he is down at the laundry room, one can hardly tell the difference between him and the people who actually do the washing. Moreover, Terry loves to have a good time and usually finds some way to have one. As a matter of fact, he has his best times during Major Silence. Terry is not as lucky as Jim; so he has had the unfortunate experience of getting caught. Getting apprehended usually produces sympathy from the remaining ship's company, but in Terry's case the fella he dragged with him gets all the sympathy. It seems that Terry cannot get into trouble without dragging someone with him. He hates to be alone. A word to the wise is sufficient: "If you want to have Saturday afternoon free, when the bell rings for silence, keep away from Terry."

Seniors 1960

Terry Maurer halts to adjust the handkerchief in his lapel pocket before joining the others. The Trojans always were sure that dependable Gyans would be surging ahead against their foes in battle. The seniors always are sure that Terry Maurer will surge ahead against his foes in softball or any sports event. Terry possesses a keen ability to play sports. He also has a quality for enkindling his enthusiasm into his other classmates. Terry has always been a valuable asset to any senior project. On this graduating morning, Terry's spark again adds zest to the lively song.

First Year College 1961,
Monroe, Virginia

To John's right, there stands with wide-eyed amazement Terry Maurer: Terry, too, has drifted down amid that sweeping snow storm of 1956 from the North. He had come as a frigid rain to harden the soul of our class which was so fresh and young. He did this, and is still doing so by putting forth his very all when he is called to the saws or to be our athletic standby. He is considered tops not only while on the diving board, but also on the basketball court. On the other hand, Terry is invariably standing in wait for any information asked him, whether it be on any advancement made by the Kennedy Administration or on a future test. It is a disposition such as Terry's that safeguards the fundamental factors in the class's unity by not allowing a speck of dirt, the tiniest speck of impurities from dissolving its united strength. Someone has just entered the room from which John and Terry were looking out the window. He seems to have doubt on his face as Terry tells him of the snow. But no, one glance and a smile instantly registers on his face. This is Roland Haag. Rol's fifth year was much similar to the preceding four; he is continually...

Recently, I came across a letter to me from Fr. John Dono, an upper-classmate of mine from the Holy Trinity days. John was the student dean of the college in 1957. I am not sure why Father. Dono wrote to me in 1984, but his letter, here in his own handwriting, tells a lot about the priests and members of the religious order to which I was connected for five years.

September 7, 1984
Shrine of Saint Joseph

Derry Terry,

May the Grace and peace of the Holy Spirit be with us forever.

What can I say except, "thank God!" After thirty-two years in the South I have now been given my first assignment up north. I must say, I found the Holy Spirit in Dixie and I shall always treasure my spirit-filled friends—South of the Mason Dixon line.

But I was born North and this is when mom, dad, and the family live. So in real sense I am home.

I praise the Lord Jesus for years, Terry. You are special in my life. A blessing to me! I love to pray and I like to be around Holy people. On vacations I seek out holy people and places. So you can imagine how privileged I feel to be assigned to work at a shrine and "what a shrine"!

The beauty, peace, joy, and quiet that's here. Wow! I have always believed God called me to be a priest the main reason so I won't quite get into so much trouble. How God has brought me to a shrine so I can become holy. He really is a loving Father.

St Joseph Shrine was started by our founder, Father Thomas Augustine Judge in May 4. He spent much time here. Another reason this is a holy place. (thank you Lord for allowing me to walk in His footsteps!)

The Shrine is perched on top of a high hill and the view from the chapel is magnificent spell finding and breathe taking. The words of a song came to my mind. "How they sing my soul, my savior God, to thee how great thou art, how great thou art!" You have to see this place! (All this and heaven too!! Thank you Jesus!)

And the people I live with are too much; priests, brothers and sisters, cheerful and spirit filled. Their names sound like a litany of saints.

Father __ Fr. Stephen or Philip, Fr. Peter, Fr. Frederick, Brother Martin, Brother Paul, Sister Anna, Sr. Agnes, Sr Irene, Sr Sophia, Fr. Norbert, Fr. Brendon, Fr. Vincent. I am compelled to say "pray for us" after each name. Truly I live among saintly people. Pray some of it rubs off on me.

You are on my mind and in my prayer today. Thank you for being my friend. Let me know if I can do anything for you!

> Your Priest—Brethren in the Most Holy
> Trinity with love and a Blessing
>
> Fr. Abraham Dono S.T.

P.S. Terry, you have been on my mind lately. I pray you, your wife and family are well. I am and I hope we can establish some kind of communication. You are a great man. Come see me if you can. God loves and blesses you.

Finally, I've included several emails exchanged between my Holy Trinity classmates (1960), Fr. Clif Marquis, Fr. Pete Krebs, and me. The first email from July 14, 2009, tells about Father Clif's fortieth anniversary of his ordination and the exchange in July 2012 discusses a reunion, which took place in Holy Trinity, Alabama, as Father Clif and I discussed several of our old classmates some fifty-two years after our high school graduation.

> First email dated July 14, 2009
> From Clif Marquis
> Re: HT reunion this weekend in Alabama

On Sunday 7 June, 2009, Fr. Clif Marquis, S.T., celebrated his 40th anniversary as a Missionary Servant of the Most Holy Trinity priest with a Mass of thanksgiving at St. Joseph's Parish in Holy Trinity, Alabama.

Fr. Bertin Glennon, S.T., was the homilist. Other guests included Missionary Servants Victor Seidel, David Sommer, David Hamm and Guy Wilson as well as family members and childhood friends from Illinois, Nebraska and Colorado. Terry Maurer, classmate of Fr. Clif's graduating high school together from St. Josephs's in Holy Trinity in 1960 and his wife, Mary Ann, from Michigan made the trip. Over forty parishioners from St. Mary's Parish in Americus, Georgia, where Fr. Clif had most recently served as pastor, also joined him to celebrate.

Chaplain Thomas Taylor and Warden Swinton, their wives, and other staff members from the Stewart Detention Center in Lumpkin, Georgia also shared in the Eucharistic celebration as well as the fiesta following Mass. Chaplain Taylor recently retired from his position at Stewart, and now Fr. Clif is the chief chaplain for the almost 2,000 mainly Latin American immigrants awaiting deportation.

Following the Mass there was a beautiful banquet prepared by the members of St. Joseph Parish and an official "roast" of Fr. Cliff.

Second email dated July 14, 2012
From Fr. Clif Marquis
Hi Terry,

Your choice was right. The men here are way behind "our time." Mike Keon is here and his classmates, Jerry Cieslinski and Tex Wiltrakis. I have seen Tex a couple of other times because of Sr. Christine, M.S.B.T. is his younger sister.

Haven't seen Jerry since '64 or '65 when he left from Winchester Mike Keon left from Novitiate. Today I am giving a brief presentation on deportation ministry and Rudy Breunig (Wisconsin) is talking about he developing apostolate to Hispanics in the Deep South.

Terry, Father Vincent, and Father Breunig in front of Father Judge. Portrait in 1990.

Third email dated July 16, 2012, 4:30 PM
From Terry Maurer
To Fr. Clif Marquis

Thanks so much John! I know you as both John and Clif. I have a photo of myself with Rudy Breunig and Fr. Vincent taken around 1990. I will try to copy it and send to you. Deportation ministry sounds very interesting. I expect that some of our high graduation class of 1960 would try to contact you. Lopata, Skifton, Seeba, Cummings, Haag, Maurer, Marquis, Krebs, Hendrickson, Putnam, Schoesow, I know I am missing at least one. Maybe Fisher or Alan Preuss. Just joking about the last two. Does Cieslinski still live in Michigan? Later, Terry Maurer.

Fourth email dated July 16, 2012
From Fr. Clif Marquis
Hi Terry,

Just for the record Bruce Cummings and Dave Lopata not only do not make contact, they avoid it. Joe Murphy ran into Bruce at a D.C. Sports event and Bruce made it clear he was not interested. I was part of that "classmates" group and wrote to Dave a couple of times and he never responded. Bertin Glennon ran into Dave at a psychologists' gathering and Dave was not responsive. Marty Mayer left just before our graduation and he does not make contact either.

Marty Hendrickson and his mother visited me in Americus, Georgia once when I was pastor there and then nothing. I have tried to find Skifton and Haag without luck. Carl Seeba apparently does not live in Dothan anymore. He is not part of the parish. I asked.

Jerry Cieslinski and his wife live in Texas!!! Tex Wiltrakis and wife live in St. Louis.

John

From: Fr. Peter J. Krebs
To: Terry Maurer
Date: Jan 12, 2015
Terry:

So good to hear from you. I can't believe it is almost 25 years since we have seen each other We have a lot of catching up to do!!!

I am doing a "contemplative sabbatical" and really enjoying and benefiting from it. I am no longer at the Shrine—tough, at first, after 44 years—but then, as a song from our era puts it: "Put your hand in the hand of a Man from Galilee." I have been able to participate in many wonderful spiritual retreats and programs, some as far away as Ireland!

Also during this time I believe the Spirit is moving me to a new ministry. At this point I have called it "Sacred Thread Ministries." I believe, as we live our lives, and weave the particular textures of our journey, "God will provide the thread." The mission of Sacred Thread is to help people discover the "thread" God provides on all our journeys, assuring us of His steadfast presence. This ministry will be ever expanding by for now we will focus on spiritual guidance, as well as the training of spiritual guidances, retreats, parish missions, bereavement counseling etc. Where indicated I will include psychological therapy taking into account one's spirituality. Please keep this new work in your prayer and I will keep you posted.

I have bent your ear long enough but did want you to know a little bit about what is going on for me and also how much I appreciated your email. Let's keep it going.

Be well and at peace in God's steadfast love,

Pete

From: Terry Maurer
To: Fr. Peter J Krebs
Date: January 22, 2015

Good morning Pete! Great to hear from you as well!!! Very happy to hear about your new ministry ("Sacred Thread Ministries"). It is a very important thing, "to get help on one's life Journey and to get help figuring out just what that journey is." My journey now has me in California six months out of the year. Mary Ann and I spend our winters out here near our oldest daughter, Laurie and her family (Trevor 23 who is studying in Paris and Camille who is 13 going to a Benedictine school in Palo Alto). Our son Stephen and his wife Nicole and three daughters (Brianna 16, Alison 13, Colette 9) live near Ann Arbor. Also our single daughter, Karin lives in Ann Arbor. I have just finished writing my memoirs (4 years and 13 chapters). This for the benefit of my great-grandchildren someday. I will get into a final book by the end of April this year. There is a chapter about Holy Trinity. I will save a copy for you. Weather here in Napa Valley is mid-'60s. I see it is cold out East. Later.

Terry Maurer

Holy Trinity School 1957 picture, Terry,
front row, middle, with white suit.

John Fitgerald Kennedy
35th President of the United States
Born May 29, 1917
Inaugurated January 20, 1961
Died November 22, 1963

CHAPTER IV

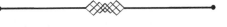

The Single Years (1961–1964)

John F. Kennedy
(1961–1963)

When I returned to Michigan in June 1961, things were changing for me and in the world. John Kennedy was still in his first year as the thirty-fifth president of the United States. Everyone in the country was excited about the future, even some who voted for Nixon. I was just as excited for my own future. I was nineteen and about to live at home again for the first time in eleven years. After six years in Catholic military boarding school and five years in seminary, I was about to be free, although I didn't know it yet in June 1961. Because I did not make the decision not to return to the seminary until the end of the summer.

So in June 1961, I got a summer job at the Mercy Hospital in Grayling. Sister Janice, the hospital administrator, thought that I would make a good orderly. An orderly was much like a nurse's aid, a respectable position in the hospital care chain. I enjoyed my job, wearing a white Dr. Kildare smock, while taking responsibility for the men's ward of four patients. I was the guy who set up the oxygen tents, discharged patients, did some of the heavier lifting, and provided the basic nursing care to my patients while sometimes making trips to the morgue and assisting the pathologist with at least two autopsies. The pay was $1.25/hour (minimum wage in 1961). The perks included working with the nursing staff, which included legends in Grayling Hospital care like Miss Mary Noa, Mrs. Redman, Sister Beatrice, Sister Janice, and Carolyn Barker. The primary doctors were Dr. Henig, Dr. Blaha, Dr. Dosch, and occasionally Dr. Oppy and my Uncle Doc Godfroy from Roscommon. In 2015 some of Grayling's leading practitioners are Dr. Eric G. Weeks, Dr. Marilyn Rosi, Dr. Lisa A. Harrington, Dr. George B. Hanert, and Dr. Michael E. Burkley.

The maintenance crew at the time was led by Mr. Dormeier and Joe Renard. Many years later, both my dad, Bernard Maurer, and my younger brother, Louis G. Maurer, worked in the maintenance department. Probably the best perk for me was the opportunity to work with the groups of student nurses led by Mrs. Hilton. I remember Rosie Schrovonich, now married to Jim Kessler, Carol Jacobs, Rosie Briley, and Pam Mauren. Others, including from the lab, were my cousin Joy (Cherven) Granland, Steve Olson, JoAnn Duby, and nurses Louise Munn and Jeannie Sloan who I remember as exceptional nurses. The main part of nursing, obviously, is the patients, and I remember a few I took care of at the end of their careers in the Grayling area. Here are five pioneers of the Grayling area, all men, probably born in the 1880s that I got to know a little bit when they were my patients at Mercy Hospital in 1961.

Frank Millikin was the grandfather of my best friend growing up, Floyd Millikin, son of Roy and Virginia. Frank made his living as I recall as a plumber. Then DeVer Dawson, famous for the Dawson drugstore, now known as Stevens-Dawson. Mr. Dawson was the pharmacist in town, and his store had a great soda fountain. It is now owned, I believe, by Mr. Bill Gannon. Mr. Dawson always hired the cutest high school girls to work behind the counter, girls like Martel Bobmeyer. Also I got to know Grant Thompson, Randy Thompson's grandfather. Randy now owns Century 21 Real Estate.

I met Tony Nelson, one of Crawford County's successful businessmen who did well with real estate in Beaver Creek Township. For many years my dad helped Jack Canfield, the tenant farmer, cut the hay, and dehorn, castrate and butcher the steers on the Nelson place. I am expecting Shell Oil or Encana to find oil there. Maybe they'll drill this year in view of the current situation in Egypt. Some of the big stories in the news as I am writing my story, in February 2011, need to be noted here. So direct from AP News, here are the headlines for six major events occurring now:

Egypt military promises no force against protests
Hamza Hendawi and Maggie Michael

Cairo (AP)—Egypt's military pledged not to fire on protesters in a sign that army support for President Hosni Mubarak may be unraveling on the eve a major escalation—a push for a million people to take to the streets Tuesday to demand the authoritarian leader's ouster.

Pro-Gadhafi forces close in on rebel-held cities
Maggie Michael

Tripoli, Libya (AP)—International pressure on Moammar Gadhafi to end his crackdown on opponents escalated Monday as his loyalists fought rebels holding a city near the capital and his warplanes bombed an ammunition depot in the East. The U.S. moved naval and air forces closer to Libya and said all options were open, including the use of warplanes to patrol the North African nation's skies and protect citizens threatened by their leader.

Massive storm paralyzes cities as it rolls east
Michael Tarm

Chicago (AP)—A massive storm billed as the worst in decades barreled into the Northeast on Wednesday, paralyzing big cities and small towns alike with deep snow and thick ice, stranding hundreds of motorists and shutting airports and schools across the Midwest. The 20.2 inches of snow that fell by midday in Chicago made the storm the city's third largest of record, with still more coming down. A foot or more was dumped on parts of Missouri, Indiana, Kansas, Oklahoma and upstate New York.

Powerful cyclone strikes Australia's northeast
Kristen Gelineau

Cairns, Australia (AP)—A massive cyclone struck northeastern Australia early Thursday, tearing off roofs, toppling trees and cutting power to thousands, the most powerful storm to hit the area in nearly a century. The eye of Cyclone Yasi roared ashore at the small resort town of Mission Beach in Queensland state, battering the coast known to tourists as the gateway to the Great Barrier Reef with heavy rain and howling winds gusting to 186 mph (300 kph)

Something in water causes diabetes

Uh oh. Even if you give up the burgers and fries and faithfully exercise most days of the week, you may still develop type 2 diabetes just by doing what's good for you: drinking water. Low-level arsenic exposure, possibly from drinking water, has been linked to this form of diabetes, formerly called adult-onset diabetes, according to a new analysis of government data by researchers at the John Hopkins Bloomberg School of Public Health in Baltimore, Maryland.

Chromium water contamination report U.S., a new report shows that scores of leaking coal ash sites across the country are additional documented sites for such contamination. Hexavalent chromium first made headlines after Erin Brockovich sued Pacific Gas & Electric because of poisoned drinking water from hexavalent chromium. Now new information indicates that the chemical leaks readily from leaking coal ash dump sites maintained for coal-fired power plants.

Cosmic census finds crowd of planets in our galaxy
Seth Borenstein

Washington (AP)—Scientists have estimated the first cosmic census of planets in our galaxy and the numbers are astronomical: at least 50 billion planets in the Milky Way. At least 500 million of those planets are in the not-too-hot, not-too-cold zone where life could exist. The numbers were extrapolated from the early results of NASA's planet-hunting Kepler telescope.

As the Book of Common Prayer expresses it so well, it is very interesting to "contemplate the vast expanse of interstellar space, galaxies, suns, the planets in their courses, and this fragile earth, our island home" and wonder how it all came to be. Now consider this: It is said that there are one hundred billion galaxies and each galaxy contains billions of stars and furthermore most of those stars have multiple planets surrounding them and that some of those planets could be similar to our Earth. Speaking of the Cosmos, I did see the total solar eclipse in Winnipeg, Manitoba, Canada in 1979. It was 53F below zero that day, but the eclipse was everything people say.

Finally, I got to meet Yalmer Morteson, a long-time farmer from Beaver Creek and cribbage partner for my dad. Yalmer lived on King Road close to our "other place" on Four-Mile Road. All five of these men were of the same age and most likely knew each other, but I never saw them together. If I had known I would write something about them in 2011, I might have asked more questions about how they came to live in Grayling, Michigan, near the forty-fifth parallel where the winters are long and cold.

I tell people that there must not have been any geography books for my dad to read in 1935 when he moved two hundred miles north of Nashville, Michigan, to the Roscommon-Grayling area, because he might have noticed that if he had gone south two hundred miles, he would have been in warmer Indianapolis or even Cincinnati. But then he would not have met my mother, and I would not be here today.

In August 1961, my old friend Ed Murphy from Holy Trinity Seminary called to invite me on a trip to Mexico City to visit another of our classmates, Xavier Milanes, who lived there. Ed said he was riding from Connecticut to Mexico City in his friend's MG. He wanted me to hook up in Mexico City with Xavier. We could stay at Xavier's mother's villa on Tuxpan Street. I asked my dad what he thought of the trip. He encouraged me to go. Dad said, "You are young, not married, and may not have another chance to travel like that." So I took money from my college savings from the $1.25/hour orderly pay and purchased a ticket on American Airlines to Mexico City via Traverse City, Chicago and Dallas.

Ed Murphy and Xavier picked me up at the airport, and we proceeded directly to a local drinking establishment and listened to the mariachi band until early morning. The party didn't stop for a month. In the day time we saw the sites: the big city with its museums, the Aztec pyramids, bullfights, jai-alai (zesta-punta), and more bars at night. Finally, Xavier, who was teaching English at a private girls' school, told Ed and me that we had to get up in the morning and teach a class, or he couldn't go out with us anymore at night. So Ed and I alternated teaching Xavier's class.

The class was easy to teach: "Just read out of the book and engage in normal conversation, they'll like your American accent," he said. One of the girls, Analana, wanted to marry me. Another invited me to her father's beach house in Acapulco. As it turned out I took advantage of neither opportunity. We did, however, go to Acapulco on our own for a long weekend. What a beautiful place in

1962! While there Marilyn Monroe died, it was in all the papers. The papers said that she had been seeing a Mexican guy, we all learned later about her connection with John and Robert Kennedy.

Marilyn Monroe, 1962, painting in Terry's collection.

One morning on the beach, I said to Murphy, "Hey, look, there is Ted and Bobby Kennedy under one of the many beach umbrellas with some other guys!"

Ed said, "Forget the Kennedys, we're going swimming."

Years later I bought yet another book on the Kennedys in a used bookstore in Petoskey, Michigan. In the center section where the pictures always are was a photo of Bobby and Ted playing touch football on that very beach in 1960. So I am sure the guys talking in unmistakable Boston accents dressed in khakis and T-shirts were the Kennedy brothers, Bobby and Ted. I just wish I'd taken a picture or gotten a little closer to the six-man conversation.

They were probably discussing how to take Marilyn out or how to cover up what they had already done. Marilyn Monroe was found dead in her Los Angeles apartment either the day before or the day after the beach scene. I did attempt to walk right up to the group of six, but it was very clear that the four bodyguards did not want anyone near. I had a chance to change history or be found dead myself at the hands of my heroes. Just kidding.

Back in Michigan, after four weeks in Mexico, gave me just two final weeks to work at Mercy Hospital before restarting my college career this time at Northwestern Michigan Junior College in Traverse City, Michigan (NMC).

My dad told me, "Terry, you will finish college. Here are a couple dozen eggs to help you with expenses." He added, "Let me know when to come to your graduation." Dad did also contribute one hind quarter of venison while I was at Michigan, but no cash. Otherwise, I put myself through college with summer jobs and all manner of part-time employment. Finally help came from the Climax Molybdenum stint as well as support from my wife. It took ten years and four college experiences. Dad came to both graduations in 1964 and 1970.

I almost stayed in Mexico City and enrolled in Medical School with my friend Xavier. However, Ed Murphy advised against that, saying that I would probably have to repeat two years of medical school in the US if I ever wanted to practice in the States.

My girlfriend at the time was Sherry Hecker, granddaughter, I found out in 1967, of my neighbor Mr. Bill Hecker. I met Sherry while working at Mercy Hospital and we stayed in touch while I was in Mexico and for a while when we both attended NMC. She became the homecoming queen in 1963, and the hit song "Sherry" by the Four Seasons was at the top of the charts. Cool, I thought. Her grandfather, our neighbor on Mixtwood Street in Ann Arbor, told me that he cut pulpwood in Nashville, Michigan, with my grandfather Lawrence and my great-grandfather Peter A. Maurer in 1909. Hard to believe I'd meet someone who knew my great-grandfather. The eleven-acre estate we bought on Scio Road in Ann Arbor in 1987 belonged to Jean Hecker, Sharon's aunt, and Bill Hecker's daughter.

One of life's twists, or is it called serendipity? At any rate, back to school in 1962, after one full year, away felt comfortable.

I took a room at 1040 Webster Street, renting from Mrs. Eva Rhiel, who worked the afternoon shift as a practical nurse at Munson Hospital in Traverse City. The first year went well, getting As and Bs in most classes. My intention was to be a medical doctor, so my classes were heavy with chemistry, math, and biology. That summer, I was back in Grayling working this time in the front office (no longer orderly) at Mercy Hospital. I would do the admitting of new patients, answer the phone, and assist with invoicing mostly to Blue Cross and Blue Shield. My job at the hospital went from midnight to 8:00 a.m. and I also worked at Camp Grayling from 8:00 a.m. to 5:00 p.m. Captain Schaible was my boss in the supply warehouse. In the first week I nearly lost both jobs. The hospital and the camp were fifteen minutes apart, and one job ended at 8:00 a.m. and the second started at 8:00 a.m. When I was fifteen minutes late at Camp Grayling on the third day, Captain Schaible was waiting for me. He said, "If you are late tomorrow, you're fired." So naturally I left the hospital at 7:40 a.m.

It only took Sister Janice, the hospital administrator, two days to notice that I was leaving early. She caught me at 7:30 a.m. on Friday of the first week of my back to back eight-hour jobs and said, "I know what you're doing. I know you're trying to make extra money for college. Why don't you leave the hospital at 7:30 a.m.? You have plenty of time to get to your camp job, and I'll just pay you for seven and a half hours." I hated to lose thirty minutes of pay per day, but it made it possible to get paid for fifteen and a half hours each day.

I made enough money to buy a car that summer, a '55 Pontiac for $600. Now back to Traverse City for my second year, this time with wheels. No more hitchhiking to Grayling (a sixty-mile trip) like I did the first year at NMC. Tony was at Central Michigan in his senior year, he called from Mt. Pleasant in early November 1963 and said, "Why don't you meet me at home in Grayling on November 14?" (the night before opening day of deer season). "We'll go to the bars in the evening and be ready for the hunt in the morning."

So after classes on the fourteenth, I filled up my tank and headed to Grayling. I had just one cigarette, so I thought I'll save it and not light up until passing the Red Barn, a few miles from home. Good idea because as I passed Dingman's Bar going at least seventy miles per hour over the rolling hills on W-72 toward Grayling I came upon a car crossway in my lane. It was already dark at 6:00 p.m. I only had time to make a quick decision, go right into the trees or left and hope I had control enough to miss the car and get back into my lane. Going straight would be instant death, I was sure. T-boning a car at seventy miles per hour without seatbelt wouldn't do. So as I went left, I thought to myself, "This is the end of me."

Going left was the only option, but my car couldn't do it, and I went into an immediate slide, hitting my passenger side into the other car's passenger side. It was the loudest noise I've ever heard to this day. I was amazed when I saw bright lights bearing down on me. I thought, *I guess I'm alive but will now die when this approaching car hits me.* I immediately tried to open my door. I couldn't because I was upside down, and every one of my windows was gone, including the back window, where I managed to climb out just as the car came to a screeching stop right up against my overturned yellow-and-white Pontiac.

Now as I stepped onto to pavement with only my socks on (my shoes were gone), it felt wet. I did not recall that it was raining. It wasn't. It was gas from my broken fuel tank. Good thing I had not had a cigarette burning when the crash occurred. It was almost a nonissue because the lady from the oncoming car was smoking her cigarette as she asked when the accident happened. I shouted at her to put her Newport out before she caused my car to blow up and burn my hunting clothes, boots, and deer rifle, not to mention my car.

The Kalkaska wrecker towed my car to Grayling. It was totaled for sure, I could tell. Fortunately I walked away with only a backache but no cuts nor broken bones. I didn't even go to the hospital. When we got to Rochette's Shell station in Grayling, Larry Lagrow, my friend and class president of Tony's 1959 high school class, was there and drove me the six miles home to the farm on four-mile road.

This was the same Larry who helped me save the brothers, John and Joe Robertson, from drowning in Higgins Lake in the summer of '62. Larry did the most to keep Joe's head above water as we swam back toward shore from a far-out diving platform. That was the third time I helped save someone from drowning in Northern Michigan.

When Larry dropped me at the farm, Tony had come and gone already. Mom and Dad did not realize the seriousness of my accident until they saw my car the next day. My mother said, "Must be God wants you to live longer for some reason." Maybe it was to produce grandchildren because Tony and Louie did not have children and my future wife, Mary Ann, and I were blessed with three beautiful children, Laurie, Stephen, and Karin. As it turned out they were the only grandchildren on both sides of the family. But I'm getting ahead of myself since I had not yet met Mary Ann.

When I returned to college after that crazy weekend, it was Monday, November 18, and on Friday, November 22, John F. Kennedy was killed in Dallas. Everything changed. Everyone knew where they were when they heard the news. I was in the NMC library studying for an American history exam when I noticed Ruth Sorenson across the way crying and telling a small study group that someone had been shot. I immediately thought that a friend of hers might have been shot while deer hunting.

Then she came over to the table where I was and said that the president had been shot. Classes were immediately canceled. On Sunday morning, Ruby shot Oswald, the alleged lone shooter of JFK. It took place on live TV. I heard the shot live on radio and then saw the first replay on TV. Many people thought the assassination was a conspiracy. There were groups offered up by the media as possible candidates. Some said it was the mafia or the Cubans (remember the Bay of Pigs and Fidel Castro) or maybe folks opposed to Kennedy's positions on the Federal Reserve or his positions on the Middle East. Kennedy was opposed to selling offensive weapons, both tanks and attack planes to Israel.

If it were a conspiracy, the perpetrators sure did a good job of covering their tracks. I find it hard to believe that Oswald had such a good position on the sixth floor of the Texas school book depository without the Secret Service prechecking such a great tree blind. I personally visited the site at least three times, and the first time a person could still stick his head out the same window which Oswald used. Having grown up around high-powered rifles with my uncles Mose and Doc shooting deer from a far greater distance, okay, they had high powered scopes, but Oswald did as well, and he was close to his target. I need to read the entire Warren Commission Report, but I don't recall hearing much about the interview of Oswald.

If he had any alibi, he certainly had time to mention it sometime between Friday afternoon and Sunday morning when Ruby, the bar club owner and friend of the Dallas Police shot him in the police station. The only quote I know from Oswald is that he said, "I didn't shoot anybody. I'm just a patsy." In 2010, I did meet and ask the grandson of Chief Justice Earl Warren (Earl Warren chaired the Warren Commission Report on the Kennedy assassination) about any transcripts from the Oswald interviews. He told me that tape recorders were not readily available in 1963. It makes me wonder all the more. So I believe Oswald could make the shot alone, but I am not convinced he acted alone (that is without being set up by the CIA or the Mossad). Needless to say, I too felt terrible about losing JFK. Everyone knows how much I admired the entire family.

I graduated from Northwestern Michigan College in Traverse City, Michigan, in June 1964. NMC had many positive benefits; not the least was excellent, fully experienced professors, small classes, and reasonable fees. One disadvantage of a junior college, at least for me, is that you are not there long enough to make many long-term friends. Larry Hunter from Grayling may be the only NMC classmate I see. Larry's wife, Gail, knew my dad when they both worked at Mercy Hospital in the '80s. Dad was in maintenance and Gail on the nursing staff.

I also do remember at least five classmates who I later saw briefly again at the University of Michigan. It just happened they were all girls: Jeannie Stephens, Beth Alway, Ruth Sorenson, Beth Rokus, and Bonnie Alpers all transferred to the University of Michigan in Ann Arbor for their junior year. Maybe I remember them because they were a few of the more popular and better-looking girls. Now most likely hot grandmothers. My summer of 1964 was productive as I earned tuition money for premed at the University of Michigan. In the daytime, I was a clerk for Captain Schaible again, and in the evening Tony and I tended bar at the officers' club. Three incidents stand out about that summer job at Camp Grayling.

First, Captain Schaible gave me a project of keeping the master inventory list for a major construction project on the camp that summer. Every day someone would drop off the daily list showing what was removed: 2×4s, shingles, nails, rafters, and a variety of building supplies. I would subtract them from my master list so that the captain would know what was going on. In mid-August he said, "Hey, Terry! Why don't you take my jeep and your master list and see how close your list is to the actual physical inventory." Well, when I got to the big warehouse on the south end of the camp and walked through the side door, I was staring at the nearly empty building. My master list showed the place should have one half of everything still there.

There was a guy way over in the corner stacking 2×4s. He hollered, "What do you want?"

I said, "I am here to check the remaining inventory."

He said, "You can see it's all gone, now get out of here!"

His language was more colorful than I am reporting here. So I drove back up front to building 5 and told Captain Schaible the news. I said, "I guess you have been paying me for nothing all summer because my inventory is way off."

Well, in the Ann Arbor News one day in late September (now I am attending classes at the U of M), the headlines read, "Governor George Romney fires General McDonald and General Neifert of the Michigan National Guard for real estate fraud."

It happens that I was the "deep throat" exposing the deed through my supervisor, Jack Rasmussen and Captain Schaible, that the lumber was missing. Both generals appeared to be in on the fraud, a swindle where state lumber was being stolen from the camp to build lakefront cottages on lake Margrethe on lots traded for useless swampland in the upper peninsula of Michigan. General McDonald was reinstated. But I don't believe General Neifert ever was. Makes one wonder about the possibilities for any fraud or waste in the broader military-industrial complex.

The two other memorable incidents occurred at the officers' club. Bartending was relaxing—relaxing, that is, until one evening, someone stole the cigar box holding the poker money. General Neifert came late to the game, and when he went to buy chips, the banker discovered that the cigar box on the inside window ledge was missing. Apparently someone on the outside was able to open the screen and walk off with the kitty. When the proprietor and my boss, Mr. Bob Hayes, heard about this, he became worried about the warehouse full of booze in the same building. It is interesting that fifty years later, Mary Ann and I would meet Bob's daughter, Susan Hayes, and her friend Rick. The four of us would regularly connect with Larry and Terry Paxton at Spike's Keg of Nails for dinner. Larry Paxton is the civil engineer who helped me with the addition to the Avita Water plant, and he is an avid hunter who regularly visits my brother in Alaska for hunting and fishing.

The commissioned officers could order cases of scotch, bourbon, gin, vodka, and all types of hard stuff, and take it home without paying state tax. Their orders had just been delivered to the club, and Mr. Hayes was worried that the cigar box thief would be back during the night to steal the entire stash of tax-free liquor.

So Mr. Hayes asked me to sleep with the booze on a cot and guard it. He said he'd pay me to sleep in the back room. I asked for a revolver. He said that would not be necessary. All I needed to do was make some noise, and the thieves would get scared and leave. No thieves came, and if they had come, they could have emptied the entire warehouse, and I would not have heard anything. The good news was that I got paid for thirty-eight straight hours when you add up the two shifts back to back plus getting paid for sleeping.

The third incident occurred on Governor's Day later in the summer of 1964. Mr. Hayes asked me to set up a special bar area for Michigan's Governor George Romney. The governor and his aides would be in a receiving line at the officers' club and they'd need their own special bar. George Romney came over to my bar and said, "Young man, I'd like a glass of milk."

I said, "Governor, I don't have any milk."

He asked me to look in the kitchen. There was no milk. I came back and asked if he'd like orange juice. He said, "No thanks. I'll just have a glass of water."

It was years later that I learned that, as a Mormon, George Romney did not drink alcohol. It was normal I heard for him to drink milk at public functions. That way no one would think it was an alcoholic drink. His son, Mitt Romney, is my preferred presidential candidate for the 2012 elections coming up in less than two years now.

It was in September 1964 when I started my junior year of college at the University of Michigan as a premed student. Zoology, organic chemistry, physics, and English literature classes were too much for me as a transfer student in a new town and a playboy roommate (in Traverse City I had my own room—no distractions). At the end of the semester it was over. My good friend Lance Nelson recommended I stay in Ann Arbor and try to get back into school. "Don't go home to Grayling," he said. "You'll never get out." So I stayed in Ann Arbor and got a commission job selling stereos. Life got more interesting. I moved into a house on Radcliff Street on the southeast side of Ann Arbor with two resident doctors, Dr. John Kaufman and Dr. George Matula.

The doctors were about to graduate, and when they did, they both took jobs at Kaiser Permanente in San Francisco. I never saw them again. Actually, I did see Dr. John Kaufman on Walter Cronkite's CBS Evening News sometime in the early 1980s. John was in the front line of picketing doctors at Kaiser Permanente, holding a sign "Unfair to doctors."

I never sold a stereo either, but I got a good lead according to my boss. "Mary Ann Horning bought some pots and pans once," he told me, according to a national sales lead outfit in New York. She may be a good candidate for a stereo sale. Mary Ann told me she bought the pots and pans for when she would get married someday. So who would have thought that it would me?

So here's the story of how I met your great-grandmother. Carrying the Mary Ann Horning sales lead in my billfold for over a month, I finally went to make the sale at her apartment on Pauline Boulevard in Ann Arbor. She wasn't home and had gone skiing, said her roommate. I was busy making other calls; selling stereos door to door on commission was not easy. Courage was required to knock on a door and ask permission to come into someone's house or apartment and make a demonstration, pointing out how great the sound was when a bowling ball sound could be heard hitting the floor on one speaker and pins could be heard hitting the gutter on the other speaker. Before I got the courage to come back for a second call to Mary Ann, I did manage to get an interview for what sounded like a "real" job at Detroit Edison, downtown Ann Arbor.

I had time for a few dates with a sweet little blond whom I had met on the stereo circuit. I even took Carolyn to Monroe to meet my old friend from military school, John Vandegrift. She passed that litmus test. So life was improving. Looks like I'd be offered the job at Edison by Paul Rogers as night time and weekend dispatcher (the guy who takes the calls from Edison's customers when the power goes out during a storm or to dispatch a serviceman to fix a customer's electric appliances—that doesn't happen anymore). And now I had a cute girlfriend to go with a real job while I worked to get back into the university. Lance was right: "Stay in Ann Arbor." However, I made one more sales call to Pauline Boulevard. I figured I could make at least one stereo sale before I started at Edison, and Mary Ann was likely to buy one since, after all, she did buy some pots and pans once.

On my second sales call I was met by the landlord, who told me that Mary Ann had broken her leg skiing and was not at her apartment. Again, I was relieved thinking I tried and now could soon concentrate on my expected new job at Edison. I had a final interview there, and when I walked through the front door, there was Judy Goetze, the Edison office manager, Mary Ann Horning's roommate whom I had met on my first unproductive stereo sales call to the Pauline apartment. She did not recognize me. *Thank God*, I thought. The interview went well. Paul Rogers hired me and Sid Rock on the same day. You had to be a University of Michigan student to get this lucrative part-time job with full insurance benefits. Mr. Rogers knew

I expected to get back into the University of Michigan after taking some summer classes, which I did in both cases. Sid was a dental student.

So now, after a few weeks, the Edison job was working out great, and my girlfriend Carolyn wanted me to visit her parents. I even told my mother about "the blonde" and mentioned a possible trip up to Grayling for an introduction. Before going to Grayling, my housemates got invited to a party in downtown Ann Arbor. They invited me to come along. As fate would have it, the party was at an apartment on Pauline Boulevard where I had tried to sell a stereo. The resident doctors' friends were much older than me at thirty-two, but I recognized the apartment complex and think that maybe Judy from Edison would like to join the party and besides she was more my age. At least I knew her a little bit from Edison and knew where she lived from my stereo sales calls months earlier. So I walked to Judy's apartment, just four or five units down the way. It was nearly midnight as I knocked on her door.

When Judy, dressed in her chartreuse pajamas, opened the door and saw me, Terry Maurer, from Edison, she was completely surprised and asked, "How did you know where I lived?" I did not clue her in about the stereo sales calls, and it was years before she learned the truth. Judy invited me in, saying, "I can't go to the party with you. *I* have to get up early, and besides, I have a steady boyfriend." I said hello to the guy and girl on the couch. It was Anna and Ed Murphey (not my seminary friend, Ed Murphy). Judy also married her boyfriend, Jim Rhoades. It was then that I saw the first likeness of the redhead smiling in a nicely framed picture of a very attractive girl in a green bathing suit. I immediately thought that this might be the Mary Ann Horning whose name I had carried around for months but never met. And then the bedroom door opened, and I saw her face; it was the first time.

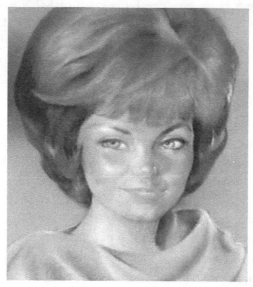

Mary Ann in 1964, painting by John Lockard.

There was an immediate mutual attraction (one knows these things). That evening Mary Ann invited me to watch the NCAA championship game with Michigan's Cassie Russell and team playing on national TV, the next Saturday. She said, "Bring one of your housemates." She had a girlfriend, and we would all four make a party out of it.

"Okay!" I said.

"That's a date."

However, on Saturday, Dr. George Matula was called in to emergency at the U of M Hospital and I would have to go alone.

The pressure was too much for me, so I stood Mary Ann and her friend up, I didn't call; I didn't go. I don't know why I didn't call. Maybe I thought I was in over my head anyway (the redhead was really pretty) and what might Carolyn think. The next time I saw Judy at Edison. She told me that Mary Ann was very disappointed, and Mary Ann told me later that no one had ever stood her up. So to make it up to her, I did finally call and invited her to a movie. We took her green '62 Ford, not my rusty '55 Pontiac (I managed to get another Pontiac like the one I crashed, but not in as good a shape).

Mary Ann wanted to keep her image up. We saw *The Man from Rio* at the campus theater on South University.

After that, we started talking on the phone almost every night, me during quiet times at my evening job at Edison, and Mary Ann as she recovered from the spiral break in her leg, and she could stay up late since she could not go back to the Tiara beauty salon until it healed. I continued to see Carolyn until Mary Ann told me she'd been asked out by some dude from Santa Barbara, California, as he was passing through Ann Arbor; for what, I did not care. Mary Ann said, "He wants to take me to a movie and I'll probably never hear from him again." Well, she told me which movie, and I took Carolyn to the same movie on the same night at the Michigan theater, never expecting to see Mary Ann. As Carolyn, the petite blonde, and I walked into the lobby, there was Mary Ann, looking very foxy, even with her crutches, seated at the lower level door into the theater.

I immediately led Carolyn upstairs to the balcony, and looking down as we walked, she said to me, "Look at that poor girl down there with the broken leg."

I said, "Oh yeah, probably a skiing accident."

I don't remember that movie. I could only think about Mary Ann sitting with the Santa Barbara dude. After the movie, while Carolyn Schray and I were having Coke, she said, "What's the matter with you tonight?"

I said, "Nothing," and that was the last time we saw each other.

Mary Ann and I drove to Grayling the following weekend to see my parents. My mother pulled me aside into the kitchen and said, "I thought you said she was blonde."

"Yes," I said, "but I brought a different girl and this one is a redhead," and thinking about her "kisses sweeter than wine," as the song goes.

We were engaged to be married soon after the visit to Grayling. Here is how the announcement appeared in the Ann Arbor News:

Betrothed: Mr. and Mrs. Edwin G. Horning, 14680
Waldo Rd., are announcing the engagement of their
daughter, Mary Ann, of Ann Arbor, to Terry Andrew
Maurer, son of Mr. and Mrs. Bernard L. Maurer, of Grayling.
The bride-elect is a graduate of Chelsea High School
and the Alexandra School of Cosmetology, Ann Arbor.
Her fiancé is an alumnus of St. Joseph's Holy Trinity
High School in Alabama, Northwestern Michigan
College, Traverse City, and is presently attending the
University of Michigan. They plan a July 10 wedding
in St. Mary's student chapel, Ann Arbor.

Traverse City, Michigan*

Life is a bowl of cherries in Traverse City, where the sweet crimson fruit is king and the outdoors are a playground ripe for exploring. Sleeping Bear Dunes National Lakeshore is a Midwest road trip destination not to be missed. The giant, sweeping sand mountain offer and enjoyable work-out as you run, climb and slide to the powerful payoff of deep blue Lake Michigan views.

The National Cherry Festival is in July. Even if you can't make it, you can still taste cherries all over town in salads, burgers and baked goods. Top cherry picks include the chocolate cherry turtle treats from Cherry Republic and the cherry crumb pie from the Grand Traverse Pie Company. Craft brews and regional wines are also big in Traverse City.

You can bike, hike, fish, swim and sail the summer days away. Located on the 45th Parallel, Traverse City's midsummer days feel especially long and bright, offering even more sunny hours for outside fun. In winter, you can downhill-ski or snowboard at Crystal Mountain or Shanty Creek Resort.

Stay at the Grand Traverse Resort and Spa, a sprawling resort with three golf courses, a private beach club and an indoor water park. Unwind in the rejuvinating spa and dine with dreamy panoramic views of the Grand Traverse Bay at exceptional Aerie Restaurant and Lounge. Get a taste of the beauty and outdoor adventure that the Midwest offers.

---

* The article was written by Cortney Fries for the USA TODAY.

Engagement photo of MaryAnn Horning

My beautiful bride. Mary Ann Horning Maurer.

CHAPTER V

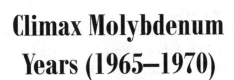

Climax Molybdenum Years (1965–1970)
Lyndon B. Johnson
(1963–1969)

The summer of 1965 was the beginning of a new life. Mary Ann and I were married at the St. Mary's Student Chapel on Thompson Street in Ann Arbor on July 10, 1965. The evening of the rehearsal dinner my dad got lost twice, trying to follow me in my old '55 Pontiac to Mary Ann's apartment on Pauline Boulevard. It was not far from the church on Thompson Street to Pauline Boulevard, but I managed to go through a yellow light on S. Main near the stadium, leaving my mom and dad stuck on the red. As I made the right turn onto Pauline, I was out of sight to my dad who was following Mary Ann and me over to her apartment. I thought that I would have to turn around and find him when I saw him coming again.

He followed me to the apartment where I asked, "Dad, how did you find me?"

He said, "It wasn't too difficult. I just pulled over to the side, shut my car off, and listened. I could hear your Pontiac without the muffler headed west. I just followed the noise."

After we were married, it was cheaper to drive Mary Ann's '62 Ford, and we got rid of my Pontiac.

The next day Father Litka performed the wedding in front of many family and friends. I was surprised how many of my Grayling friends including Steve Olson and Chum and Barb Lovely made it the two hundred miles to Ann Arbor. Our reception was held at the Knights of Columbus Hall next to the Raison River in Manchester. The Harold Mitas Orchestra was our entertainment; this was a wedding gift from my cousin Sue (Leonard) Mitas and Harold. Even then the Mitas band was well known throughout Michigan and Ohio only to reach even higher respect with their records and polka Fests in the Frankenmuth and Saginaw area. Now Harold and Sue live in McKinney, Texas, and they own a winery and events center called Mitas Hill Winery.

Around 11:00 p.m., when Mary Ann and I were saying our goodbyes, my best Ann Arbor friend and usher Lance Nelson pulled me aside to say that he would pay for his tux and get us a gift when we returned from our honeymoon. Mary Ann and I were headed for, you guessed it, Niagara Falls and returning from the north through Sault Saint Marie and then south to visit my parents in Grayling. When we got to Grayling the following Saturday, my dad said, "You missed all the excitement after you left the wedding party in Manchester."

I asked what happened and he said, "Lance jumped off the bridge." I asked, "Did I miss the funeral?"

Dad said no. He didn't die but just ended up in the river in water up to his waist.

Lance, being an ex–Green Beret paratrooper, apparently instinctively went into a roll, which protected his neck in the twenty-foot fall. It all happened because of a fight with his wife, Sherry. Lance did graduate a few years later seventh in his class from the University of Michigan Medical School. He was later on the outs with the AMA and finished his career and his life while teaching chemistry at a Texas university sometime in the late 1980s. He and I had lost contact some 10 to 15 years before the end. Sherry and Mary Ann had kept in touch after their divorce. We did go to their son Kenny's wedding and reception held at the Gandy Dancer restaurant in Ann Arbor in the mid-'80s.

We lived in a duplex near the famous Whitmore Lake while I took my summer class in industrial psychology, getting an A, which got me back into the University of Michigan for the fall semester. We moved back into Ann Arbor on Glendale Street renting a great place, a small brick house behind Mr. Van Ell's main house. I continued to work at Detroit Edison, while at the same time earning an extra $40 per week by selling my AB+ blood plasma to the University of Michigan burn center for $20 per draw twice a week. Every six weeks it would be $60 when I could also sell a regular pint of my rare blood. I stuck to that routine for eighteen months.

Mary Ann was back in her position at Tiara on Stadium Boulevard. At the end of the fall semester I was again out of school. Although my grades were all Bs, the C in rat lab was the killer. I needed a B in rat lab to stay in. The University of Michigan would not use any of my NMC transcripts toward the average; if they had, I would have been okay. So now what to do again? Mary Ann suggested I take a break from school and get a full-time job. The Ann Arbor News had an ad for a chemical technician with minimum AA degree. I fit the bill and was hired by Climax Molybdenum Company to work in the research lab. Climax had just built a new facility on Huron Parkway employed some 120 folks doing research on the element molybdenum. Two-thirds of the scientists were metallurgists with all levels of training, mostly PhD folks. The other third were chemical people doing analytical lab work and some physical testing of the performance properties of molybdenum disulfide (MoS_2). I was in the MoS_2 group reporting first to Tom Risdon and up the line to Cal Halada, PhD, and then Hank Barry, and finally to George Timmons, who reported to Al Herzig, the president of Climax Molybdenum company.

Climax Molybdenum Company of Michigan

January 11, 1966

Dear Mr. Maurer:

This letter is to confirm my telephone call of January 11, 1966. We are pleased to offer you the position of Laboratory Assistant in the

Chemistry Department at an annual starting salary of $450 per month or $5,400 per year. This offer is contingent upon a satisfactory report of a physical examination to be taken at 2:15 P.M. January 18, 1966 at the office of Dr. Edv. C. Pierce.

We are looking forward to your joining our research staff at 8:15 A.M., Monday January 17, 1966.

Sincerely yours,

Bruce C Madlock,
Administrative Assistant

During my first year at Climax, Laurie was born. Mary Ann and especially I were very happy to have a girl. My mother always wanted to have a girl but got stuck with three boys. Now her first grandchild was a girl. I figured we could always make a boy (sorry, Steve), but girls were hard to come by on the Maurer side. When I went to the nursery to see my daughter for the first time, I was apprehensive. I did not want to be embarrassed if the baby was ugly. Well, when I got to the nursery window, I saw six to eight babies. Not knowing which mine was, I kept a low profile until a man and a woman came up next to me, pointing at the baby with a full head of hair and a pink bow tied on top. "Look at that cute one," they said. It was then that I read "Maurer baby" on the bassinet. Straightening up, I said, "That would be mine." We always felt that our babies were better looking than everybody else's. I believe everyone feels that way, but in our case it was true.

Climax was a great environment both for its people (we still have alumni reunions organized by Donna Kruzich and David Sponseller every two years now some fifty-five years since I first started there) and for the physical building itself. When I first took my parents on a tour, my dad said, "You should pay the company for the privilege to work here." The brand-new building was constructed of precast massive concrete slabs with windows going from floor to ceiling. Molybdenum is used as an alloy for hardening steel, and maybe the one-story building was built to convey strength. Well, it did. The massive double front doors had huge handles made of pure Molybdenum.

My job was interesting. We would add MoS_2 to oils and greases at various percentages and particle sizes and test for its effects on lubricity. Common testing devices used were the Falex wear tester, the four-ball tester, and the stick-slip bushing machine. Sometimes we tested just the fine particle MoS_2 as we burnished it on a polished piece of steel. The coefficient of friction was the parameter we were measuring. The slipperier the product, the better the bearings and internal engine parts would perform. The better the performance of the engine oil or grease, the more MoS_2 we could sell and the happier and more bragging rights our customers could claim. The company had a marketing group headquartered in Greenwich, Connecticut, headed up by Will Tschudi and Ken Wood. Later Cal Halada and Tom Risdon took over those responsibilities and operated out of an Ypsilanti office.

After a year or so at Climax without the pressures of college, I was ready to go again, ready to continue studies toward my BS. My brother Tony, who had already graduated with his teaching certificate and BA from Central Michigan, (he later got his Masters in Micro-Biology from Michigan State) asked me what I planned to study. I said, "I'm not sure, I just want to finish my degree." His advice was to review all my credits from first year in college from the seminary, two years from Northwestern Michigan and now one full year from the University of Michigan and pick a major using most credits earned already. Well, it was chemistry, and since I was working for the chemical group at Climax, it was obvious. He told me to go to the head of the department at EMU, who was Dr. Spike, and have him sign a paper saying that when I finished the required list of credits, I would get my degree. This to prevent any future misunderstanding because it may take me three more years going part-time while working full-time and now supporting a family too.

One day, several months after Laurie's birth, Mary Ann woke up not feeling very well, telling me she would go back to bed after I left for work. Around eleven in the morning, I called home from Climax some six to seven miles from our rental house on Glendale to check on Mary Ann. Her dad answered the phone, saying immediately, "Mary Ann's dead, don't you know? Didn't anyone tell you?"

I said, "What!" And Edwin repeated what he had just said, but this time with a little more urgency. I said, "No! No one told me." And I hung up the phone, thinking to myself I didn't really hear what I just heard. So I redialed only to get Edwin again speaking in a very high-pitched excited voice, saying this time, "Where are you? Didn't anybody tell you? Mary Ann's dead. How come you are not here?" Now I was convinced that Mary Ann was dead.

I hung up for the second time and immediately called Dr. Beison's office. I told the receptionist what I knew and asked her to send Dr. Beison immediately to my house at 314 Glendale to see if he can revive my wife. The receptionist told me that the doctor didn't make house calls. I told her that her father was never married to her mother and she had better get the doctor to my house at once. Now, I needed to get myself home. But I was too upset to drive. So I found Tom Risdon, my supervisor in the Climax cafeteria enjoying the morning coffee break.

"Tom," I said. "You've got to drive me home. My father-in-law just told me that my wife's dead."

Tom was now in shock too but said, "Let's go."

On the trip across town, I remember telling Tom, "I can't believe it. We've only been married a short time and now my wife is gone."

When we finally pulled in the driveway, I was amazed that there were no cars there, not even the hearse. Tom and I immediately sprinted to the front door with me in the lead. When Edwin opened the door, he said, still even more excited than on the phone, "What's going on? The doctor just left, and now you are here."

I grabbed him by the shoulders and demanded, "Where is Mary Ann?"

He said, "Shopping with her mother. Didn't anybody tell you? I am here watching Laurie."

Now it all became perfectly clear. He was telling me "Mary Ann's dad," not "dead." I told Tom, who was speechless during this entire scene, that I needed a drink. I found my bottle of Jim Beam and proceeded to drink straight from the bottle. It was then that Mary Ann and her mother showed up at the door, all smiles with bags of new clothes.

I always tell folks that when I married Mary Ann that I married up: My dad had four cows, which were milked by hand. Mary Ann's dad had twenty cows, and he had a machine. I married way up. It's ironic that we got together because I always told myself that I would not marry a farmer's daughter, and Mary Ann said she'd never marry a farmer. I think we tricked each other: Mary Ann did not look like the farm girls I knew, and I was not like the farm boys Mary Ann grew up with.

Dr. Spike, chairman of the chemistry department at Eastern Michigan University, was happy to assist with the required courses and sign the paper. *Life is a journey, and I am on it*, I told myself. *So stay the course.* "Grab the bull by the horns," as my dad once told me in a letter at military school and get going. It did take three years. My goal was to complete my BS before Laurie started kindergarten. Well, that's the way it worked. I graduated in June 1970 with a BS in chemistry.

During that time, life continued to happen. We moved to 1131 Mixtwood in Ann Arbor before Stephen was born on September 8, 1967. Both Laurie and Stephen were born at the old St. Joseph's Mercy Hospital in Ann Arbor. Laurie's doctor was Dr. Ed Pierce, later mayor of Ann Arbor, and Stephen was delivered by Dr. Richard Beison. Both doctors were part of the Pierce, Hiraga, and Beison team of young start-ups in the early 1960s. I still use Dr. Beison in 2011 for myself. Stephen Andrew Maurer was just as good-looking as was his sister at birth. Mary Ann and I were always proud parents, and we know their grandparents, Bernard and Pauline Maurer, and Ed and Amanda Horning of Chelsea, Michigan, liked to show off their only grandkids. It was not until 1976 that our third child Karin was born. That story will come later.

Now, there were the four of us on Mixtwood, and I am working at Climax while going to college at Eastern in Ypsilanti. During the summers I organized a softball team of Climax folks, and we played in the Ann Arbor one-night-per-week fast-pitch league. In those days slow pitch was for wimps, and there were only a few teams in that group. I was the manager and the catcher. From memory I'll try to name the starters. First base was Dennis Robitaille, second base Bob Binns, shortstop Tom Risdon, third base Ron Hartman (alias Clyde Suckfinger), left field Bruce Maddock, center Cal Halada, right Dave Sponseller, pitcher Karl Kienholz, Jim Hallock, Russ Koch, Rick Gundelach was in the outfield along with Bob McConnell, Dan Diesburg, Paul Bond, and Mark Vukasovich, who was my new boss.

Climax would not sponsor us for what reason I never found out nor understood. Tom Toon, who worked in the lab next to the lubricant lab for Gene Lizlov, said that his uncle Harry Toon would do it. So we wore "Harry Toon Realty" shirts and were darn proud of it. Occasionally, especially for end of season tournaments we would get a couple of ringers to join our team. Most memorable was a guy named Al Choock, who was built like Babe Ruth and could really pound the ball. Our team never finished first in our league, but we were always in the competition and were having a good time in the process. Our families always came to the games and joined the players for a beer after the games, usually at Frasier's Pub on Stadium Boulevard.

The Climax group was a tight bunch. The second half of the sixties decade was full of depressing national news as Vietnam continued to escalate, the assassination of Martin Luther King and then of Robert Kennedy, not to mention the 1968 race riots. During this time for me at least, life was peaceful as I was insulated within my inner nucleus of Climax friendships and challenging but not stressful work while surrounded by my studies and new family. I thought for sure I would be drafted, but the Vietnam war was winding down under Nixon and I was never called. Besides I was twenty eight in 1970 and the military really wanted the younger guys.

The events in the world were very interesting but did not overpower my day to day activities. We had regular volleyball games during our lunch hour. I organized the construction of nets anchored by tires filled with concrete, tires I brought from home. We nearly always had six men to a side at these daily games on the Climax grounds. There is still the story of my running a seven-minute mile with Climax betters, betting for and against my ability to do it. We'll save that for another time.

Once a month, we had a poker night, always hosted by one of the members' wives who would provide a great lunch at the end of the evening. Life was simple but structured and fun. Reminds me of what one frog said to the other, "Isn't time fun when you're having flies?"

One time at Phil Coldren's house at the monthly poker party, Karl Kienholz arrived a little late saying he had just heard the famous radio personality Lowell Thomas crack up live on radio as he was giving the news. Mr. Thomas was telling the story of Dolly Dimples, the fat lady in the Big Top circus, who had just died. He said, "Today Dolly Dimples, the four-hundred-pound fat lady, died of a fatal fart attack." He knew immediately that he had misspoken himself and started to chuckle. Then still live on the radio, the producer could be heard starting to laugh. It really got out of control, but Lowell Thomas continued, saying she was so fat that they had to bury her off the back of a pickup truck. Now he has lost full control and is laughing at himself while trying to finish the story. Karl Kienholz lost control of himself as he tried to repeat the news about Dolly Dimples. WJR radio personality J. P. McCarthy used to replay the Lowell Thomas radio blooper at least once per year in Detroit. That was one of our more memorable nights of poker. Continuing my education was now an important part of my daily routine.

I learned how to get As in my chemistry classes, especially organic chemistry, which required plenty of memorization. First, I would always sit in the front row. Second, never miss a class, take great notes, then copy them over on index cards the same night, and finally carry the 3"×5" cards around with me until the next exam, studying them as I stood in line for lunch, a movie, or just waiting for the next thing to happen. This five-step process worked so well that I got all As in four semesters of organic chemistry. Maybe

Professor Jerry Williamson was the one who taught me to master organic chemistry that way.

Later when working for R. O. Hull (Lubrizol) headquartered in Cleveland I loaned my index cards to lab tech, Becky Zinni, who I believe got As studying my cards, which she returned, and I still have my hoard of books and papers. Dr. Ron Collins also at EMU was an excellent professor of polymer chemistry. I remember his telling the class in 1969 that the computer would be used more and more in the future in all areas of chemistry. Dr. Collins later retired as VP of academic affairs. I was also taking a computer course studying the FORTRAN language. My lab partner was a wizard at programming with this language. I've said many times that had I been more business savvy, the two of us could have given Bill Gates and Paul Allen a run for their money.

Unlike the University of Michigan, we had the full professors for daily lectures, not the teaching fellows, and these full professors were outstanding. Physical chemistry provided more of a challenge for me, and I owe my passing grade to my attractive lab partner, Jan, who was a favorite of the professor. If she got an A for our lab assignment, then I also got one. My lab grades made it possible to get through this most challenging discipline of chemistry. Kind of reminds me of the Catholic bishop who, upon reviewing his list of priests under his direction, one day noticed that one particular priest had been sent to the Congo in deepest Africa to open a mission for the church and had not been heard from for the past twenty-five years. The bishop said to himself, "I must immediately travel to Africa and offer some assistance." Arriving at the airport on the Ivory Coast, he immediately engaged a safari to take him to where the lost priest had been last heard from in the jungle of the Congo. As the bishop neared a large clearing, he could see a tall church steeple. Getting closer he saw first the entire church, then the school buildings and hospital and expansive manicured grounds surrounding the convent and orphanage. Upon entering the driveway lined with princess palms, he was beside himself in amazement. The long-lost priest, dressed in his best Sunday cassock, neatly pressed, met the bishop at the entrance gate, a gate much like the one at the Charles Krug

Winery in St. Helena, California, resplendent with waterfalls and seasonal flowers all abloom.

The priest said, "Welcome, Your Excellency. I heard you were coming."

The bishop immediately said, "How could you accomplish so much in just twenty-five years and most especially without any assistance from our diocese back in the States?" Then the bishop continued, "We are sorry that we lost track of you in our records."

"Well," the priest said, "I could not have accomplished anything without my scotch and my rosary."

The Bishop replied with a question: "Father, again my sincere congratulations, but you know I have been traveling all day now into the fifth day through the jungle and in this unbearable heat. You wouldn't have a scotch now, would you?"

The priest, extremely relieved that the bishop was not offended about the confession concerning the scotch, said, "Yes, Bishop, would you like a double?"

The bishop said, "Oh yes, Father. I thought you would never ask."

The priest shouted out, "Hey, Rosary! Would you bring us a couple of scotches?"

Having Jan as my physical chemistry partner was kinda like that.

One by one, I was checking off the classes on Dr. Spike's list. Sometimes I thought I would be an old man before I finally graduated. That's the way it feels when you're waiting for paint to dry or the dentist to finish the root canal or for the pilot to get through the storm turbulence or waiting for daylight in the swamp. But all of a sudden, it's over. But it wasn't over until June 1970.

One day in 1968, I found myself on the EMU campus waiting for Robert Kennedy to come to a rally in support of the Michigan Democratic candidate for Governor Zolton Ferency. I didn't care for Zolton Ferency, but I sure wanted to see Robert Kennedy.

Senator Kennedy was late arriving. Most of the three to four hundred students had wandered off by the time Kennedy's convertible pulled up. I was standing on the curb when the car stopped right in front of me. The senator climbed over the back seat exiting over the trunk, where I gave him a hand as he stepped onto the sidewalk. We said hello, and that's it. He spoke for about twenty to thirty minutes to the small group still there. The only thing I remember him saying is that he knew how to pronounce "Ferency," whereas President Johnson put the emphasis on the wrong syllable. I always liked the Kennedy brothers, and years later Mary Ann and I nearly had lunch with Ted Kennedy in Washington at the senate dining room. I believe that was in 1990, plus or minus a couple of years, Senator Ted Kennedy got stuck in traffic coming out of Hyannis Port and could not make our lunch engagement on that Monday.

My brother Tony and I both enjoyed politics. See this communication from George Romney to Tony in 1967:

STATE OF MICHIGAN
OFFICE OF THE GOVERNOR
—

George Romney
Governor

March 29, 1967

Mr. Tony L. Maurer
Colegio Internacional de Carabobo
Apartado 103
Urbanizacion El Trigal
Valencia, BDO, Carabobo, Venezuela

Dear Mr. Maurer,

Thank you for your recent letter and kind remarks.

While I'm not presently looking at the presidential nomination, I am taking a searching look at the possibility of doing so I am highly complimented by your confidence in my ability to provide national leadership.

I have taken the liberty of forwarding your letter to Romney Associates, a group formed to help GOP in any capacity. I am sure you will be hearing from them shortly.

Best wishes.

Sincerely,
George Romney

Speaking of my older brother, he got married in 1968 to Marilyn Elberts in Los Angeles, California. Mary Ann and I could not afford the airfare, but Tony did send a ticket for our parents to attend. Dad got a fresh haircut from Aubrey Welch or Burton McWilliams in Grayling and then drove to Ann Arbor. On the next day, we took Mom and Dad to Detroit Metro. My dad wanted a beer before boarding, and I think he had more than one because when we picked him up at the same gate two weeks later on his return from the wedding, the gate attendant said, "Mr. Maurer, did you have a good time in California?"

My dad said, "Yes I did."

And she said, "I thought you would because you sure looked like you were having a good time when you left."

Dad told me that the trip really opened his eyes to the world. I think he saw people really enjoying life out west and decided he did not have to work so hard anymore back in Michigan.

He stopped raising deacon calves (nearly always a losing venture in my eyes with the high loss rate of the fragile Holstein newborns, Dad called it the scours), and he quit his job at Stephan Wood Products in Grayling, a midnight-to-8:00-a.m. solo position making wooden picture frame molding. He immediately took a job at Mercy Hospital in the maintenance department. This gave him a chance to run for office and was elected a Crawford County commissioner. In the '50s, Dad was elected justice of the peace. Mom always wanted him to officiate at a wedding. I don't think he ever had the opportunity. My son-in-law, George Schisler, corporate attorney for Lam Research, married three couples in 2014. Dad became chairman of the law enforcement committee; essentially the sheriff reported to him. That's a long way from being the chief defendant in the State of Michigan's most publicized deer trial in the late 1940s. My dad studied law briefly in 1932 before the Depression knocked him out of college.

As graduation got closer, I began to think more about what to do with this new degree. Occasionally engineers would come to Ann Arbor from the Climax labs in Boulder, Colorado. Each would tell of sunshine and mountains and more sunshine, a commodity in short supply in Michigan. I started a subscription to the *Sunday Denver Post*, longing for graduation day and a chance to get out of Dodge. I thought I could transfer to the Boulder labs. Then I remembered that my very first boss at Climax, Mr. Jack Bacon, had taken a job at Dole Pineapple in Hawaii as director of research. Even more sunshine, I thought, so I sent a resume to "my old friend" Jack along with at least forty other resumes to companies in need of a chemist, especially one who already had four years of research experience.

I was not aware of the fact that the country was in the mid of a serious recession in 1970, the year I earned my BS in chemistry from EMU. Federal-Mogul right in Ann Arbor offered me a job as chief analytical chemist for the rubber and plastics group, part of its National Seal Division. At the same time, Climax asked me to stay on and join their sales and marketing group and triple my $5,000-plus annual salary as they would move me to the Greenwich, Connecticut, offices. I considered the move, asking Will Tschudi to describe the job. He said, "The office is in Greenwich, but you'll have to live two hours away by train because even with a $15,000-per-year salary, I could not afford to live in Greenwich." My job would require getting on a plane and flying to Los Angeles or some other West

Coast town and then work my way back across the country stopping in cities like Dallas, Houston, Chicago, St. Louis, Detroit, Cleveland, and Pittsburg before getting back to Connecticut on Friday.

I was to make presentations to oil and grease manufacturers in each city extolling the benefits of adding MoS_2 to their formulations. I took the job in Ann Arbor with Federal-Mogul. My kids were young, Mary Ann would be close to her family in Chelsea, and I really didn't like to fly so much. For the first two weeks at Federal-Mogul, the Climax gang called repeatedly saying that if I took the job, they'd set me up with an office in Ann Arbor, no need to go to Connecticut. I still did not want to fly and also thought I'd studied chemistry so long and hard, I wanted to prove to myself that I could be a bench chemist.

Climax Molybdenum Company did publish my paper at the first internation conference on solid lubrication in Denver, Colorado in 1970. The title of the paper was *The Lubrication Properties of Synthetic Molybdenum Disulfide* by H. Barry, T. Risdon, and T. Maurer.

It was nearly six months on the job at Federal-Mogul before I got a letter from the human resources manager at Dole Pineapple. I anxiously opened the envelope to read that my letter with resume had just reached his desk, and he was informing me that Jack Bacon had left the company over a year ago and further that Dole Pineapple did not need a chemist at this time.

Climax always threw a retirement going away party and presented the retiree with a scroll. Tony Deratana and I shared a party. Now here is what my scroll says:

Climax
Marching and Chowder
Michigan Society Chapter

WHEREAS having learned to jump up and down on the bank of MUD LAKE up 'ere in the Paul Bunyan town of Grayling when he was a young'un...which is supposed to make the trees on the opposite bank shake, of which this activity seems to have singularly affected his athletic prowess & his naivety-retention, by virtue of which he never could truly spike a volley ball across a blame net, but threw it, man,-threw it! **WHEREAS** with Bunyan-like spunk could harangue for hours with arch-arguer Rabbit-Tall (Bear-Cub-Bryant) & through he thought he could run the mile in six minutes, the night he ran was a nor wester blowing & he puffed in shy a bit of seven, losing thereby sums of money to ha-haers & crass Climax betting sharks... **WHEREAS**, by virtue of being the Mayo Smith of the intense Harry Toon Realty Softball team, ending up, win or lose, in spontaneous celebrations where his poker prowess would fail his purse & he would tell or Prarie Pike & Beer-bottle-deer from Grayling...**WHEREAS**, this gentle & Molysulfide-wise investigator, this most congenial family man-has some-how managed to maintain a proper hat size.

Know ye by these presents that

Terry Andrew Maurer

has been elected to the Vague Order of the Orange Fedora and is entitled to all the usual privileges and prerogatives of that ennobling office.

Given under our hand this 17th day of June, 1970
George A. Timmons, William H. Wilson
Douglas A. Doane, Mark S. Vukasivich

Here now is a postscript from one of the Climax scientists, which gives a snapshot of the caliber of research going on at our lab before it closed its doors in 1985.

Email from Anthony Bryhan
Re: Molybdenum Mosaics
April 2, 2012

Hello to the Climax Molybdenum Gang, In the vein of passing on Climax Moly history, I've a story to share:

In the early 1980's I enjoyed numerous discussions with Eric Kahns about attempts to increase the ductility of molybdenum welds. During this time Bill Hagel was having discussions with Ford Aeroneutronic about their desire for a new hot-gas valve to the Trident missile. They wanted to raise the operating temperature form 2500F to 3000F and wondered about a moly alloy that would survive the "dropped hammer" test; a Navy technician accidentally dropping a hammer on a welded moly valve. I worked for Ed Whelan at the time and I started program L216-21 to explore ppm additions of interstitial and substitutional elements to increase weldment ductility.

The Russians had two alloys, TsM-6 and TsM-10 that Semy somehow obtained. (One day months later, Doug Doane called me into his office and introduced me to two men that wanted to ask me questions-he said they were from the CIA and my first thought was "what steel company is that?") These two moly alloys were reported to have improved weldment ductility. Bob Schultz made test welds in our excellent controlled atmosphere chamber but the ductility was no better that commercial moly of TZM. I proposed we melt heats that were a bit different in composition, a Mo-Zr-B-C alloy and a Mo-AI-B-C alloy. We eventually had success with weldment tensile elongation of almost 20%. My induction into the **AMAX Marching and Chowder Society** references the "famed Bryhan drop-it-on-the-floor ductility test." Mike Ciomik and Eugene Kalil worked on a patent, Amax 997 but for reasons unknown to me it wasn't obtained.

After I left the Lab I moved to Exxon, then to TRW and next to GE Astrospace Div. I was Group Leader for Fabrication Development for the SP-100 space nuclear power program. This program was to design, develop and build a waste-basket sized fission power supply for NASA. The structural allow was Nb-1Zr selected because it was readily available but mostly because weldments did not suffer brittle fracture as did all commercial moly alloys. I visited Greenwich and talked to Steve Johnson (if I remember his name correctly) about AMAX optimizing and commercializing one of the above alloys. A weldable moly alloy would have been perfect for SP-100 since it was discovered that Nb alloys had insufficient creep strength. AMAX wasn't interested. Congress cut the funding for SP-100 in 1993.

After SP-100 ended I was asked, because of my expertise with Nb and Mo to head the fabrication development group for the US Team for the International Thermonuclear Experimental Reactor (ITER). The design was to operate at high enough temperature where weldable moly would be useful. At that time however, the US was starting one of the Mid-East wars and Congress significantly truncated funding for ITER. I moved on to become Director of Manufacturing Technology at Applied Materials, retiring in 2001.

Over the years I've been dismayed that no moly company shared AMAX's philosophy that a Core Competency was knowledge of moly metal. In 2002 I co-authored (MK Miller, AJ Bryhan, et al.) an atom probe tomography study of one half of the 19.5% ductility tensile specimen I'd been hauling around for 20 years. Quantitative atom distribution showed no oxygen segregation to grain boundaries and fracture mode was trans-granular instead of the historical intergranular. (I was very reluctant to lend my cherished moly sample to this fellow but he assured me that he would not lose it. "I analyzed fabric from the Shroud of Turin, I won't lose it." He lost it after making the first round of measurements...)

The Jupiter Icy Moon Orbiter (JIMO) pro-gram was started by NASA to again develop a refractory metal fission power system. I was part of the team. I wrote a letter to Steven Whistler, CEO of Phelps Dodge (since they now "owned" AMAX and therefore my research) telling him of the need for, and opportunity for commer-cialization of a weldable moly alloy. Phelps Dodge wasn't interested. Next I wrote to the International Moly Association in London. I corresponded with their technical representative Nicole Kinsman in 2004. IMOA I was told was happy selling moly as an alloy in 316 and thought the return-on-investment was too long to spend money confirming my observations.

Evan Ohriner of ORNL in 2006 attempted to duplicate the alloys I observed (BV Cockeram, EK Ohriner, et al. 2008). His experiment confirmed that weld DBTT for Mo-AI-B-C were consistently better than for LCAC.

I enjoy my retirement. I volunteer at the Luther Burbank Farm and tend my big garden in rural Sonoma California. My wife and I have visited most of the places we wanted to see. But, I'm still bugged about man knowing about weldable molybdenum metal. Recently I wrote to a Chinese moly company to see if they might want to have information about weldable molybdenum alloys.

It's now 30 years since I had the pleasure of working with many of you. Someday Man will "Go where no man has gone before" and a weldable molybdenum alloy, lithium cooled reactor will be an enabling technology.

Warm Regards
Tony Bryhan

Tom Risdon, Terry Maurer, Ron Hartman, Dan Diesburg,
Dave Sponsellar, Karl Kienholz and Heidi the Dog

Climax reunion in 2013: Terry wearing a hat, Ron
Hartman (Clyde Suckfinger) seated next to Terry,
Dave Sponseller seated on grass far right, and Cal
Halada seated on grass second from the left.

Me and Don Jutzi

CHAPTER VI

Federal-Mogul Years (1970–1973)
Richard M. Nixon
(1969–1974)

As I start to write this sixth chapter on March 23, 2011, from the Napa Valley, CNN has just announced that Liz Taylor has died at the age of seventy-nine. I liked her best in my favorite movie, *Giant*, with James Dean and Rock Hudson. I especially liked the scene when James Dean hits oil on his little part of the sprawling Texas ranch, Reatta. Covered with oil and drunk, he keeps saying, "I'm going to be a rich 'un. I'm going to be a rich 'un." And he did. His persistence paid off. He never quit working or looking for the oil. Liz was married to Rock Hudson but always encouraged Jet Rink, Dean's character. Mary Ann is my Liz when it comes to encouragement on the waterfront.

After working with oil and grease and MoS_2 at Climax for over four years, I was now getting to learn about the rubber business at Federal-Mogul. How to formulate rubber compounds, how to analyze competition's products, and how to test the compounds for all types of physical properties at the National Seal research labs of Federal-Mogul in Ann Arbor. The labs were located near the Ann Arbor Airport, off State Street on the southside of town.

Don Jutzi was the fellow who got my resume, interviewed me, and hired me at a salary 11 percent higher than what Climax offered me to stay in their labs. Granted I was offered a much bigger salary by the Climax marketing group to join them but chose not to move to Connecticut or even operate out of Ann Arbor with all the travel required. Don Jutzi was the manager of National Seals' rubber research operations, having moved from Chicago Rawhide, a National Seal competitor from Elgin, Illinois, west of Chicago.

Don was a fun guy, liked to celebrate happy hour daily, and enjoyed his young family. His two daughters were preteens in 1970 and his wife was close to a trophy wife. I say close because Don might not like my choice of adjectives if he were to read this. Don really pushed my career along at Federal-Mogul. Not only was he supportive in all my daily assignments, but he included me in many important corporate presentations at the Southfield corporate headquarters. I was being groomed to replace the world-renowned gasket expert, Mr. Al Gordon, from the recently acquired Vellumoid Gasket Corporation in Worcester, Massachusetts.

In that position, I traveled frequently on one of the two corporate planes visiting our plants in Worcester, Van Wert, Ohio, and Frankfurt, Indiana. There were trips to Chicago, Los Angeles, and Erie, Pennsylvania. Also, on our monthly meetings in Southfield, I'd meet and lunch with the big guys, including Tom Russell, company president, and the corporate research director Al Bearns, and the national sales manager as well as Al Gordon himself and always Don Jutzi. I was just twenty-nine years old. Who can say that completing my BS degree did not pay off? We moved to a new house, brand-new, at 1090 Wing Drive in Scio Township and the Dexter School District just West of Ann Arbor. Laurie and Stephen would be starting school soon, and we were told that the Dexter schools were superior to the Ann Arbor Mack School where they were to go.

We spent nearly six years on Wing drive, before moving north four miles to Lock Alpine in 1976. While living on Wing Drive, we got assimilated into the Dexter community, attending church at St. Joseph's Catholic Church, where Father Ted was pastor. Laurie and Steve went to Dexter schools until their graduations in 1984 and 1986. It was while living on Wing Drive that we were friends and neighbors with young Liz and Chuck McKinnon, a GM pilot, whose father we ultimately met in 2009 in St. Helena, California.

Other neighbors who were part of our euchre card group and whom we remained friends with to this day were Dave and Donna Gibson. Donna and Mary Ann were fast friends, and Dave and I briefly were partners in my first company, Green Thumb. Dave had a company called Crystal Clear, which was a water softening business. We merged our two businesses, but it didn't last.

Also part of our euchre group were Neil and Judy Gerl, Ken and Judy Collica, Stan and Donna McFadden, and for sure, Chuck and Liz McKinnon, and Tom and Barb Steffe, whom we met first in Ann Arbor on Mixtwood in 1967, and then we both moved to Loch Alpine and finally to Northern Michigan, Steffes to Suttons Bay, and the Maurers to Grayling.

I worked just three years at Federal-Mogul's Seal Division on rubber shaft seals and O-rings made of several different types of rubber base materials—SBR, Hypalon, Viton, nitrile, neoprene, silicone, and even some natural rubber. My job was primarily to break down competitive formulations using infrared, thermal gravimetric analysis (TGA), and solvent extraction analytical techniques. Also my lab did physical testing on experimental shaft seals and O-ring compounds. Don Jutzi, Bob Hinderer, Jim Hakala, John Gray, and sometimes even Bob Furhman would do the compounding of these new formulations. Testing the low-temperature properties of those elastomers was routine in my lab. I could have prevented the *Challenger* disaster if someone in authority had consulted with me. All rubber compounds have a low temperature below which the compound cannot perform—that is, below which it no longer can maintain its elasticity or flexibility.

The test is pretty simple. Allow a thin piece of the subject rubber to come to temperature in an ethylene glycol solution stabilized at a prescribed temperature with dry ice, then hit it with a pneumatic lever. If it doesn't crack in half, it can still perform at that temperature. That number is recorded in the profile for the experimental formulation, which might have a number like E1132.

This would mean that this is the thirty-second formulation attempt for the project labeled 11. So if the flight director for the *Challenger* flight had called me and told me that the temperature at

Cape Kennedy was twenty-eight degrees Fahrenheit that morning. I could have checked the O-ring low-temperature rating, and if it was twenty-eight degrees Fahrenheit, then I would say scrub the flight for today or wait till it warms up above thirty-four degrees adding six degrees to cover the margin of error. That simple. I had lab techs helping me out at Federal-Mogul; I didn't do all that hard work alone.

In August 1970, Don Jutzi asked me to hire a lab technician for my lab. I placed an ad in the Sunday Ann Arbor paper and had twenty-something responses by Wednesday. I had to interview them all. Most of the young ladies were married to University of Michigan grad students. I remember hiring Janet Hipple. Don Jutzi was so impressed with my choice that he told me to hire three more from the same group for his own lab. So I did.

Don came to me after all the new girls had been on the job for a little over a week and said, "We have a problem."

I said, "What?"

Don said, "One of the girls you hired is pregnant. She comes to work wearing a trench coat and immediately puts on her white lab coat." He continued, "It's your job to find out if she's pregnant, and if she is, you have to let her go. Company policy, no pregnant ladies may be hired. Insurance won't cover preexisting conditions."

So I asked her, "Are you pregnant?" The answer was yes. I felt bad because she said she really needed the job, but I said, "We can't keep you. Thanks for coming to interview."

Today I am sure that once a person is hired, a company could not operate that way.

While working on a gasket project, Don and I drove to Chicago to meet with engineers from a company which marketed a grinding machine called the Fitzmill. We thought that we could use this machine to grind up preformulated but uncured rubber and then roll it out like cookie dough, then punch out gaskets and cure them in a continuous oven. We got to Chicago in time for dinner at the Playboy club on Rush Street. Before finishing this story about our Chicago trip, I must insert here the latest situation concerning radiation in tap water in Japan following the catastrophic 9.0 earthquake and devastating tsunami which hit Japan on March 11, 2011, this year as I am writing.

Concern in Tokyo over radiation in tap water
Elaine Kurtenbach and Shino Yuasa
Associated Press

Tokyo—Radiation leaking from Japan's tsunami-damaged nuclear power plant has caused Tokyo's tap water to exceed safety standards for infants to drink, officials said Wednesday, sending anxiety levels soaring over the nation's food and water supply.

Residents cleared store shelves of bottled water after Tokyo Gov. Shintaro Ishihara said levels of radioactive iodine in tap water were more than twice what is considered safe for babies. Officials begged those in the city to buy only what they needed, saying hoarding could hurt the thousands of people without any water in areas devastated by the March 11 earthquake and tsunami.

"I've never seen anything like this," clerk Torn Kikutaka said, surveying the downtown Tokyo supermarket where the entire stock of bottled water sold out almost immediately after the news broke, despite a limit of two, two-liter bottles per customer.

The unsettling new development affecting Japan's largest city, home to around 13 million people, added to growing fears over the nation's food supply.

Radiation from the Fukushima Dai-ichi plant has seeped into raw milk, seawater and 11 kinds of vegetables, including broccoli, cauliflower and turnips, from areas around the plant.

The U.S. Food and Drug Administration said it was halting imports of Japanese dairy and produce from the region near the facility. Hong Kong went further and required that Japan perform safety checks on meat, eggs and seafood before accepting those products.

Officials are still struggling to stabilize the nuclear plant, which on Wednesday belched black smoke from Unit 3 and forced the evacuation of workers, further delaying attempts to make needed repairs. The plant, 140 miles (220 kilometers) North of Tokyo, has been leaking radiation since the quake and tsunami knocked out its crucial cooling systems.

The crisis is emerging as the world's most expensive natural disaster on record, likely to cost up to $309 billion, according to a new government estimate. Police say an estimated 18,000 people were killed.

Several people have contacted me and Avita Water about trying to help supply bottled water to Japan. We are in talks with Korean business people as well as potential investors from Chicago, Florida, Las Vegas, Detroit and I expect there will be others.

Now back to my 1971 trip to Chicago with my Federal-Mogul boss, Don Jutzi. As we came out of the Playboy club from dinner, we immediately encountered a man in tennis shoes and wearing a blazer offering up a host of hot watches for sale at remarkable discounts off the expected retail prices. He had watches up and down both arms and pinned to the inside of his blazer. We knew right away that the watches were for sure stolen. In hindsight, I am sure that is what the hustler wanted his customers to believe. You better make a deal quickly as he looked nervously from side to side as he was peddling his watches. Don saw him first and answered the watch hawker's question.

"Hey, do you guys need a watch?" the man nervously inquired.

"How much?" Don asked.

He said, "I've got an Omega here for twenty dollars."

I said, "Let me see it." I looked at the fancy watch and handed it to Don for his inspection.

Don said, "My wife bought me an Omega ten years ago, and I still wear it, see?"

I said, "I'll take it," and handed over my twenty which was still a lot of money, especially in 1971. But not for an Omega, which I thought could easily cost eighty to ninety dollars retail.

The rest of the night, we hit a few more Rush Street clubs I kept thinking what a deal I had made. It wasn't until about 1:00 a.m. when we stopped for a burger in a well-lit joint on the strip that I tried to set my watch. I could hardly get my fingers on the post. So I handed it to Don and said, "Here can you set this for me?"

It was then that Don took a real good look at the watch and said, "This is not an Omega, it is a Cimega."

I said, "What the heck is a Cimega?"

Don said, "Never heard of one. I think we got taken."

On Monday back at the lab in Ann Arbor Don told everyone about my purchase in Chicago. So Bob Hinderer asks to see my Cimega. He popped the back off the watch for a closer inspection and announced to those of us in the lab waiting for his scientific analysis. "It has one jewel, unadjusted."

When he put the cover back in place, the watch never ran again. But this is not the end of the story. Two years later, I was back in Chicago for another Federal-Mogul business trip and went back to Rush Street for dinner and drinks. This time it's Jim Hakala (Jim helped me move from Mixtwood to Wing Drive, he said he would not help me move my collections of **Newsweeks** again) with me, not Don. As Jim and I were walking, the Rush Street scene near the Playboy club, who do I see but the watch peddler walking on the other side of the street.

I said to Jim, "There's the guy who sold me the now infamous Cimega watch two years ago. I'm going to go get my money back." So I crossed the street and confronted the crook directly. I said, "You're the guy who sold me a watch two years ago, telling me it was an Omega and it was a Cimega, which was worthless."

He calmly said, "How much did you pay?"

I said, "Twenty dollars."

He then said, "For repeat customers, I'll give a 50 percent discount."

We both just laughed at the completely unlikely second encounter.

It was later in 1971, probably close to Thanksgiving; maybe it was the Christmas break that year that Mary Ann and I took our first trip to California. This to be my first trip West, Mary Ann had visited her cousins Kathy and Tom Kendig and Dick and Marie Powers sometime in 1962 also going to Santa Barbara and San Francisco on her first trip. For me, I was very excited to see my brother Tony and his new wife of three years, Marilyn, at their new home on Brower Street in Simi Valley, California.

We were taking Laurie and Stephen now just five and four years old. Our plans were to spend the three-week vacation seeing all that Southern California had to offer, and we did. The first thing a person from Michigan notices is the sunshine. To this day, I still tell people that on the trip I took a nap one Sunday afternoon, and the sun was shining. When I woke up, the sun was still shining. That would never happen in Michigan. We saw orange trees ripe with oranges ready to pick. In 1971, Simi Valley was still mostly filled with orange groves, so many, so full of orange oranges—I know *orange oranges* sounds redundant, but I like it like that. I could hardly stop admiring them. Then there were the mountains all around, not huge but undulating and interesting geography, again not seen in Michigan. The plant life was something to study: palms, flowering trees and shrubs, and grapes hanging from Tony's patio with a trestle. We drove to Oxnard to launch Tony's fishing boat in the Pacific. This was my second trip to the ocean having experienced it for the first time in Acapulco some nearly ten years earlier. Tony and I caught Bonita, lingcod, Dolly Vardin, sheep head, cow cod, Irish lord, calico bass, rock cod, dancing lords, salmon grouper, and some fish we could even eat.

This reminded me of the story about the young Scottish woman who recently immigrated to the US. One day she told her husband, Scottie, that she believed she might be pregnant, and she should have an exam. Well, after the exam, the doctor told her, "Ma'am, you have insufficient passage, and if you have anything, it'll be a miracle." Her anxious husband in the waiting room immediately asked her what the gynecologist said. Her English being very rough and new to her told old Scottie that she heard the doctor say, "You have a fish in your passage, and if you have anything, it'll be a mackerel."

On a later expedition, we took a thirty-person charter out passed the Channel Islands some sixty miles catching the bigger ones. My brother was the ultimate fisherman; he'd rather fish than eat or sleep. I prefer golf but never turn down an opportunity to fish on the ocean. We took the kids to Disneyland. We never experienced such a clean and entertaining adventure again. The park was still quite new. Laurie and Stephen were the perfect age to see all that Mickey Mouse had to offer, which was a lot. Pirates of the Caribbean was everybody's favorite ride, even Kimberley Guilfoyle's, I learned in 2015. Seeing Snow White, Goofy, and all the other Disney characters around the castle and the main street electric light parade in the evening were amazing.

One day Tony asked me if I wanted to see where he taught school in the Watts area of inner-city Los Angeles. I said, "Sure!"

He said, "Okay, but you'll have to get up early because it's nearly sixty miles to drive into the city, and the traffic gets pretty slow if we don't get an early start."

I think we might have been on the road headed south at 5:00 a.m. It was still dark. After about an hour of driving, Tony said, "We sure got the jump on traffic today."

I said, "What, I've never seen so many cars in my life." It was at least five to six lanes of red taillights creeping along.

He said, "We're moving, aren't we?"

It was three to four years before he got transferred to Stony Point High, a school over the hills in the next valley, Sacramental Valley, I think, much closer to Simi Valley. He told me that the switch came just before he was about to have a nervous breakdown from the daily trips into Los Angeles. I think my daughter Laurie knows what her uncle was talking about as she now makes a similar trip just once per week from her home in St. Helena some fifty miles south into San Francisco to study art at the renowned Academy of Arts in the City by the Bay, this in 2011.

I was so impressed with the weather and lifestyle in California that I started checking the papers for any company looking for a rubber chemist. Sure enough, there was an ad for a rubber chemist wanted in San Clemente. I asked Tony where that was, and he said, "Oh, I'd like the area, it's south of Simi Valley but not so faraway toward San Diego." I called for an interview.

At the interview the company manager said, "You're perfect for the job. When can you start?"

I said I had to return to Ann Arbor and give Federal-Mogul my notice, and I would be back in three weeks.

He said, "Great! But don't come back to San Clemente, we need you in Birmingham, Alabama."

That's not why I answered the add, I told him, "I've already spent four years of my life in Alabama. I now want to live and work in California."

He said he'd keep my name, just in case his California chemist didn't keep his green card or work visa from Japan. I don't know why I did not continue the job search. Probably it was time to return to Michigan. Life has a way of moving you along. You have to really, really want to change directions if that's your goal. I think the most successful people do get some lucky breaks once in a while. But a person can chart his own course. It is still best to find a mentor to help you along the way. You need to ask yourself some questions. What do I want out of life? Where do I want to live? What do I like to do? What is important? What makes you happy? Don't be a drifter. Chart your own course, stick to it, and put yourself on a schedule. Write down your one-year, three-year, five-year, ten-year, twenty-year, thirty-year, forty-year, fifty-year goals. Look at them each year on your birthday.

How about listing six key factors for a happy life: where you want to live, type of spouse you want, house style and vacation spot, salary needed, save 10 percent minimum per year, and number of children you want.

Oh, by the way, your house should have a breakfast room which catches the morning sun, it'll get you off with a sunny disposition every day. This primarily for my grandchildren, and their grandchildren, and on and on. In the future, a person born in the USA may live for 150 years. It's a good idea to plan ahead. I do expect to be around for another sixty-seven years, which would put me at 135.

So I guess I am only halfway through, so I'd better follow my own advice. Meditate at least twenty minutes per day, Father McIlmoyl from Grace Episcopal Church in St. Helena says, "Do two periods of twenty minutes per day." I say try to do just twenty once. I know you're supposed to clear your mind when you're meditating, but when that's not working, let your mind wander to your goals. That's enough time daily to map out not only your spiritual goals but also to think about your physical well-being and career goals. I read once that a dog lives five times as long as it takes for its skeleton to mature. Well, that's why my goal is 135 years. A human skeleton matures at twenty-five years, so there is 125, and I'm just adding ten more for good measure.

Grandma Maurer, Maty Ann, Laurie, and Stephen in 1972.

Bernard Maurer, Terry Maurer
Laurence Maurer, Stephen Maurer
'4' generations, dec,1971,Michigan

CHAPTER VII

Lubrizol Years
(1973–1978)
Gerald R. Ford
(1974–1977)

So now that everything seems to be in order at Federal-Mogul, it is time to make another change. At least that is what other folks think is the right thing for me. First, Dupont Chemical wants me to interview for a sales job, requiring a move to Wilmington, Delaware. Then Lubrizol Chemical Company wants me to consider selling their specialty chemicals by joining their International Rust Proof Division, the territory would be Southeast Michigan and Northern Ohio. And then Federal-Mogul, my current employer, thinks I should join their sales team in Southfield, Michigan. Even Climax Molybdenum Company wanted me to go into sales and marketing three years earlier. So I figure, maybe it's time to interview with the first three and find out if maybe sales is my thing.

First, I flew to Wilmington and interviewed with at least four or five PhD people. Since I had researched and purchased a Dupont TGA machine (thermal gravimetric analyzer) for Federal-Mogul, the Dupont sales manager figured I could sell their high-tech machine to other rubber companies.

The trip and the interviews went well, and while waiting for their offer, I came back to Ann Arbor on Tuesday and drove to Cleveland for my Lubrizol interviews on Thursday of the same week. The reason Lubrizol was interested in me for sales was, once again, I had tested their calcium zinc phosphate as a metal prep for rubber to metal bonding on shaft seals, and as a research chemist for Federal-Mogul, I strongly recommended to corporate that they should make a switch in chemistry from their current supplier MacDermid to Lubrizol. Lubrizol's new calcium zinc phosphate provided a stronger bond of the rubber to the metal.

The Van Wert plant jumped on my recommendation first, which provided annual new sales to Lubrizol of approximately 150K. So the Lubrizol sales manager figured that if he could hire Terry Maurer, I could facilitate conversion from MacDermid to Lubrizol at both the Frankfort, Indiana plant, as well as the new plant coming on stream in six months in Summerton, South Carolina. I knew why they wanted me, and I knew how much business I could bring.

Their current Detroit salesman, Bill Fast, was leaving the company to live on an Indian reservation in Arizona. I always wondered why. Of the four possible sales jobs, Dupont, Federal-Mogul, Climax Molybdenum, or Lubrizol, I felt the Lubrizol job was the least glamorous. At any rate, now I am in Cleveland talking to Lubrizol's International Rust Proof's technical and sales managers. I met with Joe McGee, Carl Varga, Howard Pekar, and the general manager, Lee Huff. I could tell they all wanted me on board, no question about it. It was getting late in the day, say about 4:30 p.m., and Mr. Varga says, "We'd like you to go down the street to Lubrizol's corporate office and talk to our human resources department before we go out for dinner."

"Okay," I said, "no problem." Well, everyone had told me what a fine company Lubrizol was, and everyone in Cleveland knew that a job there was about as good as it gets.

Great salaries, excellent benefits, fringes of travel for the sales guys, and company cars with liberal expense allowances. But it was late in the day, and I was getting tired when I stepped into the fancy office belonging to their human resources manager, dressed in his impeccable manager's suit.

It didn't take long for the interview to go south, at least from the Lubrizol guys' point of view. He said, "Hello, Mr. Maurer. I understand you are interviewing with our company. Would you please tell me about yourself."

"Well," I said, "that's true. First of all, I have a bachelor of science degree in chemistry from Eastern Michigan University." Then either by the fatigue, his attitude, my hunger pains, or irritation as to the arrogance in the tone of his voice hit me, and I snapped back. "Sir," I said, "I don't give a damn if I ever work for Lubrizol. The management at your International Rust Proof division wants me in the worst way because I can bring half a million dollars worth of new business to your company in six months." So I added, "If you don't show me why I should consider Lubrizol right now, then I'm out of here and you'll likely lose your job for screwing up this interview."

He nearly fell off his chair and immediately apologized and in the same breath showed me corporate bulletins and employee benefit brochures. I said "Thanks" and got up to leave as he put his arm around me, saying, "I'll drive you back to Mr. Varga's office for your dinner meeting. Next time you are in Cleveland, I want you to bring your wife and my wife and I will take you to dinner."

I was thinking, *This is the way I expected to be treated.*

When I returned to Ann Arbor and Federal-Mogul on Monday, I fully expected to be choosing between three job offers. As it turned out the Dupont people decided to hire a PhD chemist for their position. I needed to choose between Lubrizol's or Federal-Mogul's sales positions or remain in the lab. I chose Lubrizol's offer over Federal-Mogul's primarily because Lubrizol was recognized as more of a chemical company and Federal-Mogul more of an engineering and mechanical products company making automotive components including bearings as well as O-rings and rubber shaft seals.

It's interesting to mention here in March 2011 that Lubrizol is about to be purchased 100 percent by Mr. Warren Buffett's company Berkshire Hathaway. I once owned one share of Berkshire Hathaway in 1995. My purchase price was $18,000. I sold it for $27,000 in three weeks on the knee-jerk recommendation of Paul Seals, my Olde discount stockbroker. Berkshire got as high as $142,000 per share three years ago. It trades today in 2011 at $125,000 plus or minus. (Now on November 23, 2014, it is at $219,935.) For the record, here is the AP bulletin about the Buffet purchase of Lubrizol for $9B in cash in 2011. And now on December 12, 2019, Berkshire Hathaway class A is now at $338,000.

Berkshire Hathaway to Buy Lubrizol for $9B in cash Omaha, Neb (AP) Warren Buffett's company said Monday it will spend about $9 billion cash to add specialty chemical maker Lubrizol Corp. to the eclectic mix of businesses inside Berkshire Hathaway Inc.

The purchase may help satisfy Buffett's appetite for large acquisitions to boost Berkshire's earnings power, but the deal is still significantly smaller than last year's $26.7 billion acquisition of the Burlington Northern Santa Fe railroad.

"Lubrizol is exactly the sort of company with which we love to partner, the global leader in several market applications run by a talented CEO, James Hambrick," Buffett said in a statement.

Two years ago, Berkshire invested $3 billion in preferred shares of Dow Chemical to help finance Dow's $16.5 billion purchase of specialty chemical maker Rohm & Haas in 2009. That deal likely gave Buffett insight into the high-margin specialty chemical business.

In Monday's deal, Berkshire will pay $135 per share, a 28 percent premium to Lubrizol's closing stock price Friday of $105.44. The transaction also includes about $700 million in net debt.

Lubrizol, of Wickliffe, Ohio, makes chemicals for companies, fuel additives for gasoline and diesel and other ingredients for the transportation sector. Last month, it reported that its fourth-quarter profit climbed 17 percent because of a $19 million tax benefit and higher sales. The company's revenue grew 11 percent to $1.32 billion.

Berkshire already owns a conglomerate of more than 125 manufacturing and service businesses called Marmon Holdings that may use some of Lubrizol's products. Marmon's businesses serve the transportation, energy, and construction markets, and Marmon makes products ranging from railroad tank cars to metal fasteners.

I started work at Lubrizol's International Rust Proof division in July 1973. My boss was Don Zigmond, who had his office in Farmington Hills, Michigan. My office was, for the first time, a home office. The main products in my sales bag were zinc phosphates, emulsion oils for corrosion protection, steel cleaners, and corrosion-resistant paints. The customers were primarily job shops processing fasteners for the automotive industry. The shops themselves were required to be on approval lists by GM, Ford, and Chrysler to get the work. Part of my job was also to get Lubrizol products or systems preapproved at General Motors. We were not on commission sales in the beginning so calling on GM engineers was a welcome break from the more routine and competitive sales to the job shops. I was encouraged by management to spend money entertaining the GM engineers at fine lunches and tickets to opening day at Tiger Stadium, Red Wing hockey games, and the Detroit Lions football. Of course, I was expected to buy the tickets and go to the events myself sometimes taking Mary Ann when their wives were invited.

Good thing for the GM connection because I had second thoughts about what I had gotten myself into with this LZ sales job, especially in the first few months as I learned where the job shops were located and how much some of them were like the sweatshops in Dickens's *Tale of the Two Cities*. They were located in the poorer sections of Flint, Michigan; Toledo, Ohio; South Chicago; the inner city of Detroit; and Jackson, Michigan. In my first week on the job I found myself at Flint Chemical Coatings where the roof leaked over the zinc phosphate line. The ten- to twelve-tank line was operated by toothless, hunched-back old women who could scare you on a sunny day. I was warned by a younger version of these abused souls to be careful around the 190-degree caustic descaler tank where one of the few men in the plant cooked himself to death after he fell in head first two weeks prior to my first visit. The women got him out but should have put him in the much cooler rinse water tank instead of leaving him lying on the catwalk until the ambulance arrived. His scalding clothes and high pH skin and baking time was more than a body could endure. I was very careful as I reached into the tank to retrieve my fifty milliliters for analysis.

Week by week, I became more familiar with my sales territory, and day by day, I arrived home less and less stressed and tired from the continuous searching for addresses and driving routes to my customers scattered all over Michigan and Northern Ohio. My job and account base had three distinct areas of responsibility: first, contact job shops processing mainly automotive fasteners and various small steel parts; second, connect with captive shops (companies like Prestole Everlock and Dura Corporation in Toledo, and Kewaunee Scientific in Adrian and Tecumseh Products in Tecumseh, Michigan)—these companies actually manufactured parts and did their own coatings; and finally deal with General Motors corporate engineering, at the tech center in Warren, Michigan.

Without going into all my secrets for successful salesmanship, I'll share a key point I learned at Lubrizol through the Xerox sales training course our entire sales force took. Here it is: When trying to make a sale, one has to remember that there are always three buyers the salesperson must sell. Depending on the size of the company one person may wear all three hats, but normally in the industrial chemical sales for us Lubrizol folks, we're talking about three distinct people: *First comes the economic buyer; he is usually the owner of the company or the president, maybe the purchasing agent. Second is the feasibility buyer; he is usually the chief engineer for the project, the person who knows all the specifications required to do what it is that needs to be accomplished. Third is the implementer, the person who must make the chemicals perform on the line, the person who knows how to actually run the line properly.* If you do not have all three buyers sold on the fact that your product meets each buyer's requirements, the sale will not last very long, and you may not even get the first order.

The best example of how this works is one I've told my Maurer-Shumaker sales team many times. Mr. Zern Bigelow, chief engineer, maybe he was also the plant manager at Prestole Everlock in Toledo, told me in 1974 that I would get his business supplying all the Lubrizol products for his zinc phosphate line replacing the departed MacDermid salesperson, Tony Tranchia. This meant the cleaner, the descaler, zinc phosphate, chromic rinse, and the corrosion-resistant emulsion oil RustARest 53253, a big sale on my part. Annual dollar sales for the year for this customer would be near 75K. Here is what Mr. Bigelow told me, "Terry, you've been calling on me for twelve months. Now the MacDermid salesman is transferring to California. I'm going to switch all the business to you. I know you better. And one thing: don't ever go around me."

I had already been selling **the implementer**, and Tom Mockler, the company president, **the economic buyer** for the past twelve months. Zern was the final **feasibility buyer**. Zern also told me that one time a salesman went around him and sold directly to Tom Mockler, the president of this specialty fastener manufacturer, even skipping the implementer.

Tom came to Zern one day, saying, "I've decided to try a new supplier, and I have already ordered in two fifty-five-gallon drums of his zinc phosphate, and I want you to give it a try." Zern told me this is what happened. He said, "Yes, sir, Mr. Mockler, I'll give it a try, starting on the first of next week."

At the end of the trial week, Mr. Mockler came to Zern's office in the plant and asked, "How did that new zinc phosphate work?"

Zern said, "Well, sir, it worked very well, I've saved processed parts to show you and you can see for yourself what a nice uniform crystalline structure we got."

"Great," said Mr. Mockler.

Zern said, "But there is one problem, and it is serious and I think you'll agree."

"What's that?" Tom said.

"Well," Zern said. "I want to show you something else." He walked over to the two empty drums of the trial product, kicking them both to show that both were empty. Zern says, "Sir, we normally can do the job using one drum per week, and you can see that both drums are empty. That means we would be purchasing twice as much material with this new company as we used with the old supplier. Now, I don't think you want to do that, do you?"

"No," said Mr. Mockler. "We sure don't!"

"You had better stay with our current supplier," Zern told me.

"You know why we went throughout two drums when normally one would do?" I said no. "Well," Zern continued, "I came into the plant during the evening shift, and I dumped a full drum down the drain. So you see I make the final decision as to who the supplier will be. Don't mess with me."

I got the point and kept all the business until the plant closed some seven years later, which was two years after my friend Zern died of a heart attack.

Just a brief interruption here to share the news that my preferred candidate for president in 2012, Mr. Mitt Romney has announced he is running for president. See the email which I got yesterday!

From: Mitt Romney
To: Terry Maurer
Subject: What a week!
Date: April 14, 2011

Dear Terry,

On Monday afternoon, I announced on Twitter the launch of my Exploratory Committee for President of the United States. Click below to see the announcement on MittRomney.com.

I am convinced more than ever that the current administration has put our great country on the wrong course. But with the right leadership, I believe that America's best days are still ahead.

Together, we can get back on the right track, and move forward with a growing economy, more jobs, and serious fiscal discipline in Washington D.C.

Ann and I are grateful for your continued support.

Best,

Mitt Romney

Having seen Mitt Romney's announcement, I'm very interested in Donald Trump's intentions. Donald seems to understand business and is aware of the fact that China, Opec, and the global bankers have not been doing right by the American people for years. I think Mr. Trump could trump those guys. However, I just don't want another trigger-happy president. So it's still early in the 2012 election process. Time to study all the candidates on the critical issues of real jobs in manufacturing, increasing domestic oil or gas production, real education reforms in public school system, family values, wastes in the medical business, and stopping initiation of useless, wasteful wars.

Now, continuing with my Lubrizol years, I must tell the Dick Dorsh story. This is one I've told many times to my Maurer-Shumaker salespeople both to inspire them and to remind them of the importance of the little guy, the little customer who may one day be a big customer. Dick Dorsh, when I met him in 1974, was the salesman for one of my newest and perhaps smallest customers at the time, J. D. Plating. J. D. which was owned by my friend George Wines and later owned and managed for many years by his son, my very good friend and still customer, George "Buddy" Wines, the marathon running, hockey scoring, and devoted family man.

Dick Dorsh would always ask me detailed questions about the Lubrizol products I was selling to J. D. Plating. He wanted copies of the latest literature for IrcoBond 51800, IrcoSeal paints, and RustARest 53253, the best corrosion-inhibiting oil on the market at the time. I always spent time with Dick and answered all his questions as he would tell me thanks, saying, "Terry, someday I'm going to start my own company, and when I do, I'll buy all my chemicals from you." Well, I thought, J. D. was my smallest customer. I wonder how many chemicals the salesman for my smallest customer will buy when he starts his own small company.

But we continued the dialogue for at least a year, until one morning as I was taking a shower at 6:30 a.m. in my Dexter house, Mary Ann interrupted me, saying, "Dick Dorsh is on the phone."

I thought, *What could be so important at 6:30 a.m.?* I was surprised that Dick Dorsh even had my home phone number. Drying myself, I said, "Hello, Dick."

He immediately said, Terry, I was just told I got the job to set up a brand-new plant for Ajax Nut and Bolt Company, and I'm going to use all your Lubrizol chemicals for the zinc phosphate line and all of Bruno Leonelli's Aldoa Company's plating chemicals. Can you meet Bruno and me at 8:00 a.m. in Detroit today to discuss it?"

"Yes," I said. "I'll be there." I knew immediately the value of a new line for a company the size of Ajax, at least $100,000 a year in 1975. It would be my second biggest customer next to Curtis Metal Finishing. This was a coup for me and for Lubrizol.

The moral to the story is that a salesperson should always be polite and courteous to even the smallest prospect. One never knows who will rise to the top, taking you along. That's the selfish way to look at it. Why not just be a person who treats everyone equally because it is the right thing to do? But as you can see, it's good business too. I have many other examples I could recite. In the case of Ajax Metal Processing, which the company Dick Dorsh started up, continued as my customer for Lubrizol until 1978 when I started my own company. Then my friend Mr. Dorsh switched all his chemical supplies to Maurer-Shumaker. We kept the Ajax business until I sold the company in 1995. Sales at Ajax then were a remarkable $750,000 per year. Not bad from the salesman of my smallest company who wanted to start his own company but was tapped to run the biggest new plater in the state for the next twenty years.

I continued to enjoy success in my Lubrizol sales. One by one, I got business at most of the job shops in Michigan, taking the business from Parker Rust Proof, MacDermid, Heatbath, Detrex, and Amchem. Customers the MFSA and AESF trade associations would know include Reilly Plating, Chemical Processing, Aactron, J. D. Midstate Plating, Flint Chemical Coatings, Dura, Prestole Everlock, ITT Hancock, Cadon Plating, Kewaunee Scientific, Tecumseh Products, Commonwealth Industries, Midwest Chrome, Depor Industries, Filus Brothers in Mt. Clemens (also known as Metalcote), Rockwell International, Longworth Plating, Fitzgerald, Paul Masselink's Peninsular Plating Company in Grand Rapids, Ace Finishing, Magni, Superior Metal Finishing, Howard Plating, and of course Curtis Metal Finishing.

One day on my way home from Tecumseh Products, I stopped for coffee and to use a phone booth outside of the Country Kitchen restaurant near Clinton, Michigan. I had to wait for Chuck Gadde, a competitive salesman from Parker to get out of the booth. I said, "Chuck, how are things?"

He said, "Okay, but have you heard, my bosses are leaving Parker, and they are starting their own chemical company, and they're calling it Frieborn, German for 'Born Free.' They want me to quit Parker and join them."

"That's very exciting," I said.

It turns out there were three guys, Dave Peters, Collem Gill, and Paul Slater. Peters and Gill had interviewed me some six months earlier when they were still very active in Parker management. They wanted to take me out of Lubrizol and put me in the declining Parker organization. I surmised after hearing this news, to make it easier for Frieborn to take my business. So that evening, I told Mary Ann about the Frieborn venture, telling her that if those three guys could start a company, there should be no reason why I couldn't start a company. "There should be no reason why I couldn't do the same thing, Mary Ann," I told her.

Being the "do it now" person that she was and still is, Mary Ann said, "Do it! Do it now. Who can help you?"

Maurer - Shumaker Sales Team

CHAPTER VIII

Maurer-Shumaker (1978–1987)

Jimmy Carter
(1977–1981)
Ronald Reagan
(1981–1989)

Today is Sunday, June 12, 2011, as I begin to tell about my chemical manufacturing company. In a sidebar, I want to say that I am anxiously waiting for the Republican debates tomorrow evening coming from New Hampshire. I am cheering for my favorite, Mitt Romney. There are to be seven debaters, the other six are likely to gang up on Mitt Romney, the favorite at this early stage of the 2012 election process. I can only list five others in the debates because I can't remember the seventh person. In order of my preference the others are Ron Paul, Herman Cain, Newt Gingrich, Tim Pawlenty, and Giuliani. Also there are others still testing the waters and not debating. Of these I prefer in order Donald Trump, Sarah Palin, Michel Bachman, Mitch Daniels, Rick Perry, and finally Jon Huntsman, who served with George Bush II; that disqualifies Huntsman for me.

Now back to the early days of spring in 1977 when Mary Ann said, "Do it. Start your own chemical manufacturing company." Immediately I started planning and thinking about who, how, where, when, and why. I think Elvis Presley provided that extra push of confidence to make the big move. It came after seeing Elvis in concert in Ann Arbor, likely in April 1977. I have seen a few concerts in my time. Not many. But some of the best, for sure! I saw Frank Sinatra in Detroit, Van Cliburn in Cobo Hall, Tina Turner at the Palace in Auburn Hills, John Denver up north in Petoskey, Johnny Mathis at Meadow Brook, Celine Dion at Caesar's Palace, Joe Cocker at the Brandenburg Gate, Boots Randolph in Nashville, Tennessee, Harry Belefonte at Hill Auditorium in Ann Arbor, and Mylène Farmer in Toulouse. But none of these great entertainers put on a better show than did Elvis Presley at the House That Cazzie Built (Chrysler Arena in Ann Arbor) at one of his last concert tours in 1977. He finished with Sinatra's "I Did It My Way" and everyone, including me, walked out about a foot taller that night. "That's it," I said to myself. "I will do it my way. I will start my own company."

First, I told Mary Ann, "I need four key products: cleaners, zinc phosphates, oils, and paints. I can formulate the organics, but I need someone to formulate the inorganic cleaners and phosphates."

Mary Ann answered, "You must know someone."

Sure I do, the first name that came to mind was Gary Shumaker, chemist for Lubrizol in Cleveland who for the past three years had been formulating for Allied-Kelite in Milford, Michigan. As I write, I'm reminded of a question someone asked Gregory Peck in the movie *Mountains of Kilimanjaro*: "How's the book?"

He answered, "How's anybody's book? It isn't finished."

Harry eventually finished his first book in Paris and called it *The Lost Generation*. While I'm not finished with this book, I don't intend to stop until I finish it. It will likely be back in St. Helena in the center of the Napa Valley, later in 2011 or early 2012.

Now the how of starting my company. I knew money was needed, and I didn't have enough of my own. So again, Mary Ann said, "You must know somebody with money."

I said, "Yes, I do."

I know two people in the business who might support me: Bruno Leonelli, who owns Aldoa Company, a company which manufactures electroplating chemicals which are also used in the automotive fastener business but not direct competitors to the zinc phosphate technology I am in. The other is Mitchell Kafarski, owner of Aactron in Madison Heights and one of my Lubrizol customers.

Both Leonelli and Kafarski wanted a piece of my new company. I chose only Bruno Leonelli, who insisted that his wife, Mollie, come as his full partner. This is contrary to my attorney James Cmejrek's earlier recommendation of not involving your partner's wife in your business. Boy, was he right! Mitchell Kafarski was a great mentor to me, but I worried that the other job shops and my potential customers might not want to support a company partially owned by one of their competitors. I believe the right decision was made because we were ultimately successful.

Where to locate my new company? That was the question. I wanted my own manufacturing plant, and I wanted it close to my customer base so that they could send their own trucks to pick up the drums and totes which they'd be ordering. Banks did not want to loan to a start-up company, and we approached a few during the summer of 1977.

Finally, Bruno said to me, "Why don't you let Aldoa do your manufacturing and you can use the 20K you've raised"—10K from me, 6K from Gary, and 4K from Bruno—"for operational and raw material expenses." That is what we did but not yet. Okay, the seventh man in the debates tomorrow is Rick Santorum.

Last night the consensus of New Hampshire voters polled was that Mitt Romney won the debates with 51 percent of those polled. The remaining percentage was divided among the other six with Michele Bachmann getting second place with about 12 percent.

Continuing with *who* I needed for my company: I asked one of my customer's key guys, a Mr. David Muck of Commonwealth Industries in Detroit to take a percentage of my company and help us get started by purchasing our products while staying employed at the customer for at least a year. A second offer was made to a Mr. Ron Banc, one of the crack tech service guys at my current employer, Lubrizol. And finally, I offered a 5 percent stake for no money down to the Detroit office manager for R. O. Hull and Lubrizol, a Ms. Sally Lyon. Before Gary Shumaker and I ever got started with the new company, all three of the above rejected the invitation for different reasons. Dave Muck's family was young and considered the move too risky. Ron Banc also had a young family in Cleveland, and he learned of his terminal Hodgkin's cancer before the start date. Sally Lyon did not want to drive from Madison Heights to Livonia (some twenty-five miles) with two teenage kids still in school and a single mom.

The 1978 start-up went well anyway, and in the first six months, I hired a young neighbor, Mark Koury from our Loch Alpine Subdivision, to take Ron Banc's slot, and Sally Lyon's position was filled by using Lance Leonelli's office gal part-time. Lance, son of Bruno and Mollie, was our landlord at the Argent Ltd. building where we started on Capitol Street in Livonia, Michigan. By the way our first employee, Mark Koury, was brought to me by my son, Stephen, then only ten years old. Steve was playing catch with Mark when he asked Mark what he was doing. Mark said, "I'm looking for a job as I just graduated from Central Michigan University." Steve had good judgment as Mark worked out just fine until the mutiny. We managed just fine without Dave Muck because my old friend Dick Dorsh at Ajax immediately became our first customer, ordering a four-thousand-gallon tanker load of our heavy zinc phosphate Ultramate 1200 during our first week in business.

Dick said, "I'm going to be changing my bath chemistry over the weekend." It was normal to dump a zinc phosphate bath soon after the iron level reached ten points. "And if you and Gary can make up a fifty-five-gallon drum of your zinc phosphate and get it to me in time, I'll give it a try."

Gary and I made the product. We borrowed Bruno Leonelli's old station wagon to deliver the product late on a Friday night to Ajax on Gratiot Avenue in downtown Detroit. It worked fine, and on Monday we made and delivered the full forty-thousand-pound bulk-carrier load and invoiced Ajax for around $10,000. Maurer Shumaker Inc. was in business early in 1978.

In early 1979, Maurer-Shumaker was picking up new customers on a regular basis. Tony Kudela from the GM Technical Center had already approved our ultraseal system of corrosion protection for the GM 6174 specification. This was my reason for starting the company in the first place. It had been my job at Lubrizol to get the GM 6174 specification written around Lubrizol's polyseal process, and I had asked Mr. Kudela the $64,000 question: "If I start my own company, would you approve my own proprietary system?"

He said, "No guarantee, but I will test it, if you bring it to me."

That was all I needed to hear, so I was ready to start Maurer-Shumaker with GM's promise to test and the commitments of many other customers to try my line of cleaners, zinc phosphate, emulsion oils, and corrosion-resistant paints and coatings. So all these confidential discussions with my Lubrizol customers and GM engineers and their promise to talk to me, but no promise to buy, gave me the confidence to launch the company. Also I wasn't worried about making a living if everything went haywire. I was young, and I was sure I could always go back to some company's lab as a research chemist.

Another driving force to go out on my own came from upper management at Lubrizol/R. O. Hull (ROHCo) when my commission for zinc phosphate sales was reduced 25 percent (from 4 percent to 3 percent). When I complained to Bill Saas, the national sales manager, he just said, "Terry, you're such a good salesman, you'll increase your sales and be making the same money before you know it." I could see the handwriting on the wall. I was never going to make a real living with management operating with an attitude like that.

In my next sales review, I wrote in answer to the question about my 1978 projections, "Watch me, I'm going places." To me it meant I'm leaving Lubrizol/R. O. Hull and going out on my own. Maybe Bill Saas, Joe McGee, and John Weyls, the company president, got the message when I left the company early in 1978 to start Maurer-Shumaker in direct competition and beginning in my Southeast Michigan territory. When we obtained the GM 6174M approval for our ultraseal system, Maurer-Shumaker was the only the second chemical company listed on this fast-growing "worldwide GM standard." It wasn't very long before Pat Berry, president of Midwest Chrome in Detroit, wanted me to visit with his company's agent in Europe with intentions of signing European rights to the ultraseal process over to his agent, a certain Mr. Ruby Tubessing from Germany.

So I flew to Paris, France, to meet with Mr. Tubessing at Pat Berry's request. Rudy met me at Charles de Gaulle and gave me some advice saying, "I know you are on jet lag and really want to take a nap." It was about 10:00 a.m., Paris time. "First," he said, "I need to ask you an important question right up front: Do you need a woman for the week? If you do, she will be in your room tonight when you check in."

I said, "Rudy, It's very interesting. I've never had an offer like that in my life, but I have to pass. I don't know how I would explain it to my conscience or my wife." He apologized to me if I was offended, but he explained that many of his European business contacts expected that kind of an offer.

He then told me he'd recommend against the nap and that I should try to get on Parisian time right away. The best way is to do a little sightseeing, have an early dinner, and get to bed early, he said. We did go out to see the town but did not get back to my hotel in Neuilly until about 1:00 a.m. Paris time. With too much wine and overly tired by then, I could barely spell my name at 8:00 a.m. the next day, when Mr. Tubessing wanted to discuss business.

It was the fourth day before I felt somewhat coherent. We discussed the deal, saw Notre Dame, went to the Moulin Rouge show, visited the electroplating trade show in Paris, and visited more clubs. Rudy wanted a more exclusive European contract for the rights to our GM6174 technology than Gary Shumaker and I were prepared to release. We did not sign up with Rudy or Pat Berry's company in the US. Rudy and I did fly back to the US together. I did invite him to my house in Ann Arbor, where Mary Ann and I told him about the imminent arrival of our three-year-old Korean daughter to the United States. He asked what name we had picked for her. We told him we had not decided yet. He said to us, "I have a son, but were I to have a daughter, I'd name her Karin." We asked why Karin. He told us in the days of kings in Germany, Karin was a name given to the aristocratic, elite daughters of royalty.

"That's it," we said. "We are German, and we will name our new daughter Karin."

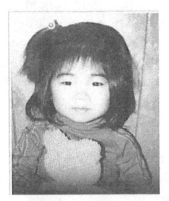

Karin Mee Lyn
In Korea 1978

Karin Mee Lyn
In USA 1982

Here now is a story which our thirteen-year-old daughter Laurie wrote describing the day Karin arrived in our family in Michigan from Korea.

Special Delivery

As we awoke that morning, the sky was just beginning to show signs of light. The clouds were thick and outlined by the sun behind them. I opened my window and was welcomed with a breath of cool, crisp air. Today was going to change the lives of both my family and me.

Unlike most mornings, everyone seemed to be up and moving. Even my brother was out of bed and in the shower. The sounds of buzzing blow dryers, the crackling of eggs cooking, and the chugging of our car as it struggled to start could be heard throughout the house. The excitement of this special day was definitely in the air. After quickly consuming our breakfast, we hurried and loaded the car, then started our journey to the Metro Airport. There we would claim a unique cargo.

As we were driving, the car seemed to come alive like the loud chirping of birds in hysterics. Everyone's pent up feelings, from nervousness to excitement, spilled forth. My brother was paranoid that we would be late for the flight, my mother sat in disbelief that the day had finally arrived, and my father and I just nodded our heads in agreement to everyone else. As we neared the airport, I again noticed the sun. It was shining very bright as if it too was waiting to welcome our package.

The entrance to the airport appeared miles from our parking place. The chill of this cool morning was felt as we ran through the lot. Upon entering the building, we were warmly embraced by some friends who had come to give us encouragement as we impatiently awaited the new extension to our family.

The room was filled with the chatter of nervous, excited people. Suddenly the loud thunder of the plane was heard. All heads instantly turned toward the window, straining to see the plane. At the realization that it was our plane, everyone's eyes lit up and their faces filled with smiles. As the passengers began to exit off the plane, the crowd became almost paralyzed in anticipation of our package. The long-awaited moment arrived. A young woman exited off, cradling something in her arms. As she walked closer, a little face could be seen peeking out from beneath her arms. As the woman came closer to us, she presented my mother with her new daughter. My eyes filled with tears as I too watched my mother confront her new child for the first time. I felt as if I had just watched her give birth rather than receive her child from off a plane.

My mother was now the center of attention. Everyone in the area strained to see the long, anticipated delivery. She was even more beautiful than we had imagined. At three years old, she had appeared much younger. Her long silky black hair drew attention to the glimmer of her dark-brown eyes. She made not a sound and showed no emotion, except for the one big tear that slowly rolled down her cheek. Her tiny hands clutched onto her new mother tightly as if nothing had changed. She was now part of our family. There are still, to this day, no words to express our feelings of happiness at this realization.

The weeks that followed were very exciting. The entire family shared in the joy of teaching and watching Karin learn so many new things. She yearned to team everything that we did, from the way we eat, how the television works up to the most difficult, the way we speak. We all worked especially hard on helping her learn English. My mother and I would tape her voice on a recorder and then let her hear it. Before we knew it, we could not shut her up.

Remembering back to those first few days with my new sister brings back many wonderful memories. My family never imagined how much we would grow through one little Korean child. She was taught us to appreciate all we have, and she has brought us countless smiles and moments of laughter. We all love Karin as we love each other, and she is a part of our family that we could not live without.

Business at Maurer-Shumaker came as planned. The first successful start-up of Ajax Metal Finishing in Detroit was completed with the strong support of Dick Dorsh, Frank Buono, and Ernie Dunn. We continued to grow by adding the complete line of our own proprietary cleaners, phosphates, oils, and paints at J. D. Plating, Fitzgerald, Cadon, Prestole Everlock, and others. Bruno was doing a fine job at Aldoa, manufacturing all the cleaners and phosphates. We blended the oils at Argent Ltd., where Gary and I made our offices. Gary and I made the ultraseal paints ourselves in the evenings at the Argent location in Livonia.

Now Mark Koury and his bodybuilder friend Stephen were on board, Mark as my salesman trainee and Stephen our all-purpose shipping and receiving man. Sometime during our second or third year the attempted mutiny occurred. Here is what happened, apparently Gary Shumaker and Mark Koury convinced themselves probably with the help of Mollie Leonelli and Josie Shumaker that the company would be just fine without one, Terry Maurer, the founder, the president, the idea man, the contact man, the person who had the vision for the company, the one who hired all the rest. I never really found out who was the Judas behind the attempted coup, probably Mollie Leonelli, who was married to Bruno and did the books for their family company Aldoa.

I believe Maurer-Shumaker had a payable bill to Aldoa of about 70K at the time. Mollie was worried about another depression during the late '70s and early '80s. She did not want to get stuck with debt from Maurer-Shumaker if the poor economy put us under. So I'm sure she convinced Gary Shumaker that he could go alone without me, especially since I had now trained Mark Koury in the basics of customer service and some sales.

One day Mark Koury did not show up for work. He called around 10:00 a.m. disguising his voice and asking for Gary Shumaker when I answered the phone. I recognized who it was and asked, "Why are you late for work?"

He finally admitted who he was and said, "I'm buying your stock, and I need to talk to Gary."

I was stunned and said, "My stock is not for sale."

He hung up and I went into Gary's office and told him about the call. Now Gary told me, "That's right, Mark is buying your stock."

Well, I told Gary the same thing. "It's not for sale."

Gary told me that he and Bruno were taking over because they had 57 percent of the stock between them; Gary had 32 percent, Bruno had 25 percent, and I had 43 percent. I told Gary he could never take over because if he had read the company's by-laws, it clearly stated that no change in officers or company control could be made without a vote of 66 percent of the stockholders. I would have to vote against myself, and I said, "That will never happen." I wrote the by-laws and decided who would get how much stock. I only gave up more than 51 percent of the stock so that Bruno and Gary would realize a higher percent equity in future distributions. I was looking out for their interest but had no intention of ever giving up control. The way it was written, I could remove either Bruno or Gary with the vote of one of them; they together could never vote me out.

Once I made this clear to Gary, who was obviously in shock, disbelief, embarrassed, and now clearly unsure what I would do. He apparently called Mark Koury the next day and told him the gig was up. "Our takeover cannot work." So then on the third day Mark and Stephen came to my office to apologize for their role in it.

Prior to that Mark Koury's father called me and said he would not consider loaning his son enough money to buy my stock. John Koury had ethics, basic morals, and he recognized the under-handed action his son was attempting and told him it was not right. Nonetheless, when Mark and Stephen came to my office, I asked Mark, "What would you do if your employees pulled that on you?"

I knew what Mark's answer would be. He said, "I'd fire them."

I said, "You're right: You and Stephen are both fired!"

Gary did not show up for work for the rest of that week. He didn't call either until the following Monday. He then asked me if his wife, Josie, could come into the business and do the books. I reluctantly agreed after thinking about it for a few days. I regretted that decision through the next fifteen years until we sold the business in 1995. Although Josie did a good job on the books, she had more influence through Gary on basic company decisions and had a philosophy of business that for the most part was contrary to mine. I wanted to grow the business, and she wanted to spend the profits. We coexisted, but it was a struggle for me. I felt undermined on many issues over the years. Josie, I felt was my cross to endure. There were times when we had a meeting of the minds. However, just couldn't see how to separate myself from Josie without alienating Gary, her husband and my partner, the chief formulator for the oils, phosphates, and cleaners in our business. When Gary came back to work a week later, he was hiding behind a newly grown beard.

I accepted Josie into the company, and Maurer-Shumaker continued to add new customers and personnel. I now did sales and delivery of many drums myself from the back of the company heavy-duty pickup. The first new employee was Lynn Wacht. Lynn came in response to an advertisement in the local paper. She assisted the part-time Josie as our shipping and receiving clerk and secretary to Gary and me. Lynn proved to be a great hire, a very capable, loyal employee with a pleasant manner and appreciated by our customers, our vendors, and all the Maurer-Shumaker employees to come later and especially by me. The next person hired was Bob Barach. We enticed Bob, a chemist at Fitzgerald Plating, to join me in sales. Like Lynn, Bob remained with the company until we sold out to Novamax, a Molson Beer subsidiary in 1995. Again the company was very fortunate to get a man of Bob's character and knowledge and also respected by our customers. We never lost a customer assigned to Bob nor any new customers brought to the company by Mr. Barach. Bob remains in the industry yet today managing a sales territory for Heatbath Corporation, the company (now DuBois Chemical in 2015) which owns the Maurer-Shumaker customers and formulations. These assets were acquired from Chem-Tech, who purchased them from Henkel, who got them from Novamax/Molson Beer, our buyer in 1995.

Sometime in 1982, Bruno Leonelli's Aldoa company had a chemical explosion at its plant in Livonia. Aldoa was the contract manufacturer for most of our products. The high-pressure reactor making some kind of zinc plating brightener blew the roof off half of Aldoa's building, destroying the lab and literally knocked Bruno off his office chair some three interior walls away from the reactor.

Fortunately, no one was killed. The two guys overseeing the reaction process realized that they had lost control and escaped to the outside just in time to save their lives. This was both bad news and good news for Maurer-Shumaker. The bad news was we had just lost our manufacturing; the good news was that we were forced to find our own home with our own manufacturing. For two months we used our Canadian distributor, Harshaw Chemical, headed up by my good friend, Erich Knebel, and later to be member of our board of directors. Erich set up limited manufacturing of our products in Toronto. Freight back to Michigan was costly, but we never lost a customer during the time it took me to get a bank loan from NBD (National Bank of Detroit). I found a site on 37025 Industrial Road in Livonia. At the same time Gary located blenders, mixers, and storage tanks and laid out the floor plan for our own production of chemicals in our very important looking and newly leased twelve-thousand-square-foot building. Within two months of Bruno's explosion, we were up and running on our own.

Now we needed to hire our own production crew. The very first guys were Kevin Sykes and Al Benoit. Kevin only twenty-one years old with a new family on its way was a neighbor to Lynn Wacht. Al Benoit nearly twenty-one himself was a production line worker we recruited from Stahl Manufacturing, one of our phosphate customers in Plymouth, Michigan. Both Kevin and Al were the best: hardworking, loyal, very knowledgeable, eager to learn everything about our industry and fun to be with. Al Benoit later became our key tech-service man eagerly traveling to our customers in New Jersey, Cleveland, Chicago, Cincinnati, Nashville, Dallas, and cities in between. Many times he was alone and others with me and occasionally with Gary or Chuck Cosner. Kevin stayed with production while training the new guys, then as Gary's right-hand man in our lab doing quality control and manning the Harshaw Salt Cabinet for accelerated corrosion testing. After we sold the company, Kevin made his career in technical sales and management.

It was also during this time that I started to run. I ran to clear my head and relieve tensions and stress from the rigors and demands of starting a brand-new business. First, it was the Dexter-Ann Arbor 10K, and soon thereafter my friend Judge Karl Fink had talked me into running the *Detroit Free Press* Marathon. Karl and I ran together in 1980. My time was a few seconds over five hours. I ran again without Karl in 1981, this time training more and finishing much better at four hours and thirty minutes. And finally, the third year, I thought I could repeat it without much training, but I came in slower at five hours and some seconds once again. "That's it!" I said and did not run another marathon, just like Forrest Gump. My son, Stephen, did run the *Detroit Free Press* Marathon in an excellent time of three hours and twenty minutes in 1986, just missing the qualifying time for his age for the famous Boston Marathon. Maybe it was good enough, I can't remember.

During those early years of Maurer-Shumaker (1978–1987), Mary Ann and I continued to live in Loch Alpine near Dexter, Michigan, in the middle of the Ann Arbor Country Club. Here we made many of our lifelong friends: Jim and Jan Balcom, a businessman who later became kinfolk; Tom and Pat Burke, a dentist; Ed and Vi Kokmeyer, American Broach owners (Vi is older than me and still good-looking); Dave and Pat Navarre, an engineer; Ken and Judy Martin, a businessman; Frank and Judy Fike, a banker and Paul Ewing's cousin; John and Barb Rutz, a GM engineer; Nancy and William A. Hardt, who is completing his book on American politics (the title is *Real Change for These United States—What Must be Done to Get Our Country Back on Track*); Andrea and Dick Mielstrup; Donna and Dave Hobgood (both Dick and Dave were military and commercial pilots); Neil and Judy Gerl, a fighter pilot in the Vietnam War, (landing on an aircraft carrier 69 times). Each time, he told me, was the scariest landing ever! Gloria and Amin Almuti, the retired president of Bechtel North America; and finally Karl and Nancy Kienholz, Climax research chemist. Karl was one of the best athletes at Climax and a superb ping pong player, beating me one evening at my own table twenty-five out of twenty-six matches. I was good, the high school Ping-Pong champion in 1960 (losing the all-school playoffs to Ed Murphy, the college champion).

Laurie, Stephen, and young Karin all swam during the summer on the club swim team. The swim team coach for the Ann Arbor Country Club in 1984 was Scott Mansfield. In high school. Laurie was active in the band playing clarinet. Stephen also played tenor sax (my old instrument). Karin was learning the ropes and making lots of friends in her new country. Later, Karin attended Interlocken Academy for the Arts in Traverse City, playing both the piano and the flute. Steve excelled in high school both as co-captain of Dexter golf and state-recognized wrestler, finishing sixth in the state in his senior year. Steve graduated from Bowling Green University in 1991. Laurie graduated high school in 1984 and was off to Michigan State. I guess she wanted a college in Colorado, but her request went over my head.

Maybe I was more focused on Maurer-Shumaker and also Mary Ann's early stages of what became full-blown kidney failure, resulting in her first kidney transplant in 1987. It took nearly three years for her kidneys to fail and the only thing that the University of Michigan Hospital and the neighboring St. Joseph Hospital doctors could say during that time was that she had nephrotic syndrome. They didn't know what caused it nor how to treat it. When her kidneys finally failed, it was dialysis and ultimately a kidney transplant. Here is the story of Mary Ann's first transplant in her own words:

It was Christmas break in 1986 for our children, and I had just picked up our daughter Laurie from Michigan State University. I wasn't feeling well because of a flu virus, and our neighbors had planned a farewell party in honor of our moving to the country. As a result of the move, plans were made for the family to spend the holidays in a nearby hotel while the movers transferred our things. On the night of the party, it was decided that I was too ill to attend because I was having difficulty breathing. We decided that I should go to the Chelsea Hospital for help. I had not planned to stay because I thought that all I needed was a bit of oxygen. While waiting in the emergency room, a two-year-old girl was whisked by on a stretcher. She was dying of burns from the explosion of a space heater. My heart went out to this stricken child and her family. As a small child, I too was seriously burned by scalding water. My own illness suddenly seemed less important.

Not long after, I was called into the examining room, and after briefly observing my condition, my husband, Terry, was told I was near death and needed to be sent to a larger medical facility without delay. I had pneumonia and a white count of forty-five thousand. My kidneys had shut down completely. I was taken by ambulance to St. Joseph Hospital in Ann Arbor and was sent directly to the intensive care unit. I was not fearful during this time. It was a very peaceful time for me. I stayed there for two weeks. Sixty pounds of fluid were removed from my body by dialysis. I was put on a breathing machine, and a catheter was placed in my heart. An incision was made in my side, so a tube could be inserted to drain fluid, and a second one was made in my back for the same purpose. The three nurses assigned to my care were from my neighborhood. This gave me spiritual support. Terry left my side only for short breaks to finalize the purchase of our new home.

I remember Christmas Day, looking through the doorway of my room and seeing poinsettias at the nurses' station. *Christmas Day is here*, I thought. Later that day, my family arrived, dressed in the outfits I had purchased and wrapped for them to open on Christmas eve. They were so excited to show me; Laurie, my nineteen-year-old daughter, Steve, my seventeen-year-old son, and Karin, our ten-year-old daughter, who we had adopted from Korea seven years before.

At the end of my stay in intensive care, as I was about to be wheeled from the unit to a private room, I heard clapping in the hallway just outside the door. Two priests and a doctor stood clapping. I had made it! With the help of prayer chains and prayers of friends and family throughout the US, the doctors were given wisdom, and I was strengthened.

During Holy Week, Dr. Paul Smith, my nephrologist, determined that I had reached total kidney failure. It was time to make the decision of dialysis. I felt as if a part of me had died. I would have to carry this cross alone, and I was frightened. What were those machines? Lazy boys? Televisions? What kind of world was this? I cried for weeks. Then I decided that I couldn't go on like this. I had to accept my new life. I began reaching out to people while on dialysis. For four hours three times a week, I became a support for the other dialysis patients. I tried to throw humor into the treatments. I dressed up for Halloween and would tell people in the waiting room outside the dialysis center, "No one really knows what we do behind those closed doors." I planned my time on dialysis as I did at home. I would bring a pack of things to do—books to read, letters to write, etc. These things plus television (each patient had his/her own television) and resting all filled my time. I also traveled with my husband on business trips to Florida and California. This took a lot of planning since our travels had to include access to a dialysis center. I found a life for myself within the center. I felt that God had placed me there for a reason. I would have to do the best that I could.

After four or five months on dialysis, Dr. Smith suggested I consider a transplant. He felt I would do well if I received one. In November, I went to the University of Michigan Hospital in Ann Arbor and had a transplant evaluation. The blood type classified the waiting period for a transplant. The U of M Hospital checked with the blood bank at St. Joseph's Hospital, where they held my blood. They found my blood to be AB positive, which was good news because this is a rare blood type and therefore the waiting list was much shorter. I was told the wait would be about six months. I was scheduled for several examinations, from dental to gynecological to determine if I would be a good candidate for a transplant. It is very important to be examined well because of the antirejection drugs that must be taken after a transplant and affect the immune system. The doctors felt that I was a good candidate.

After a staff meeting, I was approved for the list. My blood was taken monthly for tissue typing in order to assure a good organ match.

The goal I had was to receive my organ on the Easter of 1987, exactly six months down the road. I told my daughter Laurie that I felt God would give me a kidney in the spring and we could plan for her wedding in August. I told her that by then I would be well and ready for the task.

Spring arrived! On a Friday, I told Katie, my medical technician at dialysis that I sensed I would get my kidney that weekend. Katie simply nodded her head in affirmation. She, too, had strong faith, and I know she did believe me. That evening, Terry and I took a walk around our lake. I mentioned to him that I didn't really know how I deserved this kidney that I was getting. He questioned my confidence in receiving one. The following morning, Terry called me outside to see the buds breaking on our pear trees. A message sang through my soul. The time was here. I then went inside to pray. I felt God's loving presence as I asked again for my kidney. God had told me his answer would come in the spring, and the spring had finally arrived. I whispered the words, "I'm ready, God, if it's Your will." Then I went outside to help clean out many flower beds. This job took all day. As I worked, I was struck with the idea to forward our calls to our friends' house, the McClungs. We were going to a comedy show that evening, and their daughter, Merissa, and our daughter, Karin, were going to be at the McClungs' house. This idea struck me as a wonderful plan, although at the time I was unsure as to why.

We arrived early at the comedy show and picked just the right seats in the center of the room. The room slowly filled with people. I felt great, and I enjoyed popcorn and a drink during the show. About three-quarters into the show, the name Mary Maurer was repeated in my mind three times. I didn't understand this because I usually went by the name of Mary Ann, but I accepted this change. I thought it had a nice ring to it. Moments later, when I was attuned to the show, the bartender interrupted the comedian's routine. He seemed disturbed. The words "Is there a Mary Maurer here?" rang out, just as the voice in my mind had forwarded me! The man then said, "You have a phone call." As I walked to the phone, I wondered if the call was from Karin to ask about a movie she wanted to watch.

When I got there, the bartender was white with stress. The person on the other end was a good friend of mine, Andrea Meilstrup. I asked her why she had called me and she replied, "Mary Ann, the hospital called your mom, and she called me. They have a kidney for you. You are to call Maureen at the hospital as soon as possible."

Tears welled up in my eyes. "Thank you, Lord Jesus, I'm ready!" I prayed silently.

I arrived at the hospital at midnight after a phone call to my daughter Laurie in Florida to tell her the good news. I wanted to tell the world. Blood tests were done in preparation, as well as a hot shower. The gown went on, and I was ready for the big event. A box on the nurses' station read "HUMAN ORGAN." It had arrived by taxi. We were soon to be united. My thoughts centered for a moment on the grieving family and the loss of their eighteen-year-old daughter. I will forever be grateful to them for the decision they made to allow their daughter to live on in me. It was indeed a precious gift, a gift of life. My son, Steve, arrived with his friends Dave and Eric. They had heard the news and wanted to share the excitement with us at the hospital.

At 8:30 a.m. on Palm Sunday morning, I was in the waiting room for one hour as the team of doctors organized and conferred. The anesthesiologist suggested an epidural. I would be numb from the waist down. That had been my desire and I consented. I would be awake for the transplant. For three and a half hours I listened to rock music as Dr. Marion and his team performed their miracle. They explained that as soon as the kidney was removed from ice and placed in my body, the organ would become very active; in fact, it was difficult to connect the ureter and the bladder. A miracle was indeed taking place. I told myself that I would bond to this organ in a way similar to the way I had bonded with my adopted daughter, Karin. The good Lord had seen us through those difficult times, and he would help me through this one as well. The following day the kidney went into a resting stage called ATN. This sometimes happens as a result of the kidney being out of the body and kept on ice for an extensive period of time. It proved to be a very difficult time for me. I was so excited about this new kidney, and it had worked so well at the time of the implant that I wondered why it now seemed to regress. Because there was little function of the new kidney, I had to continue dialysis.

The fistula, an artery surgically surfaced and connected to a vein for the purpose of dialyzing, had clotted off at the time of preparation for my transplant. I felt this was a good sign and that I would never dialyze again. I clung to this belief even though I had to dialyze for the present time through a new access. Days went by and still no function. The doctors looked doubtful. But Dr. Campbell came by on Easter Sunday and said he still had faith in the kidney. He commented that it was large and had good color. This assured me. I decided that I should make daily goals and long-term goals for the future of my kidney. After two and a half weeks, the doctor did a biopsy on the kidney. I will never forget the look on Dr. Campbell's face when he came into my room to tell me the good news. New cells were found in the kidney, and all signs looked good. It was waking up! I was so happy that tears spilled down my cheeks. About a month from the time of the surgery, the doctors let me go home. The kidney was still waking up, but the function was much better. I made visits to the clinic twice a week until everything stabilized.

The goals I set did work for me. I try to live one day at a time to the fullest. I have enjoyed sixteen years of new life to date, 2003. I thank God daily for having given me this second chance.

As I look back on this experience, I think of it as a journey I walked with Jesus, a spiritual journey I will cherish and remember forever. I was carried and cared for by Christ when my own kidneys failed. I can recall vividly his presence throughout my intensive care confinement during the Christmas holidays. Holy week was a death experience for me as my kidneys failed. One year later, I was called three times by a voice that would put me in touch with my new organ on Palm Sunday morning. I would rise to a new life, as Christ did on that special day of Easter.

Palm Sunday will always be special, a day that lives in my heart because of the decision a family made to donate their loved one's kidney, a true gift of life.

Jesus, painting by Mary Ann Maurer.

Terry and Mary Ann Maurer, Mollie and Bruno
Leonelli, and Josie and Gary Shumaker in 1992.

CHAPTER IX

———◈◈◈———

Maurer-Shumaker
(1987–1995)
George H. W. Bush
(1989–1995)

While Maurer-Shumaker Corporation continued to grow, we experienced the passing of my dad on April 24, 1985 (he was born on January 17, 1915), from Lou Gehrig's disease (ALS), and the high school graduations of Laurie in 1984 and Stephen in 1986, both from Dexter, Michigan, and Mary Ann's 1987 kidney transplant. My mother died on October 23, 1990, at the age of seventy-nine (she was born on December 26, 1911).

At this time, we hired Chuck Cosner from United Paint Company. We now had our own expert industrial paint chemist, and we immediately set up our own blending operation, together with the lab equipment needed for Chuck to do the research needed for competing in the corrosion-resistant automotive coatings business. I myself previously formulated coatings for Federal-Mogul fifteen years earlier, so I was of some assistance to the master, Chuck Cosner.

Following Chuck was Joy Daudlin. Joy was young, newly married to her husband, Dan of Wolverine Oil Co., and very experienced in marketing. We needed someone to promote our newly packaged WD-40, competitive product, to the hardware chains. We called our product Wax-Oil but changed the name to Ultramate 2800 after being challenged by a Swedish company which claimed to have trademark rights to Wax-Oil. Joy was instrumental in placing Ultramate

2800 into nearly 1,400 retail outlets in chains like Canadian Tire, Damon Hardware, Meijers, and many other outlets. Our product had superior corrosion resistance and penetrating qualities but was not as user-friendly around the home because of its amber color. We had a nonflammable product, using a chlorinated solvent instead of mineral spirits like WD40.

Despite our advantages, Ultramate 2800 did not fly off the shelves, and within three to four years, Joy and I were lamenting its slow movement while drinking Perrier in a joint in Cleveland. I said, "What we need is something like this Perrier, you drink one and tomorrow you need another, unlike our spray aerosol corrosion inhibitor which can sit on someone's garage shelf for a year." I said, "Joy, do you think you can sell water? My family has twin artesian wells in Northern Michigan."

She said, "Let's give it a try." So we made a label deMaurier premium artesian water.

Stephen Maurer at the Avita source in 1987.

It wasn't long before we dropped sales efforts for Ultramate 2800, but Gary felt he did not want to get behind the water business. It sat in limbo for some time. We shifted Joy's sales and marketing efforts to the Maurer-Shumaker core business. We were now attending more trade shows and events sponsored by the AESF (American Electroplaters and Surface Finishers). Joy made the arrangements for our attendance at these annual events as well as taking responsibility for certain key customers in Ohio.

Next to join the company was Jan White, a chemist from one of our Canadian accounts. Jan had a talent for working with the automotive specification engineers with all the testing and follow-up required for getting products added to the key new specs, being written in the industry for extended hours of corrosion resistance. New specs were being written all the time by GM, Ford, and Chrysler. Engineers like Kudela and Shubert at GM, Jerry Gira at Ford, and Jeff Zotech at Chrysler were happy to work with Jan White.

Shortly after Jan White joined the company, I hired my daughter Laurie. Except for my son, Stephen, who had worked for Maurer-Shumaker as a lab technician during summer breaks from Bowling Green University, Laurie was the first family member of mine and Gary Shumaker's to work full-time for the company. As it turned out, she was the only one. I had instituted a company policy that no children of the owners could work for the company until at least five years after graduating from college. This was a recommendation I picked up at an entrepreneur's seminar during our second year in business.

The thinking was that the children should get some outside experience first, then they could contribute right away and not be resented by the other employees. Also, if they did not like working for their father's business, they could return to the general workforce with confidence in their own previous accomplishments. So that's what I put in place. In hindsight, I'll never know if it was the best. At any rate, Laurie, being the oldest of both families, was the first to qualify and asked to join the company.

I created a position for Laurie in our sales team. Being a quick study, she picked up on the technical end of the business right away.

Her territory, she'll tell you, was in some of the roughest places. The southside of Chicago had a job shop called South Holland where even in daylight was not the best place to be. Warsaw Black oxide in Warsaw, Indiana, had its challenges for a pretty young blonde technical sales agent. Laurie told me later that she thought I was trying to get her to quit the job. That wasn't the case. It was just as the newest salesperson, she had to carve out her own territory, doing what's called missionary work while starting out with some of the less-desirable accounts.

To be truthful, many of our job shop customers were located in the heart of the dirtiest sections of the industrial Midwest car towns. Phosphating and electroplating was and still is in 2013 not the cleanest industry. It's not the high-tech computer industry or the neat and tidy banking environment we're talking about here. I've already mentioned that in my early days in this plating industry, one of my first customers was Flint Chemical Coatings. After eight years working in the spotless research labs of Climax Molybdenum and Federal-Mogul, I found myself titrating the phosphate line at Flint Chemical Coatings where the roof leaked, toothless women worked the line, steam was everywhere, dirt and grease covered the plant floors, the titrating "lab" was in the broken-down women's bathroom. A man had been burned to death after falling in the hot caustic stripping tank a week earlier. I thought to myself, *What am I doing here, doing this type of chemistry work?*

Although Laurie's customers were more advanced, you can see why I was not anxious to introduce my children to this work environment. Laurie's job did have its more pleasant side with an occasional round of golf with customers, some nice conventions in warm places, and visits to GM and Ford headquarters working on new specifications where dining at the best restaurants was expected. Scallops at the Schmidt House across from the GM Tech Center were tops. Laurie turned out to be a very effective paint salesperson. Together with Chuck Cosner's OD bore sealant formulations, Laurie and Chuck closed some very big and profitable accounts with Federal-Mogul, Chicago Rawhide, and another customer in Detroit who purchased many barrels of our specialty blue paint.

While the sales were increasing and new automotive specifications were being written around Maurer-Shumaker products, we had good backup people in the office and the lab. Bill Henderson, retired Commonwealth chemist, worked in our lab for seven or eight years. No one could maintain a better salt spray test cabinet than Bill. His lab work was meticulous, and his sense of humor kept everyone in a good mood. At the same time Bill's daughter, Gail, was our receptionist for several years. I think office politics and Gail's exceptional good looks interfered with some of our employees' work, and Gail left the company, something I was disappointed in. It divided the close work cooperation between those involved.

Following Gail was Barbie Ash. She was remarkable in her ability to keep me current in my letter writing and overall organization. Barbie was the office mom you often hear about, organizing company picnics, remembering birthdays, and greeting visitors to the company. I used Barbie again in my Maurer Coatings business after we sold to Molson Beer (Novamax) in 1995.

Walt Kacher came to Maurer-Shumaker, much like Kevin Sykes and Al Benoit before him, as a production man. Walt was a classic success story, working his way through production, then quality control, then tech service on the outside, and finally as a highly technically trained salesman. Walt suffered a scary production-related accident during his first year with the company when a one-ton shipping container crushed his hand. I managed to remove his wedding ring from his finger before the almost immediate swelling would have made it impossible and even more painful than was his mangled left hand. The ambulance arrived soon enough thanks to Barbie's 911 call but not soon enough for those of us present to escape the horror and pain on Walt's face. He recovered completely with the help of several steel pins placed in his hand.

We were thankfully an accident-free workplace except for Walt Kacher's crushed hand and one other nearly business ending chemical leak. The leak occurred shortly after we refused a 2.1 million offer to buy Maurer-Shumaker, the offer coming from the German company Chemetal. The Chemetal offer was presented by Bill Meyer after Mary Ann and I went to Frankfurt, Germany, to be entertained and interviewed by the home office board of directors.

Now let's back up to the chemical leak: Gary Shumaker and Walt Kacher were in the process of changing a leaky valve on our four-thousand-gallon phosphoric acid tank. The tank was full. To this day I don't know why the valve wasn't changed before the tank was filled. Maybe the leak was not noticed until after the filling. At any rate I was in my office that morning (normally I'd have been out seeing a customer by 10:00 a.m.) when I heard Barbie page Gary to the phone. Gary told me later that he had asked Walt to wait for him to come back into the plant before removing the old valve.

Apparently, Walt went ahead with the job, assuming he'd have it finished before Gary returned from the phone call. Then I heard Walt or another production worker rush into the office hollering for Gary. Then I heard Gary shout, "Oh, sh——!" I knew immediately something very serious had occurred because Gary did not swear. I ran into the plant to find Gary now behind the cement block retaining wall on his knees holding multiple rags up against a two-, maybe three-inch-diameter pipe trying to hold the acid in. It was obvious he was not containing the acid as it was spurting around the rags, and he was already up to his ankles in acid.

I said, "Gary, can you get the shut off valve back on the pipe?" He said, "No, the pressure is too strong." He said, "Call PVS, the acid supplier, and ask them to send a pumping truck to empty the tank."

I called and they said it'd take an hour to get from Wyandotte to Livonia. I was told, "You'd better call the Livonia fire department." Immediately and reluctantly, I called the fire department knowing things would get worse very quickly.

When you say "chemical spill in progress," the fire department responds fast. Within ten minutes, three trucks were at our plant with sirens blaring. At least five firefighters in full hazmat gear rushed in through two different plant doors. "Evacuate the plant, everyone out!" the lead fireman shouted. I knew if Gary left his post holding the acid back (now the acid was above his knees and now acid leaking through the cement block wall cracked by our own forklift getting

190

close to the leak in a desperate effort to do something), we'd be finished as a business. The whole twelve-thousand-foot plant and office would be covered with four to six inches of acid, destroying multiple drums of oil, paint, caustic, and even the more hazardous nitric acid bulk storage tank.

In response to the order to evacuate, I shouted back at the fireman barking his orders, "We can't leave. If Gary stops holding the acid, we're done, finished, out of business." I continued talking to the firemen, "You guys, start pumping the four-thousand-gallon bulk tank."

One fireman said, "Get out of here. I am in charge now."

I told him his mother was not married to his father (you've heard me say that before), and we are not leaving our position at the valve or the building. I asked to speak to his boss. The chief showed up just in time to understand the situation. He said, "We're pumping now, and I think we'll save your building if Gary can hold on just a while longer." And he did hold on long enough to prevent a total meltdown.

Yet when the immediate emergency was over, we still had to deal with the mess caused by the acid, which had leaked onto the plant floor. I asked the hazmat cleanup manager what the cleanup cost would be. He told me, "Twenty-five thousand dollars." I thought he was crazy, and I told him so. He got arrogant, and he told me to sign on the dotted line, authorizing his cleanup expenses, which I had to do. Meanwhile the TV helicopter was still circling the plant hoping as they do for a bigger story, and now Gary Shumaker was being hauled out on a stretcher into the ambulance with chest pains. All of this was captured by the TV crew, something we all saw again and again on the local news that evening at 6:00 p.m. and 11:00 p.m. Thankfully, Gary was okay and not admitted to the hospital.

The hazmat bill came in the mail a few weeks later. The total was $125,000. Obviously, we couldn't pay it and we didn't pay anything. We were sued for the money, and prior to the court, date we met the owner of the environmental company and his attorney. Gary and I and our corporate attorney, Mr. James Cmejrek, were all there. I explained to the company president that I thought the cost should be ten to fifteen thousand and that had I had a .38 revolver the day in which I dealt with his manager and was forced to sign his paper I would have taken him out.

The company owner said, "I wished you had because my manager has cheated me and caused untold grief to my company." He continued, "I'll take $50,000."

I said, "No way, we'll see you in court."

On the trial date, the judge asked both sides to try and settle. I then told Cmejrek to offer $35,000. They said okay. I responded, "Thirty-five thousand dollars it is. But we will pay no interest and need five years to pay." They accepted that, and we all walked out of court.

Following the near business ending chemical spill, which occurred within weeks of our rejecting the Chemetal offer to purchase Maurer-Shumaker for 2.1 million gave me something to ponder. Yet we were all happy not to have sold and continued forward with business as usual. Yet there still was one additional distraction coming in the form of another overture to purchase our company, coming this time within months of the spill. It was Al Reid, owner of Mangil Chemical in Cleveland who made an offer. Gary, Josie, Mary Ann, and I visited with Mr. Reid at his sprawling estate in rural Cleveland, only to hear his offer of just one million, exactly half of what we had rejected months earlier. With our rejection of two offers to purchase the company behind us, Maurer-Shumaker increased in sales and reputation.

Following a regional metal finishing trade show in Detroit just ten days before the county elected the first George Bush, president of the United States, I met the VP and candidate at the Renaissance Center.

Gary Shumaker and I were entertaining Bruce Kafarski, president of one of our customer's Chemical Processing, and his wife for dinner at the revolving summit restaurant on the top floor at 11:00 p.m. Dinner was nearly finished when we saw six to eight very athletic young men surveying our table. I noticed that they all had a spring-like wire hanging from one ear. My first thought was that these fellas were either hockey players or part of a gay convention. I thought no more about it until about thirty minutes later when someone from our chemical group came by our table telling us, "George Bush is up here having dinner, and I just got his autograph!"

I immediately jumped to my feet telling Gary, "If the vice president is here, I'm going to get his autograph too!"

I asked our excited associate how to find Mr. Bush. He said, "You can't miss him, you walk around the circular restaurant, and you'll see some Secret Service guys wearing earrings. That's where he is."

So it didn't take me very long to come across three agents guarding an entrance into the restaurant. I asked, "Is George Bush here?"

They looked at me poker-faced, saying, "What are you talking about?"

I remembered that I had pinned a four-inch "Bush for President" campaign button to the inside of my blazer. So opening my blazer to show them, I said, "Is this the right guy for president?"

"Okay," they said. "You can go to his table."

Now I was in view of the man seated at a table for six. But just Mr. Bush and a young lady were at the end near the wall. As I approached the table, maybe six to eight feet away, I was abruptly stopped with a firm hand on my shoulder. "Why don't you let him finish his dessert?" the agent growled.

I looked to my left to see at least a dozen of the ear-ringed Secret Service watching me. "No problem," I said and stopped in my tracks.

Just then, a friend of mine, Alex Maderal, the Cuban salesman from Aldoa Chemical, howls to me, "Hey, Terry! The vice president is here and I got his autograph!"

Alex was seated in a place where he could see me but not Mr. Bush. I said, "Yes, Alex, I know, and I am trying to get an autograph myself."

So as it appeared to me that the VP had now finished his dessert, I took a step toward him. Immediately a much bigger agent stepped between me and Mr. Bush, stopping me for the third time. A quick command from the fella who had had his hand on my shoulder, "It's okay," he told the guy in front of me.

I reached my hand out to meet the extended hand of Vice President Bush as he said, "It wasn't easy getting here, was it?"

"No, sir. It wasn't," I said. "I'd just like you to autograph my [Maurer-Shumaker] business card.

Taking my card and studying it intently, he said, "Let me keep your card. I'll sign one of mine for you." Reaching for his wallet, he pulled out an oversized card which read, "Vice-President of the United States."

So now feeling more relaxed myself (the earlier scotch and water probably helped), I asked, "Mr. Vice President, would you please date your card and spell my name M-A-U-R-E-R?"

He then asked me about the convention and how business was in Detroit. We were having a nice conversation when I now noticed the young lady sitting across from him smiling broadly. So now, with my confidence in overdrive, I said, "Mr. Vice President, maybe you'd like to introduce me to your dinner guest?"

He said, "I am sorry, Terry. This is my daughter, Dora." (Dorothy is her full name).

With that, I'm thinking those Secret Service guys are probably wondering how long I'm going to hang around. I had better say good night and get back to my own dinner table with Gary and Bruce. So I did, telling Gary about my experience and showing off my autographed VP card.

Gary said, "I'm going to get his autograph too." I told him where to go, but he was back in five minutes, saying he couldn't find anybody who looked like Secret Service and Bush was nowhere to be found. Gone on the elevator down just as soon as I'd left, I'm sure. He had finished his dessert.

Spending fifteen minutes one-on-one with the vice president of the United States, a man just days away from his election to the highest office in the land, was a day I'll always remember. I felt like I was in the presence of Abe Lincoln himself. The vice president was relaxed and confident of his imminent and certain election in ten days.

However, I can say that I was totally opposed and profoundly disappointed in President Bush when he invaded Iraq in 1991. That decision and his son's decision to do it again has left the Middle East and the world in the mess it is in today.

Mary Ann and I traveled to Charlevoix, Michigan, several times each summer, mainly to play golf with my good friend, Rob Elzerman. Rob was the owner of one of Maurer-Shumaker's customers, Superior Metal Finishing, in Detroit. He had memberships at both the Charlevoix Country Club and the Belvedere, where Tom Watson learned to play while visiting his grandparents as a kid (at least that's what I've been told). Mary Ann and Joyce would shop in the tourist town, sandwiched between Lake Michigan and Round Lake, while Rob and I played one of the courses. Sometimes we'd see Harvey Witherspoon, the legendary one-hundred-year-old from town still playing a round of golf at Belvedere. Arriving in Charlevoix a few hours early on one particularly hot day in July, Mary Ann and I stopped in town to buy some fudge for the Elzermans. Mary Ann went into Murdick's Fudge shop while I waited on the grassy knoll with our puppy. As I relaxed with my newspaper, a woman in tight-fitting spandex interrupted my reading.

She said with a strong accent, "What kind of dog you have there?"

I looked up and answered, "This is an American Eskimo."

She said, "In Russian, we call that breed a Russian spitz." She continued, "I believe your spitz would like to go for a ride on my sailboat."

Getting her drift, I said, "You're darn right, my Russian spitz would love to go sailing with you, but here comes my wife." Mary Ann was just coming out of the fudge shop.

When I told Rob about the Russian beauty, he knew exactly who she was. The locals knew her well too. All summer, she dove off her sailboat docked nearby, and on hot days, she skinny-dipped. She had a great following.

Maurer-Shumaker purchased 5.5 acres of industrial property directly behind our rental location off Farmington Road in Livonia. It was an old pallet manufacturing site having for me the added attraction of a working railroad spur. I could visualize railcars loaded with twenty-five thousand gallons of oil for our Ultramate line of corrosion inhibitors as well as tank loads of liquid caustic for our heavy industrial line of cleaner products being received from rail deliveries. This would make us more competitive and profitable. I'm just saying that is what I was thinking. Even tanker loads of artesian water from Roscommon were part of my dreams. We could set up our water bottling on this five-acre site and save considerable costs in freight. This was not to be. We made land contract payments for nearly three years before selling out to a weasel of a real estate agent who was double-dipping on commissions as he sold our property twice within a month—the first time to his lumber dealing buddy outside of the Schostak Realty Co. and then again to the California Mini Storage company, this time going through the realty company.

We were too anxious to sell as Gary Shumaker once again became nervous, fearful, and impatient with the long-term plan for the company and hounded me to sell the property. There was a chance within the first year of our ownership to perhaps build on the rail site property. Josie Shumaker brought her neighbor, Bob Demadia, an up-and-coming commercial real estate developer and builder into a meeting at Maurer-Shumaker. I take full responsibility for not moving forward with hiring Demadia Construction to build our own plant on our own property. Bob Demadia's project engineer scared me in his verbal opinion as to the cost of the project. He said they could duplicate our twelve thousand square foot building for $220K or $250K, depending on the work required for the foundation. I thought he was not presenting the facts clearly. So for a mere $30K, I said we're not picking you, at least not yet. But we never got that close again and likely that explains Gary's loss of interest in the project.

J. P. McCarthy at the WJR radio St. Patrick's
Day Party in Detroit, Michigan, in 1988.

Nevertheless, Maurer-Shumaker continued to grow, but the missed opportunities, either through my leadership or the Shumakers' overly cautious approach to business growth, was building in my subconscious. I wanted to be free to grow as big as my dreams. Patience is the word for me. Optimism is the word for Gary. We both needed some of each.

On February 24, 1991, the day the US led ground war was launched against Saddam Hussein and Iraq, I was attending the Detroit Tigers baseball team's spring party hosted by team owner Tom Monaghan. As a member of Mr. Monaghan's Nicaragua's cathedral building committee, I was a guest.

So I'm enjoying the party when I notice J. P. McCarthy, famous WJR radio personality, and Bo Schembechler, the former University of Michigan coach, now the Detroit Tigers general manager. As I approached to say hello to J. P., I could hear J. P. ask Bo, "Just why did you fire Ernie Harwell?" Ernie was the beloved voice of Tiger baseball for the last forty-two years, and Bo had just ended his career with a surprise firing. No one knew why, and J. P. was trying to get the story out of Bo.

I decided not to interrupt the intense questioning, so I stopped in my tracks. However, another individual approached J. P. and Bo when I stopped. J. P. turned to say, "Hello, Governor!" It was our newly elected governor of Michigan (the forty-sixth for Michigan), John Engler. J. P. gave the governor about ten seconds and then turned back to questioning Bo Schembechler. The governor and his wife were left standing alone, so I made my move toward John Engler. I approached Mr. Engler, saying, "Congratulations on your recent election!"

He was very happy to talk to me about the other big question of the day: Did I think he did the right thing about refusing to activate the Michigan National Guard to patrol the Ambassador Bridge connecting Detroit and Canada since the first ground war had just started that day? I told the governor that I thought he did the right thing by not activating the guard. He seemed happy that I agreed and then introduced me to his wife, Michelle. Michelle Engler had triplet girls in 1994.

No sooner did I say hello to Michelle than as it often happens at cocktail parties, somebody interrupted my conversation with Michigan's first family. Then I recognized the intruder as the defeated Governor Blanchard, saying to Engler, "Congratulations on your victory. You ran a fine campaign, and I wish you all the luck as the new governor of Michigan."

For sure, we were having fun in the business. We could now afford three major trips per year. The annual AESF (American Electroplaters and Surface Finishers) SurFin convention held in the industrial Midwest, the annual pleasure rendezvous conventions now held in exotic places like Hawaii, Puerto Rico, Mexico, California, and Florida. Also, Maurer-Shumaker was capable of hosting its own annual distributor meetings in places like the Bahamas, Marco Island, and the Bear Resort in Traverse City, Michigan. Everyone within our company profited from the exchange of new technology and bonded with our distributors, which increased the cohesion of the entire organization, providing synergy in the process.

On one of these trips, I witnessed my good friend, Maurer-Shumaker, board member and president of Harshaw, now Atotech, of Canada, Mr. Erich Knebel, get his first hole in one. It was a 190-yard shot on the Wailea Course on Maui. I remember Beth Daniels, the lady golf champ at the time, had just won 75K on the same course the previous weekend.

Erich didn't think the ball actually went in the hole, but I saw it disappear. I said as it traveled in the air, "Great shot, you're going to be on the green. It will be real close to the pin. Holy cow, it went in the hole." We were a foursome. I believe the other two guys were from Chicago; one of the two also saw it go in, and the other guy missed it, as he was putting his driver back in the bag. It was quite a day on Maui, seventies and sunny on the golf course, snowy and icy on the mountain for the biker outing, and rough seas for Mary Ann, Gary, Josie, Bruno, and Mollie for their deep-sea fishing day. Only Mary Ann and Mike Phiaff of McDermid were not seasick. The lady captain told Mary Ann it was her roughest day on the ocean in seventeen years.

Erich had already given a hundred-dollar bill to a lady in the golf course parking lot, saying, "Drinks are on me, I got a hole in one." And that evening Mary Ann and I were enjoying the Luau dinner with our friends Clif Roy, Fred Gumm, their wives, and of course Erich and Ann Knebel.

The maître d', prior to introducing the entertainment for the evening, said, "Let's get the hole in one guy up here to tell us about it."

Now Erich, who had not stopped celebrating, took the stage and said, "I'm fifty years old and today was the most exciting day of my life. Nothing I've done has been more exciting, I mean nothing." Everyone laughed, including Ann.

My friend J. P. McCarthy, our Ultramate
2800 spokesman in 1995.

Erich nominated me to be a member of the industry's chemical trade board, known as MFSA, Metal Finishers and Surface Finishers Association. It was an honor to be representing all the companies which supplied and promoted our industry. I believe there were a dozen board members, all of whom were required to be presidents of their respective companies. Erich was on the board, being President of Atotech of Canada. Bob Sizeloff, president of the Frederich Gumm Company, was chairman of this group of industry leaders during the four years I was a member.

Also, on the board was a certain Thad Piatkowski, president of Novamax, chemical division of Molson Beer. At one of our meeting, Thad said to me, "I just bought one of your competitors."

"Who?" I asked.

He said, "Detrex Chemical."

I said, "Why don't you buy Maurer-Shumaker in about ten years?" I thought I may be ready to sell when I turned sixty-two.

At about fifty-one to fifty-five years of age, many people begin to get restless in their careers, and I was one. They start to think, *Will it be twenty more years of the same thing? I don't have any more to prove to myself or others in this career. I need a change or a sabbatical or just something different. Maybe I just feel trapped.*

At this junction, you should take a break—hire your twin to run things, become the chairman of the board, play more golf, write a book, start a new division with the old challenges (no need to cash out of the number one venture).

As you will read in the coming chapters, this is my advice, which I didn't get or listen to if it were offered. I did play more golf, write a book, and start a new company, but I also cashed out—it was difficult for me to live with that.

I know I will miss old friends and distributors, especially Tom Riley from Elco/Textron, Jerry Rzeppa from EM/Tiodize, and the distributors, Erich Knebel, our Canadian distributor in Toronto, Dan Stanton from Deveco in Chicago, John Murphy from Techmatic in Nashville, Frank Dunigan from Abrite in Dallas, Louis Candeil from L.C. Systeme in France, and finally Heinz Kyburz from Kyburz Company in Switzerland.

Thad said, "I can't wait that long. I'm buying companies now."

So I said, "Why don't you come over to our offices in Michigan next week and let's talk about it."

He said, "Okay."

He told me that Molson Beer had a billion dollars in beer sales and another billion in sales from its Novamax chemical division, but that the Molson board wanted to grow its chemical group, and he was buying up certain additional smaller chemical companies in the metal finishing supply side in order to round out the Novamax product line.

Hence Maurer-Shumaker Inc. was a good fit with its cleaners, zinc phosphates, oils, and paints. "How much do you want for your company?" he asked. Never be the first to give a figure, I knew that, but to get the conversation going, I did tell him the dollar figure which we had rejected some five years earlier. "Let's have another meeting in a few weeks," he said, "and I'll bring the chief financial officer down from Toronto."

Gary and I both went to that meeting at the Crown Plaza Hotel near Metro Airport. At that meeting, we told Mr. Piatkowski more about Maurer-Shumaker. He already knew our company. Here is actual write-up from *Finishers Management Magazine* about our company in 1990:

Maurer-Shumaker, Inc.

On almost every GM, Ford, or Chrysler car today, a careful observer can find Maurer-Shumaker chemicals on one or more of its nuts and bolts or other fasteners. From its plant at 37025 Industrial Road off Newburgh, this small but fast-growing firm manufactures industrial chemicals, including cleaners, oils, coatings, and phosphates (zinc, iron, and manganese) for many large and small metal-treating companies that supply the auto industry, including Masco Corporation, the Cold Heading Company, Federal Mogul, and many others.

Founded in 1978 by two seasoned chemists, Terry Maurer, president of the company, and Gary Shumaker, vice president, the firm employs other experienced chemists in product development, manufacturing, and service. Maurer-Shumaker is regarded as a specialist in heavy zinc phosphates, although the firm manufactures a broad range of products including cleaners for steel; various phosphate coatings; organic coatings such as paint, pigmented oils, and primers, which are all applied over phosphates; and oils that inhibit corrosion. One or all of these products can be applied on small metal fasteners that go into cars, appliances, and buildings.

Today the market for metal fasteners demands finishes that are more corrosion resistant, nontoxic, and reliable than ever before. Because of size and experience, Maurer-Shumaker can move quickly to develop new products and get them into the market.

"One reason our business is growing is that we try to out-service our competitors," Terry Maurer says. That commitment to service, together with on-time delivery, fair prices, and high quality products, add-up to an unbeatable combination.

Maurer-Shumaker, Inc., serves the U.S. and international metal-finishing market through its manufacturing centers in Livonia; Toronto, Canada: and Toulouse, France, with several other licenses under negotiation. The company has also established and extensive network of North American and European distributors and a sales force of more than 30 engineers who promote and service Maurer-Shumaker chemicals around the world.

Terry and Erich Knebel in 1992
after his 'hole in one' on the Wailea course in Maui, Hawaii

Terry and Erich Knebel in 1992 alter his "hole in
one" on the Wailea Course in Maui, Hawaii.

Domino Pizza girl, Tom Monaghan, Eric Kafarski, and Stephen Maurer at our Plymouth House in 1990. (Tom sold Domino Pizza to Mitt Romney's Bain Capital Company for one billion dollars and founded Ave Maria School of Law in 1999 in Ann Arbor, Michigan, and moved it to Naples. Florida, in 2009).

CHAPTER X

Novamax, Henkel, Chemtech, and Maurer Coatings (1995–2001)

William Jefferson Clinton
(1993–2001)

We did it. We all three did it, Gary, Bruno, and me. We sold our baby to Novamax, a division of Molson Beer. I had second thoughts about the sale and nearly called it off just days before the closing scheduled for the first week of January 1995. The first of the New Year was to delay the tax bill for a full twelve months.

Immediately following the closing, I felt a sinking feeling of loss in my life. Maybe I had sold too soon, for too little money, and for sure, I had turned over my life to others. Things did not seem right. Had I done it to myself, and did I really have to live with the decision I made?

The night following the sale, I had a nightmare: I had two days to undo this terrible decision. In the dream, I was told that I could renege on the deal. So first thing in the morning when I woke up, I called my attorney and told him to undo the sale immediately. My attorney told me that, unfortunately, the deal could not be reversed. It was a business sale, not a realty transaction.

The second night I had another dream, another nightmare: This time Bob Grayson, CEO of Curtis Metal Finishing, our biggest potential customer, called me to say that he was giving me 100 percent of his business. I was so happy and dumbfounded: I had worked hard at getting his business, and now it was a reality! It was all mine! Millions of dollars. But then I woke up. It wasn't so at all. I had no power. I had lost it all.

I was happy, then sad because I realized I had sold the company two days before. But then relieved too, as I realized that it was just a dream that Mr. Grayson was not really giving me all his business, actually none of it.

One other incident happened within days of the sale that drove home what had occurred. I was having lunch with one of the GM fastener engineers and my daughter Laurie. "Terry, now, you are just like the rest of us," he exclaimed.

"What do you mean?" I asked.

He said, "You now work for someone else, just like the rest of us."

Suddenly I understood my pain: I had been the boss of my own company for eighteen years, and now I was reporting to Thad Piatkowski, the president of Novamax. Quite a different ball game: no more board of directors, all chosen by myself; no more bankers always eager to listen to my latest business ventures.

Here is what my daughter, Karin, sent me from Michigan State a few days after my sale. She so kindly felt my pain and tried to cheer me up.

January 25, 1995

Dear Dad,

Thanks for the little note and the $ it's good to hear that you think of me. I heard you missed me (by people whose names I won't mention), and at odd times, believe it or not, I miss everyone too. I always brag about you and Mom because everyone else complains about their parents, and I guess knowing so many dysfunctional families really do exist has put me in my place with my views about you two. But I don't want to get too mushy and anything because I know that

Mom will read this and start crying or something cheezy (Provolone) like that.

School's going OK, I think I did really terrible on my first French test, but I'll give that one for the sake of adjustment. My professor just automatically thinks that everyone in the class was in her first one and is totally used to how she teaches, but she's mistaken. Oh well, I'll get the hang of it soon. I was thinking about taking some German this summer, and minoring in languages, and majoring in International Relations (aka IR). Anyway, it would allow me to be able to work and live anywhere I want, well depending on the languages I learn, and beyond that I have no idea.

Regarding Maurer-Shumaker, think of it this way. Had you not sold the business, you would have used the past fifteen years of your life creating something that wasn't using your full potential. The only thing you would have gotten in the end was money. This way, you see your business grow symbolizing its potential to go on beyond what it could have in your complete ownership. Now, not only can Maurer-Shumaker expand, but so can your mind. You are such a business genius that to have withheld all your ideas this long has probably been torture. Your heart always misses things, yet you constantly make decisions that make your mind not miss anything. The heart will heal, but to waste a mind is a pity. The heart simply misses out of attachment, but the mind misses out of uselessness. So, let it go. If it was meant for you to have it, then it will make its way back, but by then you won't need it. See, right now, you think you need it, but you don't, you need the security the company gave you, and that security can come with your other ideas.

Well, I wish I could write more, but I just wanted you to experience how my computer is doing, so thanks again, say "hi" to everyone for me, and take care.

Love,
Karin

Between January and August 1995, Mary Ann and I managed to sell Maurer-Shumaker, take a cruise to the Caribbean with Novamax managers, sell my stocks in Berkshire Hathaway and other stocks (another decision I soon lived to regret), preside over our son's, Stephen's, wedding to Nicole Balcom, and take a two-week trip to Homer, Alaska, to visit my brother Tony. We went with our friends the McClungs and the Jacksons. Here is a write-up of a very similar trip to Homer taken by our friends Ed Murphy and Wayne Jeronimus. Wayne writes for the Calistoga Tribune in California; hence, his story has the look of a polished writer. Yet we experienced everything that Wayne wrote in his story.

Homer Spit

Homer Hemingway Hero
by
Wayne Jeronimus

After an all-day, intermittent drizzle, the sun broke through at six o'clock as I took the first sip of my cocktail. Droplets hanging on the tall timothy grass and sedges became instant jewels, refracting the sun's rays among the field of lush green. I sat on the weathered wooden steps overlooking the meadow; swallows swooped low over the grass, darting back and forth at a stunning velocity. To my right, a pair of bald eagles watched from their aerie at the top of a dead tree. To my left, cargo planes—Coast Guard, National Guard—mimicked the swallows, swooping low for touch and go, practice landings at the airfield.

I was staying with my friend Tony at his house located on a broad meadow above the town of Homer, Alaska. Below, the Homer spit, a narrow spike of land housing commercial buildings and a marina, glowed in the sunlight, pointing to the mountains and glaciers of the Kenai Range, across the now-blue waters of Kachemak Bay. Cocktails in hand, halibuts on the grill, all's right with the world.

Homer has a rugged, "last frontier" feel to it. I didn't spot one metrosexual in the entire week.

My friend Ed and I were both the beneficiaries of Tony's hospitality. Tony is everything that I'm not: a fisherman, a hunter. A Hemingway hero. He's bagged deer; elk; caribou; moose; a bear, once, with a single shot. It was only natural that he'd have a boat (Maurer's boat, not Hemingway's).

We took it out, one afternoon, for a shakedown cruise. The boat was thirty years old, stuffed to the gunwales with fishing gear and spare parts and nuts and bolts in coffee cans and cans of oil and lines and floats and bumpers, but a worthy craft she was.

Another afternoon was devoted to fishing. We set two troll lines for salmon and caught a halibut. Then we anchored and let out lines for the bottom-dwelling halibut, and caught nothing. The most excitement was generated when I, holding a pole in choppy seas, was knocked flat to the deck by a rogue wave, narrowly avoiding the ignominy of landing in the bait bucket.

Another day we set sail to Gull Island, a seabird rookery and sanctuary on the far side of the bay. Gull Island was aptly named— there were hundreds of thousands of seabirds perched on the craggy rocks and endlessly circling around them, their cries filling the air. There's a live, remote-controlled television camera mounted on top of the island which beams back to a screen in the Pratt Museum in Homer, which we later visited. There, the camera could be manipulated a full 360 degrees around, up or down, and could zoom in and out of vistas of the whole island or a close-up of a single bird's face. I spent a good deal of time at the exhibit.

After Gull Island, we sailed on to the Halibut Cove, a secluded collection of rustic buildings clinging to steep rocky hillsides above the water. Over half of the twenty-three residents are artists. There was a coffee house with a dock where one could stop in for a latte, but it was closed. A latte? Maybe this was where they kept the metrosexuals.

We spent a manly week, three men in a house. There was a daily morning routine: Tony would arise early, take Jake the beagle for a walk to the end of the long driveway, retrieve the newspaper, and settle into a stuffed chair (all chairs in the house faced a wall of windows which faced the bay) to take a crack at the crossword puzzle. He would then hand it off to Ed for a second crack, and study the bridge column. "I play duplicate bridge over at the senior center on Tuesdays," said Tony. "On Thursdays, we play party bridge. Interested?"

Was I ever. I learned to play bridge in college, got pretty good playing every day during lunch hours at work, but hadn't played in nine years. It came back. There were four tables of us, there at the senior center on Thursday afternoon. I held my own against some pretty stiff competition. And I got the impression that a couple of the ladies took a shine to me.

The antithesis of playing bridge with seniors would be hiking through forests teeming with grizzly bears. That's what we did another day, driving as far as possible in Tony's old jeep, then hiking into Tony's "moose camp," state-owned land where he has pitched a tent since time immemorial during moose hunting season in the fall. Before we set out, Tony loaded his 30.06 hunting rifle and slung it over his shoulder.

"Just in case we run across a bear" he explained. "And I want you two guys to carry these," he said, handing automobile emergency flares to Ed and me. "Light 'em up and yell and wave 'em in the bear's face." Right, I thought. And click your heels and do a jets, and the bear will bolt. But I guess Ed and I couldn't be trusted with firearms.

"So if we see a bear while we're still pretty close to the jeep, I'll shoot it," said Tony. "Then we'll have to drive back home and get all the butchery equipment, skin it, gut it, and haul out the meat." I thought: Please, Lord, let us not see a bear.

We didn't. We did, however, get to fire the rifle. At a beer can, not at a bear. I remembered what my father had taught me; steady the stock, sight slowly through the scope, squeeze—don't jerk—the trigger. The gun kicked, the shot was deafening, the bullet hit its mark.

"Wow!" said Tony. "You can be in my army anytime."

I walked a bit taller on the hike back. My pratfall on the boat was history.

Tony and Madeleine Maurer, Ed Murphy and Trish, Ginny and Wayne Jeronimus, and Mary Ann and Terry Maurer in 2010.

There was a reason for the sale of Maurer-Shumaker, and I was now about to pursue that, and that new passion was to bottle and sell the artesian spring water from my family's estate, now owned by my mother's brother. The high-pH, ultra-pure springs were in Beaver Creek Township, Crawford County, in northern lower Michigan. Before I could really begin, I had agreed to manage Maurer-Shumaker for Novamax for the next three years. In hindsight, this was a big mistake. I was not happy reporting to Thad or anyone for that matter. Watching incompetent managers in production, sales, and marketing who did not report to me was pure torture. I should have given them three months, not three years. Thad's plan, unknown to me when we sold, was to sell the Molson Novamax chemical division to a much bigger German chemical company, Henkel, and he did sell to the billion-dollar Henkel Corporation within two years.

Within twenty-four months, I now had another new boss, now from Henkel, North America. Not knowing exactly how to absorb Maurer-Shumaker, Henkel kept us as a separate division, I was now VP of the Maurer-Shumaker division. During this time, I tried to buy back at least the paint portion of my old company, nearly had an agreement, but Henkel management decided to sell the entire Maurer-Shumaker group, together with some electroplating chemistry which came with one of Henkel's earlier purchases to two attorneys in St. Louis. With this sale done, we were back to being a small chemical company again, now being called ChemTech.

I was asked to head it up, but deferred to Paul Frank, since I was still planning to leave and do the water project. It was clear to me that Paul Frank didn't know how to manage a company, but I had other plans for myself. It didn't take long, maybe two years for Mr. Frank to bankrupt the company for the clueless St. Louis attorneys. What was left of Maurer-Shumaker, now ChemTech, was sold to Heatbath Chemical, Tripp Whalen's family company, from New Jersey. Heatbath was sold to DuBois Chemical in 2015.

At our first ChemTech meeting, one of the folks on our new team, Ed Budman, formerly with the Fred Gumm Chemical Company, asked the group if there was any interest in some German technology around zinc-rich coatings. I spoke up immediately, saying, "It sounds like the kind of technology Maurer-Shumaker tried for years to develop but unsuccessfully. We should license it for the US if possible." So it was agreed that Ed Budman, Chuck Cosner, and I should travel to Frankfurt, Germany, to explore a license. Zincrich, chrome-free coatings would compete with the chrome-containing resins being supplied to the US auto industry by Magni Corporation, a spin-off of David and Pat Berry's family companies, Midwest Chrome and Depor.

We met with Herman Donsbach and Volker Kunz as well as James Amigo from Sidasa Corporation of Barcelona, Spain. These two European companies had already formed a joint venture around this new promising chrome-free, corrosion-resistant dip-spin coating for fasteners. Their joint venture was called UCI (Units Coating International).

While all these chemical moving chairs were going on, our son, Stephen, married Nicole Balcom, daughter of our family's long-time friends Jim and Jan Balcom of Loch Alpine. It was a big wedding held in Ann Arbor on August 5, 1995. Then on January 25, 1997, our daughter Laurie married Tom Shelton in an intimate and most memorable ceremony with the best wines at the Joseph Phelps winery in St. Helena, California, the heart of the Napa Valley wine country.

At Tom and Laurie's wedding, Joe Phelps announced his promotion of Tom Shelton. Here is a copy of the actual press release:

Tom Shelton named President and CEO of Joseph Phelps Vineyards
KK Dirickson and Monique Nelson assume additional sales responsibilities

At a winery-wide staff meeting on January 23, 1997, Joe Phelps announced the appointment of Tom Shelton as president and chief executive officer of Joseph Phelps Vineyards.

Tom joined JPV in 1992 as vice president and national sales director and in December 1995 was appointed president and director of sales and marketing. Joe will continue as chairman of the winery, which he founded in 1972.

Citing benchmark sales in 1995 and 1996 as evidence of a dynamic renaissance of the Phelps brand, Joe attributes the winery's success to the combined efforts of Tom Shelton and Craig Williams, Phelps's winemaker and vice president of production. "This team assures our position as a producer of premium Napa Valley wines well into the twenty-first century," Joe explained.

In fact, here is my favorite wine story about my son-in-law, Tom Shelton, a story with more than one twist and a humorous ending. Tom was not only president of Joseph Phelps Vineyard but also president of the Napa Valley Vintners Trade Association. A true leader in the Napa Valley Wine Business respected and liked by all wine connoisseurs.

On one of our visits to St. Helena in the heart of the Napa Valley to see our daughter Laurie and her new husband, Tom Shelton, we had this encounter with a certain very old bottle of wine. Mary Ann and I arrived at Tom and Laurie's Silverado Trail house via limo courtesy of Tom.

We arrived minutes ahead of Tom and Laurie, but time enough for me to check out Tom's wine cooler. The first bottle I pulled out was obviously an old one, then I read the label: "1915 Bordeaux." Mary Ann said, "Put that bottle back in the cooler now. It is obviously a rare and expensive bottle." For sure, I had no intention of opening it. I was just very impressed that Tom would be in possession of such a bottle and I wanted Mary Ann to just see it.

The first thing Laurie said when they arrived at the trail house minutes later was to tell me what Tom had expressed to her as they were driving fast to get home before we arrived from San Francisco. Tom said, "I sure hope your dad doesn't find and open the 1915 Bordeaux before we arrive." The bottle was safely back in the cooler before the owners got home, but shortly after the hellos and "welcome back to the wine country," Tom told me the story of how he bid $7,000 at a charity wine auction at Meadowood (just to get the price up) and got stuck with the bottle. From the day of the auction Laurie was bugging Tom for "blowing" seven grand and trying to get him to resell the rare wine in hopes of recovering some of the money.

Now came their friend and renowned wine auctioneer, Mr. Fritz Hatton, to inspect the bottle and perhaps auction it off at his next event. Fritz told Tom (without knowing what Tom paid for the gem, I presume) that he could likely get at least, at auction, $2,000 for it. Tom said, "I'll think about it."

So fast-forward a few weeks, and Tom still in possession of the now-infamous Bordeaux is entertaining a few winemaker associates, one for sure (Tom told me this on our next visit from Michigan, when I asked "Whatever happened to the old bottle you had?") was Dan Duckhorn. Dan was the founder of Duckhorn Vineyards and also present was the winemaker from Caymus, and likely Craig Williams from Joseph Phelps. Tom told me, "You won't believe what happened: Well, Dan Duckhorn opened my cooler, like you did, and pulled out the old Bordeaux bottle, saying, 'What have we here?'" Tom told the wine aficionados, "Look I paid $7,000 for that bottle, it's only worth $2,000, let's drink it!" So they did. I never heard how that ninety-four-year-old bottle tasted. But there is still more to the story. It seems that two weeks after the drinking, Tom got a call from the auctioneer, Fritz.

"Tom," he said, "I've been doing more research on your special bottle of wine, and I'd like to come over and take some photos of your bottle and put it on the front of my next auction bulletin. I think I can get you $20,000 for it."

Tom responded, "It's too late."

The postscript to this story takes place in St. Helena in December 2008, some six years later, at the home of Janet and Lester Hardy, friends of Laurie's. It was a very nice Christmas party with lots of good wine and delicious hors d'oeuvres. In the course of the evening I found myself telling the 1915 Bordeaux wine story to a fellow I bumped into at the wine bar. We started talking before any real introduction. I think I said that I was Tom Shelton's father-in-law, and boy, did I have a good story for him about Tom's "old wine" fiasco. The fellow let me tell the whole story as I'd just told it, when I said, "By the way, my name is Terry Maurer. What's your name?"

He said, "I am Dan Duckhorn, and I opened the old bottle you're telling me about." He also told me he remembered the bottle as an 1895 Chateau Lafite Rothschild. However, I am sure it was the 1915 Bordeaux. In fact, recently Fritz Hatton and I were retelling our versions of this story, and Fritz remembered it as a 1915 Musigny Tagot, which is a pinot noir from Burgundy.

The joining of the Maurers and the Sheltons brought many trips to Northern California, as well as an appreciation for fine wines for everyone in our family. Mary Ann and I heard Tom talk wine at a number of special dinners and events, and I can still hear him describe a wine something like this: "It has flavors and aromas of blackberry, blueberry, plum, dark cherry, and a hint of mocha. The wine is elegant and rich in texture, with plush, round tannins, and finely integrated oak characteristics. Final flavors of black spice and maple combine to create a long, velvety finish."

Late in 1997, my grandson Trevor was having some difficulties, believe it or not, in kindergarten. His mother, my daughter Laurie, asked me to give him a grandpa talk. Here is my letter to Trevor:

Octobers 1997

Dear Trevor,

Tonight your mom told me that were having some trouble in Kindergarten. Don't worry about it. Things will get better.

I remember when I had trouble in school, my Dad (your mom's papa) wrote me a letter telling me to "take the bull by the horns" and get the job done. It means "work hard" at doing the right thing. Well it seemed to help me, because I always thought about what your great "papa" told me when things get tough.

So I'm asking you now to "take the bull by the horns." It's an old farm expression, you remember I grew up on a farm in Grayling, Michigan, way up North near "Trevor City."

Remember to ask God to bless each day "every morning" for you—then thank God at night for your "great day." You will grow up to be a very important and much respected adult, I know that because we all have lots of confidence in all your abilities, after all you have some great-grandparents on both your Mansfield and your Maurer side who love you greatly.

Trevor, always obey your Mom and Tom, and obey when you are with Nana and Papa and your Dad too. Your teachers at school want the best for you, that's why they're called teachers. So listen carefully to what they ask you to do. Then do it to the best of your ability.

Like my Dad told me when I got this kind of letter, I've got to go to bed now"—he had to get up early to put the lights on in the chicken coop so the chickens would lay lots of eggs. I have to go sell some chemicals early tomorrow morning so I'm going to bed now too.

I will be picking your Nana and great Nana up at the airport tomorrow and I'm anxious to hear about all the fun things they did with you in California on their visit. Nana will probably tell me all about how great Nana got lost walking from your school and how she herself cut her leg on a wisteria vine and how you helped out.

Well good night, Trevor. Papa looks forward to seeing you and your Mom next month in Michigan. Much love and encouragement!

Papa Maurer.

P.S. Please say a short prayer every day for your Papa and I'll say one for you. Also—no one ever

said things would always be easy. It's how we react
to things that show what we're really made of.

By the end of 1998, I had resigned from Henkel with intentions of working Avita Water full-time. It never happened that way.
As soon as I resigned from Henkel, the Kunz group from Germany
wanted me to market their zinc-rich coatings. Soon after leaving
Henkel, I negotiated an exclusive distribution contract for the US
and nonexclusive for Canada and Mexico between Kunz and my new
company Maurer Coatings (a name change from Maurer-Shumaker
to Maurer Coatings). The sale to Molson was an asset sale, so I was
left with 100 percent ownership of the new shell company Maurer-
Shumaker Inc.

Now I was running two new companies, Avita Water and
Maurer Coatings. I thought I could do it, but to be successful, I
needed a quick and significant breakthrough with at least one of the
enterprises. This did not happen. No large profitable water sale came
through, not John Deere, not Eden Foods, not Avita itself. No breakthrough zinc-rich customer for Maurer Coatings, not Curtis, not
Ajax, not Marty Straus's company in Chicago, not Torcad in Toronto.
Although the Kunz technology was the first to be hex-chrome-free,
the European Union of Automotive Fastener Engineers delayed the
mandated conversion to hex-free for three years. The storm was coming, I now needed something in the water business for sure. I didn't
see how I could keep the new chemical business going for three years
waiting for the opportunity to sell the key Kunz products. The incen-
tive for the industry to change to Maurer Coatings' licensed German
technology was put on hold. The three years gave Magni and the
German Doerken Co. time to catch up to Kunz. Doerken had even
contacted me through a headhunter saying that I was the perfect
guy to run their US operation. They were authorized to pay 150K
with full expenses and benefits if I would set up headquarters in Ann
Arbor. I turned them down, convinced that my US exclusive with
Kunz was the best opportunity.

In 2001 I was on yet another business trip to Switzerland to
visit Kyburz Electroplating in Stein am Rhein, a unique and beauti-

ful little village some sixty to seventy kilometers from Zurich. Stein Am Rheim is also home to the 1200th Century Castle, Hohenkligen, a tourist attraction and great restaurant which I've enjoyed. Despite the delay in making the switch to chrome-free coatings Kyburz was still considering taking a license for the Zintek/Techseal coating system, which my company, Maurer Coatings, was handling for Kunz GmbH. While there I decided to visit the world-renowned Evian bottled water plant.

I asked Katarina, Heinz Kyburz's office manager, if she would help set me up with a plant tour. She was happy to do it and even said that Kyburz offered me his Mercedes for the four-hour drive from Stein am Rhein to the Lake Geneva Ferry station, which would take me across the lake (about one-hour boat ride) to Evian on the French side. However, later in the day, Katarina told me, "Bad news, Terry, Evian is done with tours for the season, but I know that I can get you into another water company."

"No thanks," I said. "I really want to see Evian because it is the world's most popular 'still' water bottling operation. I'll be happy just to drive by it."

"Okay," she said, "but you may prefer to take the train since you've never driven in Switzerland before."

So the next day, Katarina dropped me off at the local train station, and I proceeded to the edge of Lake Geneva, caught the ferry, and arrived in the town of Evian at quarter to five on Friday afternoon. There was a queue of taxi cabs waiting for the ferry passengers. Speaking my best French, I told the first driver in line that I wanted to get to the water plant. The first driver either didn't understand my French or didn't want to, so as I am trying to rephrase my request, the third driver in line spoke up and said, "Get in my car! I know where you want to go!"

We took off with some degree of urgency since the driver reminded me that it was late on a Friday afternoon. I could tell we were starting to head out of town, so I questioned, "I thought the Evian plant was in the town of Evian?"

He said, "Why, yes! The old plant is right up this street on my left, but I thought that you wanted to see the new plant."

"Let's see the old plant first," I said.

So within minutes we were parked at a closed gate with guardhouse and a clearly visible operating bottling line behind a very large viewing window. My driver immediately got out, leaving me in the back seat of his cab, and hurried to the guardhouse where I could see him gesturing toward me and obviously telling some kind of a story. Pretty soon he's waving me up to the guardhouse and said there was a lady on the phone who would talk to me. As I picked up the phone, a pleasant young lady's voice was speaking perfect English and laughing with her French accent, telling me, "The tour season is over, but if you come to Evian in six months, you'll get a great tour if you tell the folks that Mr. Baud sent you."

Now we're really off to the races as the driver said, "We'll now go to the new plant." It was only ten minutes or less before we pulled up to another much-larger guardhouse at the front of a very long, flowered, and tree-lined drive, ending at I'd guess to be a million-square-foot modern plant with multiple rail sidings. My driver (you'd think I'd know his name by now) was immediately out of the car again, outside the guardhouse, explaining to the guards as I could pick up 80 percent of his French, telling them that he had an important visitor from the USA, and I heard Mr. Baud's name. Before I knew it, the driver was back to the cab telling me that a tour of midwives was about to start and that if I didn't mind touring with twenty to twenty-five women, I should get up to the main entrance at once. I said, "Let's go!" Soon we were stopped at the main entrance and a gentleman looking very spiffy in a three-piece suit greeting me at the cab.

I really hope I tipped the driver well, as the spiffy suit said to me, "I am Dr. Williams, and I will be conducting the tour of midwives today, and you are welcome to join us."

"I will be very happy to join you," I said.

The tour began with a twenty-minute movie about Evian, which laid out the benefits of this ancient Alpine spring water for infants, toddlers, and expectant mothers. Then we began the tour, walking along an elevated viewing area, looking down into the actual bottling plant, watching bottles being blown, filled, capped, labeled, packed, and palleted and moved toward multiple truck-loading docks or directly onto waiting railroad cars. At least two times during the walking tour, Dr. Williams drifted back to ask me about Mr. Baud. I really deflected his question, not knowing exactly what the clever driver had told the guards who then told Dr. Williams about the American man who needed a tour.

When the tour was over, my guide asked me where I was staying. I said that I didn't have a hotel reservation yet, but I was sure that the next cab driver could take me to one. He said, "Don't get a cab! I'll drive you to a hotel on my way to the restaurant where the midwives will be having dinner. After their meal, I'll be giving a short talk about Evian. But first, let me drop you off at the casino downtown. You'll have time to get a drink and play some blackjack. Then after I get the ladies situated at their event, I'll come to get you and take you to the hotel. I'll be back in thirty minutes."

I did not expect to see Dr. Williams again, but I was grateful that I got to Evian, France, and experienced an exceptional, almost-private tour of the Evian water bottling plant, and now I was ready for a scotch on the rocks. Like my son, Stephen, would say, "I am now just going with the flow."

However, true to his word, Dr. Williams found me in the intimate Evian Casino, and he said, "Are you ready to go? I told the ladies I would be back very soon."

"I'm ready," I said.

Back in his car, we drove to the top of the hill and passed a remarkable golf course, all just above the town of Evian. We stopped right in front of the Evian Hotel. Both of us were escorted directly to the front desk by the doorman. The doctor, without introducing himself to the most attractive, beautiful young hostess, politely asked for a room for Mr. Maurer.

She responded, "So sorry, Dr. Williams. The Evian Resort Hotel is full for tonight. We have no rooms available."

The doctor then said, "Mr. Maurer is here to see Mr. Baud, can't you find a room for him?"

The smiling beauty then said, "Yes, sir. We most certainly can. How many nights will Mr. Maurer be staying?"

Then Dr. Williams said, "Merci beaucoup and au revoir" to me, telling me he's got to rush back to the midwives.

Now, as I was checking in, the young hostess informed me that Mr. Baud would be arriving at the hotel any minute, and perhaps I would like to wait for him at the fireplace. *Holy cow*, I thought. *What will I say to Mr. Baud?* And furthermore, I didn't even know what Mr. Baud's position was at Evian. So I discreetly asked the hostess, "Can you please tell me exactly what is Mr. Baud's position at the company?"

She said, "Mr. Baud is the number two man at Evian."

"Thanks," I said. "I'll be waiting at the fireplace."

So now, I thought, what to say. After all, I never wanted a meeting with Mr. Baud! Suddenly it came to me: I would tell Mr. Baud that my family had some of the best water in the world, analysis very close to Evian's, and should Evian ever need a water source in the United States, I would be happy to discuss the possibilities.

Well, I waited at the fireplace for perhaps thirty minutes. Then I went back to the front desk and told the hostess that I would move to the dining room, and maybe she would be so kind as to direct Mr. Baud to my table for our meeting, a meeting that she presumed had been set up previously. I had a very nice dinner alone, except for a glass of French red for company. Returning to the front desk, it was 11:30 p.m., I explained to the mademoiselle that I was going to my room without seeing Mr. Baud. She said, "I saw him come in some time ago. I know he's had a very busy schedule tonight, speaking to several different groups. He must have walked past you at the fireplace." Then she added, "Why don't you leave him a note? I'll make sure he gets it."

So I did. My note described the Avita source in Michigan, and I explained that we might have something to talk about. The next morning, the same young lady was still at the desk; she told me she was working a double shift. She said to me, "Oh, Mr. Maurer! I have a note for you from Mr. Baud." The note was a short apology for missing me, especially in view of the fact that I had traveled all the way from the US. He wrote that he would refer my note to his manager in New York who handled such matters.

As I retraced my journey across Lake Geneva, then the four-hour train ride back to Stein am Rhein to Herr Kyburz's office that day, I could hardly wait to tell Katarina about my good fortune in getting an Evian tour.

It was some weeks after my return to Michigan that I received a letter from Evian's office in Montreal in touch with Mr. Baud, saying that they were not looking for a US water source at this time, but they would contact me and Avita if the situation should change.

I did receive another letter from my daughter Karin about this time, which put me in a good mood, and here it is:

November 27, 1996

Mom & Dad

    Just a small reminder that I think you are the best parents on Earth. (Even though the Earth may sometimes seem insignificant on the whole scale of things, the sun, other galaxies, etc.) Also just to let you know, you two have handled all the major & minor adjustments to having an adopted daughter quite wonderfully. You have been and are the embodiment of the perfect parents. I know I sometimes don't act in accordance with that view but I wouldn't want too many people knowing what I think of you. Lest there be babies being handed to you from all parts of the world! You might think that you were lucky to get a cute one but all in all, I'm positive I got the lucky end of the deal.

    Thanks for a great anniversary and holiday. Have a splendid weekend and I'll see you on Sunday.

Lots and lots and lots of love.
Karin

P.S. Drive safely.

Mary Ann and Chuck Haltiner were doing what they could in Northern Michigan. Chuck, my brother Louie's stepson, proved to be the best Avita employee through the years. Chuck can fix any and all bottling machines, and in 2015, he managed Avita production together with another dedicated and reliable manager, Mr. Kim Dake. I was taking jobs for folks wanting private labels of pallets of water, e.g., banks, real estate offices, 10K run ventures, and others who thought having their own label on a bottle of water was the hottest new promotional tool. This a time-consuming, unprofitable way to sell the world's best artesian spring water. Bob and Pat Millikin were the first dedicated plant managers at Avita, but we needed a better plan to stay in business. The big guns of Pepsi and Coke also wanted into the new beverage market with their own water.

See this bulletin in *Beverage Digest* in February 5, 1999, announcing Coke's imminent entry into the water business. This fact confirms what I recognized in 1987 when Joy Daudlin and I were drinking Perrier in Cleveland, but it also adds a serious competitor for all US small pioneer water companies. We all have to struggle with the new competition.

From Beverage Digest, Bedford Hills, NY
February 5, 1999

Coke Likely Near Announcement
of Dasani Bottled Water,
Big Shakeup of Category Ahead.

Coke bottlers say company close to announcing introduction of new bottled water, named "Dasani" (BD 11/6/98). Product is reverse-osmosis purified water with minerals/salts—"concentrate factor"—added to enhance taste. Bottlers say product will be sold initially in 20-oz PET. Several bottlers says Dasani's proprietary package will likely be "very light blue" transparent PET. Other bottler says, "it's clear or faintly light blue, but it will be recyclable." Bottlers report seeing two prototypes. One is round, with horizontal ribbings, "the other is more exotic." Bottler says initial limited introduction may not use final version of proprietary package. Label said to be dark blue with gold print; stated "A Product of the Coca-Cola Company." Bottler: "It's attractive." Bottlers says Dasani—after debut in 20-oz—will also be sold in 1-liter and 1.5-liter. Category. BD estimates in 1998, overall bottled water category grew about +8%. PET segment—1.5-liter and under—up 20+%. Dasani and Pepsi's reverse-osmosis Aquafina bottled water compete in PET segment.

Impact on other waters

Coke bottlers now sell other waters, including Evian and Naya plus regional brands like Vermont Pure. Nava. CCE handles 60+% of Naya's US volume. Under current contract, CCE distributes Naya through may 19 (BD 12/11/98), though discussions could alter that. Several executives predict CCE ultimately drops Naya in much of its geography. Bottlers say if CCE drops Naya, distribution via 3rd-tier bottlers/ warehouse likely. Another executive suggests possible Pepsi system role for Water executive: "Pepsi is pushing Aquafina, it's a successful brand for them." Major 3rd-tier bottlers: 1) "I'd sure take a look at Naya." 2) "We might be interested, but only if we got in for (all channels)." Vermont Pure. CCE sells Vermont Pure in northeast. Vermont Pure on short-term termination basis with CCE. Vermont Pure likely switches to East Coast Snapple distribution system, including Triarc-owned Mr. Natural in NYC area. Pepsi

Honickman NY sells Evian and Aquafina. Evian. Bottlers envision two-tier water strategy for Coke system, with Dasani at lower-mid price point and premium spring water, like Evian, at higher price. Predict: 1) "You'll see more and more Evian in the Coke system." 2) "Don't be surprised if Coke (eventually) buys Evian."

Spring vs purified

With Pepsi/Coke systems selling national brand purified waters, many industry executives see showdown ahead between spring and purified waters. One spring water company executive predicts consumers will prefer spring water. But Coke bottler says consumers will favor purified water, "as they won't have to worry about the source." Senior industry executive: "Coke and Pepsi will give spring water a bad name. (Reverse-osmosis waters) are purified and the same in every market." Like teas? Other industry executive says Coke and Pepsi "will do with the water business what they did with teas." Today, Pepsi Upton and Coke Nestea cold-filled teas lead category (BD 11/20/98).

While Avita Water and Maurer Coatings were struggling to find their place, bigger worldwide issues were festering, especially in the Middle East after George H. W. Bush's ill-advised entry into Iraq after Saddam's invasion of Kuwait on August 2, 1990. See this short email from our Montreal friend after the 9/11 attack.

Date: 9/23/01
From: Serge Archambault
To: Terry Maurer

It has been quite a while since we saw each other in Oakville last May. We hope all is well with both of you, healthwise and business (Avita in particular) wise also. I seem to recall you were embarking on a new career with a German organization in your area of direct expertise. The sad and tragic events of Sept 11 caused me to think back about the many American friendships and colleagues I was fortunate enough to build during my 31 years in our industry. I pray God you were not directly impacted by the acts of cowardness and terrorism.

Give us news about all of you and tell me if you are planning a visit to Montreal sometime. Maybe we could host you or meet you in town for dinner.

We look forward to reading your reply at your convenience.

Best regards,
Serge A.

In addition to the email from Serge A., my old friend from Erich Knebel's group at Atotech Canada, here is another email from my buddy Ed Budman, marketing manager from ChemTech and Fred Gumm Co. Ed's email sheds light on progress or lack of progress of what became of the former Maurer-Shumaker company, now called ChemTech.

Subj: Happy Holidays
Date: 12/15/01
From: Ed Budman

Hello Terry,

It has been quite a while since we spoke or wrote, and I hope that everything is going well with you. Chemtech made a big move months ago, as you must be aware. We moved from Farmington Hills to the plant in Warren. Actually the job was quite well done, and the owners have been absolutely splendid. The warehouse looks completely different, as the stocking arrangements have been arranged for maximum efficiency. The Lab makes best use of the space needed to QC, R+D, and routine lab work. Conrad Berube is back with us, as QC person. He seems to like it and has adjusted to it quite well.

I seem to be the last of the mohicans regarding marketing. That does make one want to look over their shoulder a bit. I sure hope nothing does happen in a bad nature job wise. Right now, no one seems to be hiring and if you are unemployed the chances are you will be that way for a while until the economy straightens out, and confidence is restored.

The MacDermid website indicates that they are suspending manufacturing in Waterbury, Ct., and all production stateside will be in Michigan. Atotech has let a bunch of people go, mostly McGean folks. They have not been thrilled about the income that McGean has brought to the table with regards to sales. Hasn't anyone told them that this is a shrinking market?

How is your work going with Kuntz I hope that Volker and all the folks are doing well. Maybe I will see them in Chicago at SurFin next June. It sure seems odd, never to be travelling to either Europe, Brazil, or Japan any more. Maybe that is a blessing in disguise, as international travel is not what it once was.

I would like to close by wishing you and your family a very merry Christmas, and a

Happy, Healthy, and prosperous New Year. Terry, if you get a chance to write, please do. I will be in Michigan this coming week…Maybe we can have a dinner together. Most times I eat simply at the ChiChi's at the hotel.

All the best to you,
Ed

On March 19, 2003, George Bush II, ignoring his father's advice and certainly mine if I had been asked, initiated the second war-mongering attack, with Dick Cheney's prodding, against Iraq. I just want to include my comments as expressed in email to my brother, Tony, prior to the attack.

March 1, 2003

Hey Tony! I don't see the moral justification for an invasion of Iraq. We have Sadam Hussein contained and can do this cheaper than an invasion and the repercussions. Also I see very little correlation between now and 1944. The USA has never been the aggressor in my memory, except after our Civil War when the white folks killed the Indians in this country. I don't think we want to go back to that way of living, that's what the Israelis and Palestinians do to each other every day and by the way is the source of all the MidEast problems. If it wasn't for the oil in the region we would all ignore the local problems there much as we, the USA, and the rest of the world ignore all the things which go on in Africa. Let's just go get the oil in Alaska and also stop shipping US Alaskan oil to Japan. Let Japan make their own oil deals with the oil producers who have a surplus. We also have more oil in Crawford

County and the Gulf of Mexico which could be harvested and let's get serious about alternative sources of energy for our cars. We have enough natural gas in this country to heat all the homes. Bush's war posturing is all about the price of oil in my opinion.

Regards,
Terry

Also, I think this person expressing his feelings about the pending attack in a *USA Today* editorial on March 15, 2003, raises more questions and offers another side to this ongoing saga.

Attack on Iraq would spur worldwide terrorism, war

Young Americans are rising up to voice their opposition to a military strike against Iraq, and we really need to listen ("Debate over Iraq fires passions not seen since the Vietnam War." Cover Story News, March 6).

Preemptively annihilating Iraq likely would be the beginning of worldwide terrorism and war, especially in light of the fact that for years America has been planting seeds of despair, pain and righteous outrage in the Arab and Muslim world by arming and empowering the Israelis in their conflict with the Palestinians.

Anne Selden Annah
Mechanicsburg, PA

As long as I am discussing the heady topic of war in the Middle East, I'll remind everyone to study up on the Balfour Declaration of

1917. It is the document that has had the most influence on Middle Eastern history.

Also, one more extremely important historical fact which everyone needs to know about is the Glass-Steagall legislation. The Glass-Steagall Act of 1933 passed during the Great Depression prevented commercial banks from trading securities with their clients' deposits and created the FDIC as a guard against bank runs.

According to some people, the repeal of the original Glass-Steagall Act by Bill Clinton in 1999 was perhaps the single greatest criminal act committed against the economic welfare of the American people in the twentieth century. In the election of 2016, I do not think the country can afford to gamble with another Clinton presidency, beholden to the big bankers and special interest groups.

These two things, the Balfour Agreement and the repeal of the Glass-Steagall Act, have created great misery, hardship, and sacrifice for US citizens. We should all get informed.

Laurie and Tom Shelton and John Cogan at
2000 Napa Valley Wine Auction.

What's happening now.

CHAPTER XI

The Perfect Storm
2002–2008

George W. Bush
(2001–2008)

By now, my company had changed names three times: From Maurer-Shumaker Inc. to Novamax Technologies, to Henkel Corp, to ChemTech Industries. I resigned from ChemTech to work only on Avita Water (at least that was my plan). However I reactivated my original company, changing the name to Maurer Coatings, when I inked the deal to be the exclusive USA distributor for the small German company, Kunz Electroplating. Kunz was partnered up in a 50/50 venture with the large Spanish chemical manufacturer, Sidasa. Their combined venture name was UCI (Units Coating International), and that is technically who Maurer Coatings Inc. was now representing exclusively in the USA and nonexclusively for Canada and Mexico.

To clarify the players in this international group, I'll use actual press releases from the companies themselves.

First, about Kunz:

> Founded in 1988 Kunz GmbH develops and distributes general metal finishing products for electroplating and zinc flakes. Kunz has gained global market acceptance for high corrosion protection solutions and holds major approvals for the automotive industry.

Second, about Sidasa:

> Sidasa started its activity in the field of chemical processes for electroplating of zinc, nickel and chrome in 1952. Sidasa's electroplating and zinc flake business has achieved a major market position in the countries of Spain, Italy, France, Portugal and Brazil.

And finally, about Maurer Coatings:

> There are three key players: Terry Maurer, Chuck Cosner, and Dr. Tarek Nahlawi. Terry Maurer is the Managing Director. His experience in corrosion resistance coatings goes back to 1965. Most recently 1977 to 1995, he was president and founder and 57% shareholder in Maurer-Shumaker Inc., the predecessor to Maurer Coatings. After an asset sale of Maurer-Shumaker in 1995 to Molson Beer, he stayed on first as president of the Maurer-Shumaker Division and marketing manager for the next three years. His responsibilities were to secure automotive approvals for new coatings while serving as CEO and Chairman for Maurer Coatings.

Chuck Cosner, the coatings chemist, has worked in the automotive area for twenty years. Chuck is responsible for assisting the applicators with start-ups and leading the UCI internal audits.

Tarek Nahlawi, PhD, chemist from the University of Michigan, class of 1994, heads up the promotion of the inorganic side of the license agreement signed with Units Coatings International GmbH. Dr. Nahlawi has worked as a research chemist for Maurer-Shumaker in this area for five years, traveling many times to China. Dr. Nahlawi is also fluent in German.

Also, the press release put out by Maurer Coatings clarifies the products, services, and marketing plans for these new hexavalent-chrome-free, low-VOC, and PTFE-free (therefore environmentally safe) coatings for the automotive markets.

Products and Services:
Maurer Coatings, Division of Termar Inc. is now ready to license applicators in the U.S., Canada, and Mexico who will purchase these new environmentally friendly coatings and apply them using special "Dip-Spin" machines. The coating will be applied to automotive fasteners and other small parts including springs, clips, wheel weights and sub assemblies of all sizes and shapes. In addition, the two major coatings normally both applied to the same part can be sprayed on break calipers, fuel tubing as well as hub caps and we now know on reinforcing rods used in cement work for bridges and highways—a potentially huge market for non automotive work. The key (2) coatings are sold under the trademarks Zintek and Techseal.

Marketing:
The Marketing plan for Maurer Coatings is simple and straightforward: We will license 6-8 key applicators in the U.S. and 1-2 in Canada and at least 1 in Mexico. Since the North American automotive giants of General Motors, Ford and Daimler Chrysler are all going to World Wide Specifications for their coatings for the car industry, only a handful of top quality established ISO approved automotive applicators are needed to handle the work. Most of these applicators in good economic times will run this "Dip-Spin" machinery 2 or 3 shifts 6 days per week. They

will use in each case approximately 1,000 gallons of (Units Coatings) Maurer products per month. The average price per gallon is $95. Therefore we expect each applicator to do $95,000 per month with our company (that is over 1 million per year). For 10 applicators then we expect to gross over $10,000,000 per year. This doesn't include the opportunities for captive shops and spray shops as well as nonautomotive areas like coating reinforcing cement rods now being coated with inferior epoxies.

Here is an example of a Maurer-Coatings monthly sales report which shows our progress in promoting the units coatings zinc flake and electroplating activities for June 2006.

To: Hermann, Jaume:
From: Terry Maurer and Robert Anderson Date: June 29, 2006
Subject: Monthly sales report for 2006, January-June 29:

We are making progress on the Zintek/Techseal and expect significantly more sales with E/M and Torcad in the 4th quarter of2006.

Also we expect sales with Curtis once the GMW 3359 Black approval is complete. Progress is being made with Bosch and Allegheny, now that the sale of two Allegheny plants is complete. Curtis-Wright is the buyer, the same company which owns E/M Coatings.

We continue to follow the APGE testing at FORD through Adrian Cockman.

Our expected sales to Maurie Constantine of the electroplating Zn-Ni process is expected to kick in the 4th quarter of 2006.

We expect to make new sales at ACE Metal Finishing., Roy Metal Finishing, and to increase sales at JD Plating and Ajax Metal Processing for electroplating once Robert Anderson completes his training at Kunz in Germany later this month.

Roy Metal Finishing and Greystone continue with regular purchases of Sealer 300 W CT.

We have hopes of increasing our sales with Tinnerman-Palnut with the dip spin coatings, and have had a good response with Dynamic Coatings and J and M coatings in the Chicago area.

At the present sales rate, Maurer Coatings expects to end the year with sales in excess of $800,000 USD. Also, we look forward to both Hermann and Jaume participating in the International Fastener Show in Las Vegas, where we are already registered to exhibit (November 15–18, 2006).

We are immediately following up with the meeting we had with Muli Prasad at GM, and will be contacting the small fastener manufacturers, themselves during the month of July. We are hopeful that we can sell Sidasa machines to some of these manufacturers. Also JD Plating is interested in the Sidasa automatic Zn-Phos line, similar to the one he saw at Paulstra in Grand Rapids.

Finally, Robert and Terry expect to make a presentation directly to the GM and FORD fastener committees about the benefits of the Sidasa Planetary machines, and all the products which we represent on behalf of UCI.

In summary, interest in UCI products has picked up significantly now that we have entered the final year of the mandatory switch to trivalent or chrome-free coatings.

During this time, there were yearly trips to St. Helena, California, to visit Tom, Laurie, and our new granddaughter, Camille Elizabeth Shelton, born on October 9, 2001. Camille's birth was anticipated by everyone in the family, even Tom's friend, the governor of New York, George E. Pataki, offered his congratulations on her coming birth in a letter to Tom:

March 27, 2001

Dear Tom:

Thank you for your letter. As always, it was good to hear from you.

I was very pleased by the news that you and Laurie are expecting a baby in October. Congratulations!

I have passed your letter along to my staff so that they can be advised of the issues you mentioned of concern to grape growers.

As for the specifics of my visit to California, I would encourage you to continue to work with David Metzner on that. Above all, I look forward to seeing you and Laurie and toasting to the coming addition to your family.

> With warm regards,
> George E. Pataki
> Governor of New York

While working 80 percent of my time promoting the Maurer-Coatings chemical business I was also spending considerable time growing the Avita Water business. Robert Anderson was my right-hand man in both ventures: we operated first out of an office in Dexter, Michigan, which we shared with our CPA, Victoria Staebler, and then from a larger office with a chemical laboratory in Ann Arbor, off Baker Road. Here is a summary of our progress and plans for rapid growth in the water business as things were on January 25, 2007.

At this time, we were considering Totally Organica's request to have Avita Water get into the carbonated flavored water business. Robert Anderson introduced me to his old acquaintance, Ken Burke, from his college days at Eastern Michigan University. The summary here was likely prepared for Ken Burke's benefit.

AVITA Artesian Water LLC

Avita Water, a Michigan-based water bottling company, is approved in all fifty states as well as New York City. Avita is also certified by the NSF organization and is certified Kosher by the Circle K Rabbinical Association. Avita Water is also approved by the US Department of the Army allowing sales directly to any US government agency.

Avita Water has been bottling artesian spring water since 1987. In 1998 a new, modern six-valve filler and complete system were installed with capacity to do forty bottles per minute. Avita has established eight to ten steady customers purchasing mainly 500-ml sizes. Avita is not profitable at this sales level, because of the high overhead associated with testing required to maintain our fifty-state and NYC approval permits. Also high labor costs associated with our current slow bottling equipment contribute to profit erosion. Customers include Eden Foods, a natural food company in Clinton, Michigan; the John Deere Corporation (distributed by 2-B Global Company); Deja Vu Consulting, a private chain of clubs; Arbor Springs Bottling Company of Ann Arbor; Shay Water Bottling Company of Saginaw, Michigan; and Avita's own brand to several distributors. However, faster equipment is needed to be more competitive and original in our packaging.

Avita is talking to several new potential customers who expect to obtain some significant business. To obtain this new business, Avita needs to purchase about 1.4 million dollars of new and faster equipment. With this new equipment for which we already have firm quotes we can bottle about 120 bottles per minute, a threefold increase in our speed. With this new equipment, we not only save money for the total package but become more competitive and more profitable. Also we will have packages which will be much easier to sell namely 24- and 12-pack shrink-wrapped products with a new colorful label. In addition the new equipment will allow Avita to offer a mildly carbonated flavored water for which we have been asked to quote. Our plans are to use $200K of the $1.4 million for a warehouse addition of approximately five to seven thousand square feet. This would be built very early in the spring of 2007 and be attached to our existing five-thousand-square-foot bottling plant.

While we were talking to Vic Trutanich and Dan Gorham at Totally Organica from Las Vegas about their carbonated flavor project, others were interested in purchasing Avita Water for sale in many other countries, including Japan, Dubai, Netherlands, Spain, Korea, and Mexico. A few emails here show the level of interest in this high-purity, high-pH (7.9 to 8.2) artesian spring water from Northern Michigan.

The first email is from one of Tom Shelton's wine contacts, Mr. Ted Meegan, who has contacts in Japan interested in bottled water.

> From: Tom Shelton
> To: Ted Meegan
> Date: April 4, 2008
>
> Ted:
>
> It is great to hear from you. My father in law is making several available waters and is interested to hear from you if there is any interest. Let me know if you like to reach him.
>
> All the best,
> Tom

From: Ted Meegan
To: Tom Shelton
Date: April 4, 2008

Tom,

Please send me some info on your father-in-law's water. Afterwards, we will require some samples to test the market, etc.

Keep up the fast recovery so we can get you back in the business world. Looks like I will be in NYC on May 1 for a couple days so I will give you a call.

Regards,
Ted

Probably as a result of Avita Waters' bronze and silver medals at the Berkeley Springs International water-tasting contests, I was invited to speak at the first international water forum in Dubai in 2008. All expenses paid.

From Zafar Khan
To: Terry Maurer
Date: April 10, 2008

Dear Mr. Terry Maurer,

We take great pleasure in announcing new date for the Almiyah-Arab Bottled Water Forum. The forum now would be held at the Dubai World Trade Center on the 17th of June, 2008.

The Almiyah forum would begin immediately after the Arab Beverages Forum on the 15th and 16th of June, 2008 and would concurrently run with the Ingredients ME Expo at the same venue.

"Qatrah Awards," recognition of excellence in various categories of beverage industry, would be held in the evening of the 16th of June 2008. The award function would be followed by gala dinner at the prestigious Madinat Jumeirah Hotel and resort, with a night of social networking and live world class Arabic entertainment.

The forum will feature case studies, industry related papers, and interactive discussions that will bring together broad knowledge and experience in applying global innovations and strategies in the Arab beverage industry.

As we are working to ensure the best line-up of speakers for the event, we are considering your presence. Your presentation could be an invaluable addition to this year's event, which is why we, the organizers, request you to kindly summit proposed paper titles for the review by our steering committee. Your paper should be related to the theme of this forum, and in-line with your area of expertise.

Please include a brief outline of each paper, as well as your professional background so that we may better understand the value that your papers will bring to the forum. A committee will be meeting to review and approve the papers for this event.

We at the Almiyah Forum feel that your attendance would be a positive experience for all involved, and look forward to your response. We hope that you share our enthusiasm for this meeting and favorably consider this invitation.

Please let us know as soon as possible, if you are able to accept this invitation. If you would like additional information or have any questions, please do not hesitate to contact us at any time.

Forum Schedule:
15th and 16th June Arab Beverages Forum
16th June(evening) Qatrah Awards and Gala dinner
17th June Almiyah-Arab Bottled Water Forum

We look forward to your reply and, hopefully, to seeing you in Dubai.

Thank you and best regards,
Zafar Khan

From: Robert Anderson
To: Zafar Khan
Date: April 10, 2008

Hello Mr. Khan!

Thank you for the updates on the new date for the Almiyah-Arab Bottled Water Forum. Terry A. Maurer is honored to accept your invitation. We sent all the requested documents as a prerequisite to being a guest speaker in March. Do you need us to resubmit the documents again?

Thank you for this invitation and best regards,
Robert Anderson

From: Zafar Khan
To: Mr. Anderson
Date: April 13, 2008

Dear Mr. Maurer:

We would highly appreciate if you could email all documents at your earliest. We suggest you book airline for Mr. Maurer to avail the best rates. As mentioned in my earlier email, the forum is only for one day i.e. 17th June 2008. However, Mr. Maurer is requested to arrive a day earlier to be present at the Gala dinner and Qatrah Awards on the 16th June 2008. Thank you and best regards,

Zafar Khan
Projects Manager
Dubai, UAE

From: Zafar Khan
To: Terry Maurer
Date: April 18, 2008

Dear Mr. Maurer:
We would reimburse roundtrip coach airfare and would arrange accommodation in Dubai for 2 nights, during the forum.

Thank you and best regards,
Zafar Khan

In the end, Robert Anderson went to Dubai and presented Avita. I did not go but instead went to California to see Tom. One more email here to show the level of interest in Avita Water worldwide.

From: "Arie Sibonney"
To: Avita
Date: April 7, 2008

Netherlands order first.

I may be sending you Spanish bottles for Spain order next week.

Can you give me an estimated time to complete Netherlands order? They want to pick up urgently.

Thank you,
Arie

From: Avita
To: Arie Sibonney
Date: April 7, 2008

Hello Arie!

The Homegoods order is ready for shipping right now. We are continuing with production for the overseas orders to the Netherlands (13 x 1/2 litre and 7x1 litre pallets) and for Spain (10 pallets of each 1/2 and 1 litre).

Still waiting on response from US embassy in France.

Please let me know when the truck will be up for the Homegoods order.

Best regards,
Robert Anderson

Camille, Laurie, Trevor, and Bella in 2005.

While Avita Water was growing, there was still time to travel west to see Tom, Laurie, and the kids. We all know that our grand-children are special, in our case, starting with Laurie's oldest Trevor, and her second, Camille and then Steve and Nicole's three girls, Brianna, Alison, and Colette. However, when Camille was four, she told me that she knew she was very special. I was picking her up from nursery school on Niebaum Lane across from the Rutherford Grill just south of St. Helena. It was just me and Camille, and I wanted to turn left out of the nursery school drive and go west to see a few wineries, particularly Dana Estates.

Camille, now four years old, told me, "Papa, we have to turn right to go home."

I said, "Camille, I want to go left to see some wineries."

She told me, "I am a princess and my mommy is a queen and my daddy is the king. So I say, 'Turn right.'"

I responded now quite firmly, "Camille, I am the emperor and I say we go left."

She had the last word saying after a pregnant pause, "There are no emperors."

We still went to the left to see the wineries.

Even though I thought that my two businesses were about to break through with remarkable new sales and profits, we were grounded with the health issues of Tom and Mary Ann. I will let Mary Ann pick up her story in her own words written for the *Michigan Transplant Magazine*:

> My husband, Terry, and I had just returned from a family trip to Napa Valley, California. We were visiting our daughter Laurie and son-in-law Tom along with our five grandchildren. Tom had been diagnosed in June of 2007 with Glioblastoma, identified as a virulent brain cancer that is usually fatal. He went through two major surgeries and follow-up treatments of chemo and radiation. He also tried alternative treatments along with exercise and still there was no remission.
>
> During our visit, we took this time to celebrate our son-in-law. There were constant visits from friends and family and we truly enjoyed this special time together. Tom had been fighting this cancer now for one year. We had strong hopes for a miracle but the doctors said that his time was limited.
>
> We all kept very busy during our stay. Every three days I had to be driven to the nearest dialysis center to be dialyzed which took 3 hours, not including the drive, and I needed to do this 3 times a week. I would schedule these sessions prior to even leaving Michigan, and I knew how fortunate I was that the dialysis center was fairly close to my daughter's home.
>
> In 1984 I had been diagnosed with nephrotic syndrome, my kidneys were shutting down and the doctors did not understand what was going

on. I had been suffering with rheumatoid arthritis and a few years later I was treated for a tick bite. All of which could have caused my kidneys to fail. I finally reached the point of life support and left with no alternative but to be placed on dialysis. I was on dialysis for 4 months when I was approached by my nephrologist to see if I would be interested in a transplant. He thought I would be a very good candidate. Eight months after I was approved on the transplant list I was called to receive a kidney in April of 1987. My transplant lasted for 19 years.

In May of 2006 my kidney began to fail. I lost my transplant kidney, and that is why I was put back on dialysis. I did have one close call because of an overload of fluids which required life support and round the clock dialysis. Three days later I was back to my normal self. Overall things were going well. I maintained a very positive attitude and a positive spirit while once again I was placed on the transplant lists. I waited patiently for 2 years knowing in my heart that I was going to receive a new kidney; and also, knowing my new kidney would come to me in God's time. So many people were praying for me: family, friends, prayer groups, and parishioners. I knew with that much prayer support God would surely answer my plea. Six individuals, including Ed Murphy, came forward and asked to donate one of their kidneys, but they were not a match. Their generosity will be forever in my heart.

Every time we visit our daughter the air is filled with endless energy. For instance, Laurie planned a side trip for my husband and son-in-law. They went to Vancouver, Canada, to pick up our grandson, Trevor, who attended Brentwood

Boarding School and needed a ride home for his summer break. The three of them made this a memorable road trip: visiting friends of Tom's in Vancouver, taking a relaxing boat ride, shooting lots of photos, and eating out at some fine restaurants. The trip took a lot of energy out of Tom but there were no regrets. The trip was unforgettable.

We stayed on for another week to celebrate the 4th of July. Now it was time for Terry and me to leave and come back home to Michigan. I personally remember just how difficult it was to leave Tom. He was waving goodbye from the back porch as Laurie was driving us away from the house to catch the bus that would take us to the airport. He knew and we knew that he had a short time left.

Now that we were home in Michigan, my thoughts were constantly on Tom, Laurie and her family. I started to think about what I could do to help them. So I prayed. I asked God if he would move me forward off of dialysis because my family needed me right now.

The next week, God spoke to me in my thoughts. He said, "The last kidney you received you lived on Scio Rd in a farmhouse near a pond shaped like a kidney." I was thinking, yes, but I don't live there now, so how will I get a new kidney? There was a no answer.

Two days later, I got a call from Neil and Judy Gerl asking if they could "borrow back his tennis racket" for their grandson to use. Terry said he would drive me over to their house to deliver the tennis racket and it would be fun to visit with our friends. Terry wanted to drive down by the farmhouse where we used to live and where I received my first transplant twenty years before.

So we left to deliver the tennis racket. We missed the turn on Scio road and we had to turn around and head back because this was the short-cut to our friend's house and it was also the way by the farmhouse where we formerly lived. As we approached the farmhouse property on Scio road, directly in front of the one shaped like a kidney, my cell phone rang. I answered it. Terry pulled the car into the driveway. The phone call was from the transplant coordinator, and she said, "Mary Ann, we have a kidney for you."

I was so excited. I said, "Where?" I said this because I was on two different transplant lists.

She replied, "At the U of M of course." That is where I received my first transplant. "Now," the coordinator added, "we have the person on life support and a decision has to be made by you because this individual has had number one diabetes since childhood. We chose you, as we wanted someone a little older, and we thought of you as a person who has a normal pancreas and we are hopeful that the kidney will flip flop and function properly."

I looked at the house and looked at the pond shaped like a kidney and I knew for sure that it was God that had spoken in my thoughts earlier. There was no decision to make. It was a yes. God had prepared me for this entire moment in advance. Right then I gave her my answer: "Yes, this kidney will be mine." The transplant coordinator said that the donor's life support would be removed soon, the kidneys would be blown up to make sure that they were in good condition and she would call me again. Then, after a quick trip to our friend's house, we were able to share the good news and then returned home promptly to pack and prepare for my hospital stay. I was overwhelmed with joy.

The transplant coordinator called back. The hospital was ready for me. All was a go! Terry and I left for the hospital. I was fearless because I knew it was from God. I was held in the palm of his hand. I was so blessed at my age, 67, to receive a second kidney. The surgery went exceptionally well and one week later I was home again walking one mile a day. The drugs for transplants available today, twenty years later, have improved dramatically. How generous it was of the family and loving donor who shared his kidney with me. I now am able to share my new life with my family and be there to support them.

I received my kidney transplant with Dr. Diane Cibrik's help (University of Michigan) and my new life on July 13, 2008. I would be the first person to receive a kidney from a (number 1) childhood diabetic. The hope was that as soon as the kidney entered my body with my normal pancreas, the transplanted kidney would return to normal. Today, eight years later, the kidney is working better than a normal kidney. My creatinine level is always 0.9 to 1.0.

My son-in-law, Tom, passed away to his new life on July 26, 2008. The young man that gave the wonderful gift of a kidney to me passed to his new life as well. God moved me forward to help my family. I was able to be there for my daughter and my grandchildren during a most trying time.

Now both of my companies, Maurer Coatings and Avita Water, seem to be well on their way. Soon I'd be over the hump with both: smooth sailing ahead. Kind of like the captain on the Andrea Gail sailing unaware straight into the perfect storm. The sword fishing boat was loaded with supplies and a happy crew anticipating a record catch late in the season as they left Gloucester. He couldn't know at his departure that brewing out in the Atlantic was a convergence of weather conditions, which would sink his best-laid plans for success. In Sebastian Junger's classic book, it was a cold front from the northwest bumping into a high pressure in the north both colliding with Hurricane Grace coming up the East Coast—a 1991 Halloween nor'easter, a "perfect storm."

My cold front was the approaching economic collapse in the US. On October 9, 2007, the Dow Jones was at an all-time high of 14, 164.42. By March 5, 2009, the Dow was at 6594.44, more than a 50 percent fall, then dropped at 504.48 points on September 15, 2008, then again 777.68 on September 29, 2008 (the biggest one day drop in history), then a dropped at 449.36 on Thursday, September 17, then dropped again at 800 points on October 6, 2008; it was enough to shake investors worldwide. It for sure stopped my Maurer Coatings and Avita Water companies dead in their tracks or to say it another way we were capsized by a rogue wave.

The second blow came as high pressure from the wild wannabe water partner, Ken Burke. Again I'll let my February 17, 2009, summary for the judge lay out the facts of Avita's collapse:

History and Events
Related to the Ken Burke offer
to Terry Maurer
to purchase some of "his" stockholdings
in Avita Water and Maurer Coatings

An offer was made by Ken Burke to provide Terry Maurer with $400,000 to acquire the stock of Avita Water held by Eden Foods. Once Maurer owned the stock, he was to sell it again to Burke. The stock was never purchased from Eden Foods because Burke was not able to come up with the total amount, only $350,000.

In an effort to complete the deal, Burke had approached Pam Sexton, a loan officer at the UBT Bank for the extra $50,000 shortfall.

When Burke went to pick up the $50,000 letter of credit, he was told that there was a $700 fee attached. Burke said to the loan officer that he refused to pay the fee. Therefore, the letter of credit was never issued.

Simultaneously, while Burke was asking UBT Bank for the letter of credit (and before Burke learned about the extra fee), he and Maurer were applying for two loans at same bank: one for $400,000 for working capital and another for $200,000 for additional bottling equipment.

The same loan officer who neglected to tell Burke about the $700 fee stated to Burke and Maurer that the two loan applications were a "slam-dunk no-brainer done deal"; this is because of Burke's good credit and pledges of stock as collateral.

However, the loan was rejected but most importantly not before Burke had instructed Maurer to use all the $350,000 to expedite the purchase of carbonated equipment needed for the Vegas project. The $350,000 would be replenished soon enough with the pending "slam-dunk no-brainer done deal" loan.

However, they were not aware that the loan officer, offended by Burke's refusal to pay the $700 fee, had never presented the loan application before the committee. Therefore, the $50,000 small loan was never received.

The worst followed: Burke and Maurer were out of the promised "slam-dunk no-brainer done deal" $600,000 loans but Maurer had already used the Eden Purchase $350,000 advance under Burke's order. Therefore, because of the loan fallout, there was no money to purchase the Eden stock and no stock to transfer to Burke.

At the same time, another $90,000 was for the purchase of Maurer Coatings stock, but it had nothing to do with the water business. This was an entirely different matter. It was entered into because of Burke's ever-flowing erroneous business promises.

Burke was obviously a gambling man who offered enough money to his prey so as to expect follow-through, and when he decided to back away, he made sure to blame everyone but himself for the results.

The third part of this perfect storm occurred when Totally Organica was unable to raise their $350,000, which under a signed agreement with Avita Water had agreed to prepay for the first twenty truckloads of the carbonated Totally Organica water. Their concern was due to the rapidly deteriorating US economy in late 2007. Totally Organica's own investors were backing out as the markets were tanking.

By then, a shady fellow named Bob Colt called Maurer from Las Vegas, saying that he was taking over the Organica water project from Vic Trutanich and Dan Gorham and that he was going to pay Maurer's company, Avita Water only $90,000 of the contracted $350,000. "Take it or leave it," Colt told Maurer. Maurer immediately called Burke, who flew to Vegas the next day (this all happened before Burke finally quit the project) to meet Colt.

On return to Michigan, Burke told Maurer that they should continue with the project and that Maurer should relax about Burke's $350,000 intended for Eden's stock purchase and to be ready for this windfall business coming from Vegas. Burke said he'd soon close on the $600,000 loans with UBT Bank, and he was convinced by Gorham that the Totally Organica was a great deal.

In the end, none of Totally Organica's distributors were ready to promote the new product (lightly carbonated flavored Avita Water—flavors of lemon-lime, pomegranate, grape, apple, and others) because Totally Organica no longer had financial capital to support its marketing efforts as the US economy tanked.

Maurer continued to work with Totally Organica as they tried to raise new money in 2010 and 2011 to purchase 51 percent of Avita and pay off Avita's debts generated by the promise of business from Totally Organica. Unfortunately, the Vegas financing never materialized.

So it is clear that Avita Water in 2007 is floundering under Burke's pressure and poor sales from Totally Organica. At the same time, my other company, Maurer Coatings got blindsided by the Atotech acquisition of its German (Kunz GmbH out of Berlin) and Spanish (Sidasa, out of Barcelona) chemical suppliers. Atotech is owned by the 115-billion-dollar Total Final giant headquartered in Paris, France.

The acquisitions by Atotech of Maurer Coatings' source of product was the hurricane, which we were not able to weather without an experienced, well-paid corporate attorney with knowledge of international law and chemical expertise. I thought I could handle it if I could deal directly with my old friend and former golf partner (many times at the Glen Abbey in Toronto) John Kinne. Mr. Kinne, president of Atotech, USA in Rock Hill, South Carolina, was fired by Herr Schneider, Atotech worldwide CEO, before we could get our discussion started. The details of the demise of Maurer Coatings and the mistakes made in these final negotiations with Atotech, which took place in Ann Arbor, Berlin, and Rock Hill, South Carolina, is another book in itself. Suffice it to say that Atotech's Herr Schneider wanted to break up the Maurer Coatings exclusive contract with Kunz and Sidasa (UCI).

I went to Berlin within days of the acquisition announcement to defend Maurer Coatings' contract. Mr. Schneider had set a trap for me, having two Atotech attorneys, the Total Final VP of finance from Paris, Herman Donsbach from Kunz, and two other Atotech executives. I even brought a magnum of 2002 Joseph Phelps insignia for Herr Schneider as a gift from Maurer Coatings. I needed instead to have brought my Ann Arbor corporate attorney, Mr. Jim Cmejrek. Going solo was not a good idea.

I did reach out to Mr. Kuldip Jehal, John Kinne's replacement as president of Atotech USA, asking for some time and consideration in handling Maurer Coatings' trumped-up debt to Atotech. Here is a copy of my email:

> From: Terry Maurer
> To: Mr. Kuldip @ Atotech
> Date: July 21, 2008
>
> Hello Kuldip! Thanks for your email and telecom last week. Regarding the monies due Atotech: First, I need to ship the remaining inventory to Atotech in South Carolina. There

are about 10 drums and 7 pallets of obsolete materials, most of which Hermann sent over in the beginning of our association. We can not sell these materials nor can we afford to dispose of them properly nor can we afford to warehouse them while we can not sell them. We need to ship these chemicals out of our warehouse this week. Second, I sent an email to the Atotech attorney some two months ago or more asking to postpone the first installment of the stock purchase agreement. Essentially I want to skip this year's payment and put it at the end of the contract. I did not get a response to my email. Also this payment should be in USD not in euros. Hermann and I both agreed to put $150,000 USD into the company which we both did. Third, due to the extreme slow business climate in the USA and Dipsol in particular, we can not afford to make the July 31st 2008 payment on old business. Dipsol has drastically cut its purchases of the sealer, mainly because of the Atotech price increases and Tarek has told me one of his customers has gone from running 7 lines down to 2. We also miss the opportunity to sell black coatings to our biggest potential customer, Curtis, because your research department has not been able to finish developing the product according to the GM requirements as to GMW3359.

Ultimately, my company was sued for over $300,000 for old inventory disputes, stock purchase agreements with Kunz, and other issues. The suit was dropped when I countered sued for breach of contract. I wanted to go to trial, but I did not have assets sufficient to pursue it. Atotech dropped its suit against Maurer Coatings after my counter of $64 million.

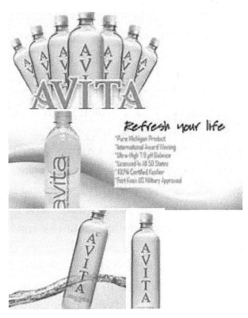

CHAPTER XII

Avita Water
(2008–2012)
Barack Obama
(2008–2012)

In the beginning, I said this book would be about the first seventy years of my life. Well, we are now into 2012, and I am approaching seventy years. I am expecting that the experienced businessman, Mitt Romney, will be good for the country and for business people like myself.

Here it is now twenty-four days before the presidential election of 2012 with my guy, Mitt Romney, challenging the sitting president Barack Obama, I voted for Barack four years ago mostly because I feared his opponent John McCain would take the country into a war with Iran. I didn't realize at the time how uninformed Mr. Obama was on what makes the economy work. It's private-sector jobs, and having never worked in the private sector, Obama doesn't have a clue. He believes it's all about the government and what jobs it creates. That's not how the economy works, and now Mitt Romney and his running mate Paul Ryan are laying the facts out for all to see. The good news is that the American people are getting the message through the presidential and VP debates. Today's polls are showing Romney climbing to a 51 percent to 54 percent lead in the key state of Florida. The Rasmussen poll shows Romney and Obama tied in the very critical state of Ohio.

As I am writing today, all is good with at least my part of the world. I have a fire going in the stone fireplace at our log house in Grayling. I just finished reading in my *Killing Lincoln* book. Abe is planning to take his wife, Mary, to the theater tonight. I think he knows what's coming. Bill O'Reilly's book is a great read, and I am looking forward to reading his next one, *Killing Kennedy*. The Birdie house is quiet as Mary Ann and her friend Jill Damon are out selling Mary Ann's artwork at the St. Mary's Church Bazaar. It's raining, which seems to have put our ten-pound Maltese/shih tzu, Katie, to sleep on the couch.

I've got a cup of strong instant regular coffee, with my shoeless feet up on a footrest and a good strong reading light over my shoulder. As I listen to Nora Jones and Edith Piaf, the WWII French singing sensation, it's now my new French friend, Mylene Farmer, who catches my ear. I spent 10 minutes (one on one) with Mylene Farmer as she was having her after concert party (there were 20,000–30,000 concert goers that night in Toulouse as Mylene Farmer was the most popular female singer in France at the time) at the hotel MaryAnn and I were staying in Toulouse, France in 1992. She was very nice and gave me two signed CD's. Only one other thing could be better, and that would be enjoying Napa Valley cabernet and Cohiba cigars with my son, Stephen, and grandson Trevor (December 11, 1991).

It is now twelve days until the 2012 presidential election, and I am determined to finish this final chapter of my seventy-year chronicle simultaneously with the election of Mitt Romney on November 6. So I've decided to write at least two hours per day if necessary to make that happen.

Chuck Haltiner, plant manager; Peter Edmonds, Michigan State inspector; and Cameron Moore, investor at AVI TA Well House.

Over the past weekend, our son, Stephen, and his bride of seventeen years Nicole and three granddaughters Brianna (March 30, 1999), Alison (November 23, 2001), and Colette (April 20, 2005) came from South Lyon to Grayling, Michigan, for a visit. We all relaxed on a rainy Saturday while watching the Michigan vs. Michigan State football game. Nicole graduated from Michigan, I earned a quarter of my BS credits from Michigan in 1965, but the majority of our family, including my two brothers Tony and Louis, graduated from State, Tony with master's in education and Louie with AA in nursery and landscaping. Both of our daughters Laurie and Karin were students at Michigan State while graduating from other colleges. Mary Ann graduated from Alexandra School of Cosmetology in Ann Arbor, and Stephen graduated with a business degree from Bowling Green in Ohio.

Most of us cheered for Michigan, but not me. Michigan did beat State 10–9, kicking a winning field goal in the final seconds. This reminds me when I was driving through Oklahoma City several years ago, I was pulled over for speeding. The officer asked me to get out of my car with my hands up and walk to his car, leaving Mary Ann behind. Once by his car, he said to me, "I see you are from Michigan, you probably cheer for the University of Michigan."

I answered, "No, sir. I do not."

He asked, "Who do you cheer for?"

I replied, "I cheer for Notre Dame."

"In that case, you're all right," he said. He escorted me back to my car and only gave me a warning. My ticket would have been $175 for speeding in a construction zone.

This week I accepted an offer to sell my bottled water business Avita Artesian Water to a couple of Detroit investors, and on October 1, I celebrated my seventieth birthday with my family. Life is good this Saturday morning.

Mary Ann, Katie, our dog, and I were preparing to fly to San Francisco on October 30, next Tuesday, when my attorney, Mr. Don Darnell from Dexter, emailed that I should stay to finish reviewing the sales documents. This will put Avita Water on a new path. So we have already changed our Delta Flight to December 5.

I was actually pleased with this change, which gave me more time in Michigan to oversee all the last-minute details concerning the closing of the sale of Avita assets (building, water, lease, goodwill, and inventory) to the new owners, Johni Semma and Taft Gaddy of Avita Water Partners, investors from Detroit.

Interesting enough, one of the other suitors of the Avita Water Company just resurfaced, injecting himself into the process. At this time, I was keeping a water company from New Mexico up-to-date on the expected closing with Avita Water Partners. The New Mexico company and I have been discussing their possible purchase of my company for over two years. Now we are fully expecting to close the deal during the week of November 26 with Taft Gaddy's people.

If my sale to the Detroit group should fall through, then the New Mexico company said it would pay 1.5 million for 90 percent of Avita and put another 1 to 3 million into the company for faster bottling equipment. The high-pH 7.9, combined with enhanced oxygenated artesian spring water, would be targeted to the health-conscious sports market. They claim to have orders for 40 million (16.9 oz) bottles for his first year with Avita. That would be five truckloads per day (TL = 1,368 cases). It's likely he'd want Avita to produce one half of the order. It all sounds good (show me the money); still, today, I was sending the company more info on Avita: the 2012 source analysis, which I just received yesterday from Eaton Analytical Formerly MWH Labs in Monrovia, California. The analysis was nearly identical to our 2006 report from NSF. We have repeated the source analysis annually since 1987 without any changes. The 2006 analysis is what I had readily available for comparison. Also, I was sending the hydrogeological report on Avita prepared by Insight Environmental Services Inc., in Howell, Michigan. The report #3765 by Mark Sweatman in 2004 is a one-inch thick document and study completed for Avita by Eden Foods about ten years ago. And finally, I was sending a rough sketch of the Avita bottling plant footprint. The New Mexico company said our fifteen-thousand-square-foot building might need a ten- to twenty-thousand-square-foot addition.

Now back to the 2012 election, with just eleven days remaining, Governor Mitt Romney (former governor of Massachusetts and his wife Ann were both born in Michigan) is surging in all the polls. Here are the latest polls nationally and in the key swing states. I believe the percentages below are a compilation of several polls, including Gallup, CNN, CBS, and Rasmussen.

Poll Results (October 26, 2012)

State	Mitt Romney	Barack Obama
Ohio	48%	48%
Florida	50	49
Virginia	47	45
Colorado	48	48
Nevada	47	50
Nationally	50	47
Independents	57	38
Female	47	47
Economy	52	43
Energized	73	66

Based on these polls, I am very happy with the prospects of Mitt Romney becoming our forty-fifth president. Possibly affecting the election in addition to the negatives of the Benghazi fiasco, and binders of women coming from the Obama campaign is the looming yet another "perfect storm" bearing down on the entire East Coast this weekend. Sandy, the hurricane in the Atlantic, is expected to be a six-day event this weekend (October 27, 2012, through November 1, 2012) and have an effect on the election for November 6, 2012. See this news bulletin from Netscape News of October 25, 2012.

NOAA to East: Beware of coming "Frankenstorm"
Seth Borenstein
AP Science Writer

Washington (AP)—An unusual nasty mix of a hurricane and a winter storm that forecasters are now calling "Frankenstorm" is likely to blast most of the East Coast next week, focusing the worst of its weather mayhem around New York City and New Jersey.

Government forecasters on Thursday upped the odds of a major weather mess, now saying there's a 90% chance that the East will get steady gale-force winds, heavy rain, flooding and maybe snow starting Sunday and stretching past Halloween on Wednesday.

Meteorologists say it is likely to cause $1 billion in damages.

The storm is a combination of Hurricane Sandy, now in the Caribbean, an early winter storm in the West, and a blast of arctic air from the North. They're predicted to collide and park over the country's most populous coastal corridor and reach as far inland as Ohio.

The hurricane part of the storm is likely to come ashore somewhere in New Jersey on Tuesday morning, said National Oceanic and Atmospheric Administration forecaster Jim Cisco. But this is a storm that will affect a far wider area, so people all along the East have to be wary, Cisco said.

It is likely to hit during a full moon when tides are near their highest, increasing coastal flooding potential, NOAA forecasts warn. And with some trees still leafy and the potential for snow, power outages could last to Election Day, some meteorologists fear.

Some have compared it to the so-called Perfect Storm that struck off the coast of New England in 1991, but Cisco said that one didn't hit as populated an area and is not comparable to what the East Coast may be facing. Nor is it like last year's Halloween storm, which was merely an early snowstorm in the Northeast.

The Perfect Storm only did $200 million of damage and I'm thinking a billion," said Jeff Masters, meteorology director of the private service Weather Underground. "Yeah, it will be worse."

My guess is that this storm will affect the turnout at the polls on November 6. I would think that a lower turnout in the heavily democratic East Coast would favor Mitt Romney. We will see. Even Michigan is expected to get higher than normal winds for this time of year.

While the campaign is winding down to its final days and the weather is ominous, we have the World Series to entertain us. In Michigan, we cheer for the Detroit Tigers, and this year our team is in the World Series against the San Francisco Giants. An offensive rampage by the Giants in the first game where Pablo Sandoval, the Venezuela native smashed three, count 'em, three home runs in one game knocking in four runs in the process, beat Detroit 8–3. Sandoval hit a solo home run to right-center on a ninety-five-mile-per-hour 0–2 fastball at the letters in the first. He reached outside and hit a two-run, opposite-field drive to left in the third on another ninety-five-mile-per-hour pitch from Verlander, the reigning AL MVP and Cy Young winner. Then added another bases-empty shot into center-field in the fifth, this time on an eighty-four-mile-per-hour off-speed offering from Al Albuquerque. When Sandoval stepped up to the plate for the third time, I told Mary Ann, "Watch him, I believe he's going to do it again." Only three others, Babe Ruth, Reggie Jackson, and Albert Pujors ever hit three home runs in a World Series game. It was something to see even on TV.

Detroit managed to lose the next three games. One in San Francisco and the next two in Detroit. The World Series of 2012 is over. Detroit could have used 'Mr. Tiger', Al Kaline, this year. Kaline was one of the Detroit Tiger's all time best players (1953–1974). Mr Kaline was my golf partner, three days in a row, this while I was playing in Tom Monaghan's charity event on Drummond Island in the mid 90s.

For those of you in Germany, Spain, England, Brazil, China, etc. who are not familiar with the world series in baseball, you may Google 'World Series', and get an explanation.

Brianna, Allison, Colette, Nicole, and Stephen Maurer in 2014.

Mary Ann and I did go downstate, as folks from the North like to say, for the weekend. Actually, we left Grayling on Sunday morning and arrived at Stephen and Nicole's in South Lyon in time to spend three hours helping Steve split fireplace wood. We split a few cords of black honey locust. This wood, according to Steve, is the preferred log due to its clean and hot burning nature, not to mention its attractive reddish appearance. Honey locust is better than white oak, box elder, or elm according to Steve's neighbors.

Mary Ann and I, Stephen, Nicole, Brianna, Alison, and Colette all met our daughter Karin the Bauma Group realtor, for dinner at Palios in downtown Ann Arbor. Palios is a great Italian restaurant directly across from the old Detroit Edison (now ATT) location where I worked my first job in Ann Arbor on weekends while a student at UM In 1964 Paul Rogers hired me and Sid Rock for this high paying customer service job, set aside for U of M Students only. I worked at Edison for about a year before getting the full-time chemical lab tech job at Climax Molybdenum in January 1965. I met and married Mary Ann Horning, roommate to the Edison office manager, Judy Goetze. I may have already told the story, but some things need repeating.

We spent Sunday and Monday nights with Mary Ann's brother Dale and sister-in-law Gaelene Horning on Waldo Road in rural Chelsea. Dale and Gaelene purchased the Horning family farm years ago. They have lived on the family homestead since at least 1980 and now lease out the acreage for corn and soybeans to their neighbor Trent Sathaway. On Monday morning, Dale took us to the edge of Sharon Township, ten miles west of Manchester on Austin Road to Horning Road in order to show us the new oil wells there. I wanted to see the wells just to have a look at what I expect to see pumping in Crawford County once Mitt Romney gets elected. Actually, the wells Dale showed us (four to five) were in Norvell Township, Jackson County, Michigan.

We stopped in Manchester at the Black Sheep tavern for lunch. The tavern located just West of the Raison River, the same river and bridge where my best man at our wedding July 10, 1965, Dr. Lance Nelson, tried to take his life by jumping headfirst into the river at about 11:30 p.m. Lance survived and graduated seventh in his class from UM Medical School in 1970. He died in Texas in 1985. He was a chemistry professor.

Early afternoon we stopped to visit Richard and Mary Dingeldey, parents of my former key employee at Maurer Coatings and Avita Water, Robert Anderson. I spent much of those three hours watching the approaching monster storm, Hurricane Sandy, on CNN and the weather channel. The Dingeldeys may come to visit us in St. Helena, California, this winter. It is clear that Sandy is not your ordinary storm. It is expected to produce tidal surges, which may flood NYC subways and strong ninety-mile-per-hour winds (category 1 hurricane) and snowfalls of possibly fifty inches in the higher elevations of WVA. Landfall in New Jersey, Atlantic City, area is projected for 8:00–9:00 p.m. in the dark.

Monday evening, we met our old breakfast group from Chelsea St. Mary's at the Breakaway restaurant behind Chelsea Lumber. It was fun to see them all again, including Larry and Peggy Grant, Roger and Linda Wiedmayer, Norm and Cathy Newman, Liz and Rich Hallo, Larry and Irene Kranich, Terri Myers, Erich and Karen Frederickson, and Al and Pat Sangara. Missing was my golf partner, Kurt and Mary Hollinger and Pam Newbury.

Gaelene, Katie, and Dale Horning on the family farm in Chelsea.

Hurricane Sandy hit landfall Monday night as projected. We learned on Tuesday about six to seven million folks were without power and a remarkably low death toll from this superstorm. Obama and Romney toned down their campaigns for a couple of days.

On Tuesday, Mary Ann managed to get to a lunch at Knights' Pub in Ann Arbor with her cousins from her mother's side of the family, the Buss group. Those who showed up numbered nine: Mary Ann (Terry Maurer), Donna (Orman Roehm), Pauline (Bob Shaeffer), Doris (Earl Roehm), Helen (Phil Bareis), Cindy Bareis, their daughter is married to the offensive line coach Greg Studrawa for Ohio State's 2019 football team (one of George Schisler's favorite teams). Ohio State is rated no. 2 in the country in 2019. Marilyn (Froda Maaseidvaag), Lillie (Bob Miller), Ann (King Hanna), and Janet Buss; missing was Gaelene, Dale Horning's wife. A good time was had by all, as they say. Their husbands are all alive and well. You can see, we made the most of our weekend reconnecting with family and friends.

By the way, Knights is where I was caught in a drug bust after my weekly tennis night sometime around 1989. My dentist friends and tennis partners, Tom Burke and Bob Brustad, and I were leaving Knights after a burger and a few beers when someone knocked on my driver's side window as I was preparing to drive off. I looked up to see a .45 revolver pointing at my head.

As I lowered my window to ask "What's going on?" I was told, "You are caught in a drug bust, put your hands on the wheel." The man continued to tell me, "We've caught five guys already and we know there are six and maybe you are the last guy."

I said, trying to have some fun, "How do I know you're not the guy? You're not in uniform."

He said, "Don't make any moves and I'll show you my badge." Now, shaking his gun in my face, he managed to produce his Ann Arbor City police badge with his left hand. Just then I saw two uniformed cops, with guns drawn, rush my car from the rear and side. Also, I now could see Tom Burke's car also surrounded by two or three squad cars with red and blue lights flashing. We were all caught up in this sting.

I was told to get out of my car slowly, keeping my hands in the air, which I did. Once out of the car, the officers started shining their flashlights in my back seat while I now had my hands flat on top of my car. Suddenly one of them says, "What's that on the floor in your back seat?" Knowing my innocence I decided to have some more fun, I said, "Those are my chemicals." They now thought they had their man.

"Reach in your car and bring the briefcase out," the plainclothes officer said.

The case was my titrating test kit used every day for checking Maurer-Shumaker Co. zinc phosphating baths.

Just then Ray Knight, owner of Knights' Inn came rushing up to my car, saying, "You've got the wrong guy. This is one of the doctors. They come here every Wednesday night."

Coming back here for Mary Ann's lunch reminded me of that memorable night at Knights.

Five days before the election now and Newt Gingrich is predicting Mitt Romney will win with 300 electoral votes and 6 percent more popular votes than Obama. Another scenario has the election ending in a 269–269 tie. This laid out by Susan Page in the *USA Today* newspaper on November 30, 2012, as follows:

Big If by Susan Page, *USA Today*

Obama wins	Romney wins
All states leaning	All states leaning
Democrat plus	Republican plus
Michigan	North Carolina
Pennsylvania	Then assume
New Mexico	Romney wins:
Then assume	Colorado
Obama wins:	Florida
New Hampshire	Iowa
Ohio	Nevada
Wisconsin	Virginia

We would get a tie, 269–269, and we have President Romney and likely VP Biden (per Twelfth Amendment) because the House of Representatives would choose the president and the Senate would choose the VP.

Today is Saturday, November 3, 2012, and we are just three days before this historic election. Already twenty-five million are said to have voted early. Mary Ann and I are among those, having voted absentee at our Beaver Creek Township in Crawford County, Michigan, some two weeks ago for Mitt Romney and Paul Ryan. The race seems to have boiled down to two different basic philosophies of government. Obama's choice is more and bigger government with its interference in our daily lives, something I believe leads to European-style and mounting unsustainable debt a la Greece, Spain, Portugal, and others.

The second and preferred choice is to have a smaller, streamlined, and responsible government with tax-paying small and large private businesses creating real jobs as outlined by Mitt Romney. I've said it before, many times, as has Mr. Romney: it is the private sector which creates real wealth. Manufacturing, farming, mining, and investing in our natural resources of oil and gas are what the country needs first and foremost.

Then we can afford hospitals, libraries, schools, and infrastructure. A great example of this came from my neighbor in Chelsea a few years ago. The lady, a medical doctor, told me that she had just lost her job in a city west of Chelsea. I asked why. She said, "General Motors closed an assembly plant in the city." So the hospital where she was employed had to close its doors. Pretty basic to me. Mr. Obama, having never held a real job and doesn't have a clue as to what makes an economy and a country prosperous.

All the polls show a tight race. Both candidates are campaigning hard in the so-called swing states of Ohio, Florida, Iowa, New Hampshire, Nevada, and Colorado. Also, three traditionally Democratic states are in play: Michigan, Pennsylvania, and Wisconsin. Mitt Romney lays out his five key points to create twelve million new jobs. Here they are just in case you missed them:

Energy independence by drilling for domestic oil and natural gas, not to forget renewables of solar and wind, which are heavily dependent on government subsidies. Mitt mentions nuclear too. I'm not convinced we need more nuclear. More trade, especially with Latin America, and crackdown on unfair trade from China.

Educational reform, improving all schools so as to provide training for the folks for the skills needed in the future.

Capping federal spending so as to balance the budget. Do this by working across the aisle with Democrats.

Champion small business by reducing burdensome regulations and making banking more friendly to small business.

The Five turns two!

My favorite soft news commentary show is *The Five* on Fox News at 5:00 p.m. Here are their election predictions. On Thursday November 1, just five days before the election:

Eric Boiling—Romney wins big.
Bob Beckel—Obama with 291 electoral votes.
Dana Perino—Romney with 54 percent of popular votes.
Kimberley Guilfoyle—Romney with 3
percent margin, 280 electoral votes.
Bob Gutfeld—no prediction made.

Looming over Obama are two major events which could pull him down. First, Benghazi, Libya, where four US personnel including our ambassador, J. Christopher Stevens, were murdered by a terrorist attack, not a random event brought on by an anti-Islamic video. Obama, not wanting to look like his Middle East policies are failing, dreamed up the spontaneous attack and video story. The truth is yet to be told by the president just three days before the election. He is trying to run out the clock. I think enough true facts will get out in the next three days to give even some Democrats time to reconsider their votes. And the second event is his response or incompetent response to Hurricane Sandy.

The monster storm hit the East Coast on Monday evening October 29, now five days ago, and there are many disgruntled residents (Staten Island especially) who are complaining loudly about the slow emergency response from FEMA, the Red Cross, Mayor Bloomberg, and President Obama.

One lady from the Duncan Hills area in Jefferson complains that today, five days after Sandy made landfall, "It's just another day, no different than yesterday." She continued, "Politicians are all for themselves, I've lost all respect for Bloomberg." President Obama is making an effort to run the clock down, just like Benghazi. If that sentiment hits the mainstream media, NBC, CBS, and ABC, it won't be good for Obama's reelection chances. The situation on Staten Island is becoming desperate as folks there are out of food and water, still no power, and hence no information coming from phones nor internet.

Already more than 169 deaths from Sandy, 69 in Cuba, Haiti, and other islands, and now more than 100 in the US. Also coming on election day, in three days is a nor'easter winter storm. If the temperature gets below freezing for any length of time, the problems will get worse when pipes start to freeze. Bloomberg did cancel, reluctantly, the NYC Marathon yesterday, which was to start in the middle of devastated Staten Island. One other casualty from the superstorm was the loss of the tall ship HMS Bounty off the coast of North Carolina. This happened just before Sandy hit shore, taking also the captain's life and one other. Fourteen were pulled from the sinking ship, a triple-mast coastal vessel. On a positive note, I've learned about the Coast Guard House restaurant in Narragansett, Rhode Island, a place I'd like to visit someday.

On Monday, November 4, the headlines on TV news was starting to report the strong movement toward Mitt Romney. The first indication came with the news that Pennsylvania was now in play: 50 percent for Romney and 50 percent for Obama. Typically, Pennsylvania is a strong Democratic state, but now the current administration's EPA policy against coal and natural gas in eastern Pennsylvania and Mitt Romney's campaign efforts there are paying off. Indications are that Michigan, Minnesota, and Wisconsin could go for Romney. Obama says he's proud of his record over the last four years, but Romney points out that the country cannot borrow its way into prosperity. The increase of the federal debt up to sixteen trillion under Obama will sink the country. I do understand fully that Bush #43 put our country in a huge mess, and Obama is trying to fix it.

At his rallies, Mitt Romney is asking the folks if they are tired of being tired, and he says it boils down to this: "Do you want more of the same or do you want real change?" He also says, "From day one, I'll help people get jobs." One of his first bills he'll send to Congress is his Down Payment on Fiscal Sanity Act. A bill laying out how to slow down spending in government but also a bill to cut federal spending. Romney says, "With the right leadership, America will come roaring back." Reince Priebus, RNC chairman, says "Obama wants to be somebody special, but Romney wants to do something special."

The predictions of victory for Mitt Romney are growing today, now the day before the election. Newt Gingrich predicts Romney wins 53 percent to 47 percent and gets 300 electoral votes (30 more than needed). Becker from *The Five* says it'll be close with Obama winning by fifteen electoral votes and only 300,000 popular votes. Sean Hannity and Karl Rove on the *Hannity Show* both agree it's Romney winning with a total of 281 electoral votes and a 2–3 margin in the popular voting. My favorite prognosticator is Dick Morris, and I hope he's right, "It's a landslide for Romney with 325 electoral votes and a 5 percent spread on the popular votes." Morris has Romney winning Pennsylvania, Florida, Virginia, Minnesota, and Ohio.

The mood in the Romney camp this morning coming from Sanford, Florida, is jubilant, excited, and talking about victory. Five hundred retired generals and admirals have come out today urging a vote for Romney. The veterans are angry at Obama over Benghazi. Senator McCain says Obama is either totally incompetent in the Benghazi, Libya, terrorist attack or covering something up. But this election really boils down to the economy and jobs. Mr. Leroy Murdock, a national columnist, gives Obama a grade of D for his handling of the economy. How can you give anything better than a D when we have 42 percent increase in food stamp recipients, 52 percent increase in the national debt, 101 percent increase in gas prices, and 7.9 percent of Americans unemployed (that is, twenty-three million people). Murdock calls it stagnation, and the president tells his supporters to go to the polls and vote out of revenge. Revenge for what? Mitt Romney tells everyone to go out and vote "for the love of Country."

Former NYC mayor Rudi Giuliani says Barack Obama is the worst president on the economy in history.

Finally, I'll give CNN the final word on tomorrow's election. Cain says, "It's a dead heat." They can't call it for Obama any longer, and this is the best they can muster as their candidate's ship slips further into the water. Romans on CNN says that the quickest way for

Obama to win is to take Iowa, Wisconsin, and Ohio, giving Obama 271 electoral votes, and the quickest way for Romney to win is to take Florida, Virginia, and Ohio for 266 votes than Colorado and New Hampshire putting Romney over the top. I can't wait for the Romney victory celebration tomorrow.

It's finally here, Election Day, Tuesday, November 6, 2012. I can smell victory for soon-to-be president-elect Mitt Romney. Switching between CNN, Fox, NBC, Squawk Box, and even Bloomberg you get a feeling that more of the talking heads now want to continue trying to prop up Obama's chances.

Late on Election day

Even last night, as Obama and Romney were addressing their supporters, Obama in his last rally in Iowa, you could tell that Mr. Obama knew it was over, he would lose his bid for a second term. No enthusiasm by him nor Michelle Obama, just a sincere thank you for past support, reminiscing about how he started there four years ago. Even the large group of Iowa supporters knew it was over, done. Today Barack will play basketball in Chicago as he awaits his fate.

In sharp contrast, Mr. Mitt Romney will continue his campaign in Cleveland, Ohio, and Pittsburg, Pennsylvania. His New Hampshire supporters last night were electric, enthusiastic, and expectant of what today will bring. Romney knows, the people realized, and I knew and am thankful that the entire country is finally getting the leader that it needs and deserves. As Ann Romney says, "I know this man, and he will not fail." We are getting a president who will go down in history as one of the greatest, the profile of #45 will be carved in stone."

At Reagan library in 2011: Laurie M. Shelton, Camille
E. Shelton, and Mary Ann and Terry Maurer.

Statue of Freedom under repair in 1994 (photo by Terry).

Mary Ann and My 5 Grandchildren
Trevor Mansfield
Alison Maurer
Camille Shelton
Brianna Maurer
Collette Maurer

CHAPTER XIII

The Future (2012–2016)
Barack Obama
(2012–2016)

The 2012 election was over two days ago. Mitt Romney lost to Barack Obama. I can't believe it happened. I was in shock, then profound disappointment, not despair, but sadness for myself and for the country not to have the leadership of this great man, Mitt Romney. Hope for the future has been replaced with reluctant acceptance of what is to come from four more years under Obama. I don't think you can change a tiger's stripes. But there is a chance, and I'll explain in a few lines.

The final electoral vote count was 303 to 206 without Florida votes. As usual, Florida still hadn't figured out how to count on time. Obama got most of the swing states, including hopefuls like Michigan, Pennsylvania, and Wisconsin. The young people, especially young women, blacks, Latinos, and newer immigrants, and government employees went Democratic. Businesspeople, older whites, mostly private-sector employees, and let's not forget the "greatest generation" (those according to Tom Brokaw, who worked and fought during WWII) went for Romney. My dad always told me, "We're all born Democrats, we turn Republican when we get a little money." Seems to me that the whole country would be richer if more of us had a little money.

Still Romney came up short 49 percent to Obama's 51 percent total popular votes. Some 118 million folks voted. Some people believe that the election was won by the Far Left, which seems to have an agenda of the following:

free stuff for everybody
legalizing marijuana
gay marriage
free birth control pills
abortion on demand and free
take God out of the country and schools
more food stamps for all
windmills and solar panels
lawless borders
higher taxes for the rich
more regulations for businesses
borrowing from China for infrastructure repairs

I understand that others believe that the Right wants the following:

dirty air and water (ask Shaun Hannity)
more wars
wasteful military spending
tax breaks for the rich
unfair immigration policies
government grants to hostile countries
abuse of women
tax loopholes for big business
excessive bonuses for corrupt bankers
unconditional aid to Israel
keep the poor, poor
backdoor-deal-making congressmen and senators

On Monday, November 4, the headlines on TV news was starting to report the strong movement toward Mitt Romney. The first indication came with the news that Pennsylvania was now in play: 50 percent for Romney and 50 percent for Obama. Typically, Pennsylvania is strong a Democratic state, but now the current administration's EPA policy against coal and natural gas in eastern PA and Mitt Romney's campaign efforts there are paying off, indications are that Michigan, Minnesota, and Wisconsin could go for Romney. Obama said he's proud of his record over the last four years, but Romney pointed out that the country could not borrow its way into prosperity. The increase of the federal debt up to sixteen trillion under Obama would sink the country. I do understand fully that Bush #43 put our country in a huge mess, and Obama was trying to fix it.

The country might not have lost the opportunity to have an honest, hardworking, problem-solving leader in the White House with Mitt Romney. But there was hope, and I'll tell you why. First of all, Obama wants a legacy for good. I do believe that. In order to get elected in 2008 he promised "Hope and Change." But in his first four years he had to cater to his left-leaning base in order to get reelected. Just like Romney had to cater to his right-leaning base to get his Republican nomination. Both parties are controlled by their Far Left or Far Right party "leaders." The people who always make the most noise. It happens, that's the way the world works.

The "far stuff" is just how the press paints each side just to stir up controversy and divide the country in order to get viewers.

Now, just to shed a little more light on my thoughts on the election, the economy and capitalism in general, I have included copies of three emails which I sent to my democratic friend, Ed Murphy, just prior to the election, as well as one from Ed, and then another email in response to an article in the Traverse City Record Eagle by a certain Mr. Stephen Dick, who was blaming the decline of Detroit City on capitalism.

From: Terry Maurer
To: Murphy Edward
Date: August 21, 2012

Ed, I blame the greedy bankers and the stupid congress and weak, incompetent presidents for not putting import limits (20% maximum imports for everything we use in this country would have been just about right) on every aspect of the US economy. Ross Perot was 100% right in 1992. He spoke of the "giant sucking noise" as jobs were allowed to leave the country back then. This country has had trouble electing "smart" representatives and presidents ever since JFK. The Detroit problem, the Chicago problem, the Newark problem, the East St. Louis problem, the problem itself is the total lack of smart leadership. Who gives a royal—about the globalization of the US economy. We elect our representatives to look out for the best interest of the citizens of the USA not to look out for the rest of the world. Other countries can look out for themselves. Our representatives have failed us big time. They all got bought out by the "globalization" bull—lobbyists who are controlled by the dishonest bankers who should be tried for treason. Terry Maurer in Michigan who has seen firsthand what dishonest stupid government leadership has done to the US manufacturing base.

From: Murphy Edward
To: Terry Maurer
Date: September 27, 2012

So how come the GOP always creates a deficit? Google Reagan and Bush, Jr. for proof. The reason is because they want to make the deficit so big that no funds are left for social programs. Revenue will have to go for interest payments. Over and over the GOP does this while saying that the deficit is huge an we must put our money into defense and cut social programs. Don't raise taxes! It's a very simple and effective strategy. Too bad for the low and middle class, invest in more and more weapons, cut taxes for the rich, and cut social programs. Finally, I think most people are now getting the picture.

Murphy, Gillin, and Father Domingo.

From: Terry Maurer
To: Murphy Edward
Date: September 28, 2012

Hey Ed! I voted for Obama last time. Mitt Romney is not the regular GOP He has a brain and moral character, different than the previous two GOP administrations. You will see. Real jobs in manufacturing, mining, farming, natural resources (like oil and gas and timber) come way before schools, hospitals, libraries, and even government armies. You need the first things and then you can afford the others. It has always worked this way and always will. Mitt Romney knows what comes first and will re-invigorate the private sector which will allow the 53% to help the 47%. He may even be able to reduce the 47%

to a more manageable %. And everyone wants and needs that!!! No question we will always have folks in the lower quadrant. But it should always be a small group.

Later, Terry
From: Terry Maurer
To: Stephen Dick
Date: August 6, 2013

Hello Mr. Stephen Dick! Your article in the Traverse City, Michigan Record Eagle paper today caught my attention. You really need to visit Detroit before you blame everything on the capita list. First of all, capitalist like Henry Ford built Ford Motor Company into the company which built Michigan and helped win WWII, not to mention at the same time providing a prosperous company for folks to work in and a great Detroit city for folks to live in, especially during the 50s. In 1977 I started an automotive chemical supply company from scratch and owned the company until 1995 when I sold it to a bigger chemical company Most of my customers were in Detroit, I know something about Detroit. The downfall of Detroit City itself is shared by an ignorant US Congress, payed off by dishonest lobbyists which allowed the Big Three to ship jobs overseas. They should have had control over automotive imports, say minimum 20%.

Also, Detroit has had a Democratic mayor for the past 50 years, I am quite sure. The pensions which the city folks voted for themselves is sinful. Chicago is next with its dishonest politicians voting themselves obscene pensions. One city manager in California gets about 250K for life and she is in her 50s. This sort of irresponsible behavior on the part of too many politicians ruins a city and a country. The unions drove the big three to search for cheaper foreign parts, but Congress should have to say it again, put a limit on cheap imports. They, the US Congress, and the Union bosses were both in it together. Ross Perot was right in 1992. "Watch out for the Giant Sucking Noise as the jobs leave the US" (Detroit in particular) under the stupid NAFTA agreement. It is not a black nor white issue as you claim. Most everyone wants all people to have a good life which comes from an educated hard working labor force showing fiscal responsibility.

Detroit and now Chicago is in the same economic mess, in no small measure, caused by excessive pensions, debt and not to mention crime. These things capitalist don't like! Obama had to save the auto industry when he did, that was good for the country, but trying to bail out Detroit does nothing for anybody. It needs to go through BR. I say, sell plots of land to a hundred thousand Chinese families if they bring 250K with them to build a house. They can earn citizenship if they stay and live in Detroit for five years. Many of them would build a business in the city, I am sure. We all know there are enough vacant lots.

We need capitalist entrepreneurs in Detroit not folks on the public dole. I agree with you about the need for entrepreneurs in Detroit, but the city could never be trusted to distribute the $300 million you mention. We need a Republican like Snyder with his manager Mr. Kevy Orr to handle any new money for the city. I also agree, let the Red Wings build their own new stadium (without public money) and not on the river blocking the beautiful view there. Don't blame everything on the Republicans. I say the Republicans are generally war mongers wasting our resources on stupid wars and today's Democrats are too liberal for me.

What the country needs is local, state, and US Senators and Congressmen who recognize the importance of "energy independence" for the US. We can't pension ourselves out of this mess, it's all about the basics of manufacturing, mining, agriculture, and the responsible harvesting of our God given natural resources. Let's support the Keystone pipeline and the new oil and gas exploration taking hold in the US. These are examples of real job creating, tax paying industries we need in order to get Detroit, Michigan, and the entire US out of the massive debt hole created by both parties.

Best Regards,
Terry Maurer
Michigan entrepreneur

From: Terry Maurer
To: Murphy Edward
Date: September 27, 2012

Hey Ed! Thanks for forwarding Joe Brooks' comments on Mitt Romney. Hey Joe, hope you and Janet are great! Come visit us in Michigan next summer. I like Mitt Romney and Mary Ann and I will vote for Mitt Romney in a few days via absentee! We will all see Medicare as we know it. Under Romney the changes to Medicare will still come for folks younger than 55 today. So, no worry! The most important thing is jobs, jobs, jobs, so that folks can pay taxes to support the 47%. Romney can produce private sector jobs! Anybody can create government jobs which gets the country nowhere, except deeper in debt like Greece, Spain, Portugal, etc. Then we will be left with a bankrupt country.

Failure to restrict imports have caused a massive loss of US jobs, raising the federal deficit to 18 trillion dollars and reducing the size of the tax-paying middle class.

The fact of the matter is that eighty (80%) percent of the country, both Mitt Romney supporters, and Barack Obama supporters want neither the 10% far left nor the 10% far right stuff. The "far stuff" is just how the press paints each side just to stir up controversy and divide the country in order to get viewers. There is no question that the dishonest media wants to divide the country, but we can win if we pay attention.

Here we are now, Mary Ann and I, in St. Helena, in the middle of the Napa Valley, some seventy miles north of San Francisco in Northern California. We live in the Valley next to neighbors like Henk and Joyce Brok, who occasionally invite Mary Ann and me to gourmet dinners. In February 2015 it was a five-course affair for eight (Henk and Joyce, Danny and Lois Bloom, Mary Ann and me, plus Paul and Rosalie Blumberg—Rosalie is first cousin to Frank Sinatra). The third course of peasant lamb pie paired with a vintage Merlot was outstanding.

Golf with my buddies, Paul Piazza, Jack Bailey, Steve Schwarz, Larry Richards, Lex Brainerd, and of course, Ed Murphy add to the California lifestyle. Golf back in Michigan sometimes will include Pat Haley, Paul Seymour, and their old Royal Oak group. It's always a special round when my son, Stephen, can play, and he does occasionally join up with Kurt Hollinger, my regular partner, and me, and now, John Bromley on Fox Run Country Club. Can't forget Tom Sommerfeldt's large group of Traverse City area golfers, of which I'm a member.

My friend Kurt Hollinger helps me with my golf game and has taught me the difference between the Iso, Drake, and Hex hatches when fly-fishing for trout on the Au Sable River. Mary Hollinger can really work a kitchen, and I am sure would impress the Sheltons' old friend and internationally-renowned chef, Daniel Bruce, from the Meritage Restaurant at the Boston Harbor Hotel. Chef Bruce is also the founder of the Boston Wine Festival. In 2008 I was lucky enough both to dine and golf with Daniel Bruce and Tom Shelton at the Mayacamas Golf Club in Santa Rosa.

Meeting Ann and Sonny Camacho while walking their dogs (Cutie and Toby) sometimes at eight thirty in the morning when I walk Katie is always enjoyable. Then there is my Friday poker nights with Warren Lechner, Bill Snyder, John Morrison, Oleta McGrath, Jenna Babin, and Carol Munro. Now, Butch and Wayne from Palm Springs have joined our poker group.

While I'm playing poker, Mary Ann is hosting a game of dominoes with our neighbors and good friends Judy Calish and Nora O'Neill. The rare but fabulous dinners with Polly Keegan and her parrot Rosie are always a special occasion.

Mary Ann and I now play bocce ball on Tuesday evenings with Jan Craven, Ann Marie Clifford, John Morrison, John Polley, Eve Breckenridge, Judith Hanley, Joan Buchholand, and sometimes Lyn Dahlberg.

It's great to have friends like Jewels Drury; Jewels is our special St. Helena friend. We met seven years ago at Grace Episcopal Church.

We have enjoyed her friendship and her generosity many times over these years. She can play golf with the best and knows a thing or two about wine, felines, and spiritual counseling.

Jewels and Carol Sanderlin join us for happy hour at the Calistoga Pacifico on many a Friday. The $4 margaritas are the best when listening to the seven-piece mariachi band. We also look forward to more dinners with our new friends, Mark and Mary Linder, especially at the Market with a couple of bottles of the dirt farmer's cabernet sauvignon. We see our close neighbors Andree Bryan and her dog Coco and also Linda Titus and Jeanne Wilson, occasionally we see Judy Greene and Laurel Giuliani and her dog, Luna. Skip and Cynthia Lane are our great next-door neighbors. Skip and I both cheer for the 49ers. We now welcome Patrick and Carol Loomis.

"It's heaven here," says my neighbor, Daniel Bloom. How could you not love living in a place with lots of everblooming roses, camellias, orange and lemon trees, stately Italian cypress, and lots of redwoods? And did I mention, the sun shines most of the time. All this in a valley full of vineyards and wineries. This is our winter retreat.

Summers are spent in Grayling, near Avita Water. It is here in Grayling that we enjoy Sunday coffee with folks like Butch Feldhauser, Sammie Williams, Barbara Whittaker, and her mom, Nancy Hoffman (the widow of my first optometrist, Dr. Ralph Hoffman), Bob and Lu Davis, Diane Doremire, Sharron Nanney, J. C. and Liz Millikin, Rita Schlehuber, Juan Decker/ Renier Construction the Dayton Freight contractor, and another golfing buddy, Marlyn Neuberger and occasionally Fr. Robbie Deka himself.

And at my second hometown of Roscommon, we can connect with Larry Paxton at the Roscommon Farmers' market. Larry is the civil engineer who helped with the Avita Water building expansions but is also an accomplished craftsman and gourmet jam and jelly confectioner who sells his wares at the farmers' market. While visiting with Larry at his booth in May 2015, I ran into another old Avita connection, attorney John E. Rosczyk. Mr. Rosczyk was just appointed Roscommon village manager and was telling me about the town's brand-new library. I even bought a bunch of green onions from Mr. Bill Smith. I know a thing or two about green onions from my days back on the farm just northwest of Roscommon. We get to see Julie DeWitt occasionally, our builder from Birdie Circle.

Not working is not the same as working. A person misses one's life career. However, most of us who get seventy years do ultimately accept the change of pace. Living in Napa Valley during the winter eases the transition for me. Slowly I am removing myself from the business world, which I was wrapped in for over forty years. Oh sure, there are still weekly dreams about tanker loads of zinc phosphate, lost sales opportunities, employee issues, Federal-Mogul OD red bore sealant, which won't cure and all manner of chemical manufacturing issues, and old friends in the business, like Bill & Kitty Ifkovits, Dan Stanton, Pat Billinge, Bob Grayson, Joe McGee, John and Pat Murphy. I still keep an eye on my second company, Avita Water, now managed by a talented group out of Los Angeles and Florida.

There are things to do, which take the place of daily business dealings. Christmas 2012, we spent at our daughter Laurie and George's ocean cottage in Watsonville, south of Santa Cruz. A week at Pajaro Dunes on Monterey Bay, a place known for its many native birds is good for the soul. It's a place our friend and nationally recognized bird artist, Catherine McClung would find inspirational. There were osprey, double-crested cormorants, snowy egret, northern shoveler, willet, and black-necked stilt. Cathy recently painted the thirty-three birds species mentioned in the Bible. I haven't checked if any of these birds, local to Pajaro Dunes, are mentioned in the Bible. We took long walks on the beach with the dogs Katie, Cleo, and Calypso.

Euchre games and discussions with George about politics and my favorite subject, the need for US energy independence. I told George there is much progress being made with new discoveries in the Bakken oil fields of North Dakota and the fields in the Eagle Ford, Barnett, and Permian regions of Texas as well as the Marcellus basin in Pennsylvania which extends west to Ohio and north to New York. Southern Illinois has its new Albany shale deposit. Colorado and California have lots of oil and gas yet to be tapped. According to the experts US oil production has grown by 1.1 million barrels per day in the twelve months from November 10, 2013, to November 20, 2014, and we now produce 9.1 million barrels per day and consume 19.05 million per day. And there is no sign of slowdown yet. Encana Energy Company is even drilling the Collingwood shale in Northern Michigan.

Let's also get the Keystone XL oil pipeline through the House and Senate and signed by the president. We are well on our way to a prosperous long-term US economy all because of these booming oil and gas production figures. The following end-of-year (2014) opinion page by James Bloodworth in the *Wall Street Journal* really explains the positive benefits of our good fortune resulting from the shale-gas and hydraulic fracking revolution going on in the US. Here is the article published in the *Wall Street Journal*, December 30, 2014, by James Bloodworth, which tells the fracking story:

Christmas came early for the world's liberal democracy this year, with news in mid-December that repressive regimes from Russia to Venezuela and From Iran to Belarus are tumbling down an economic spiral. Who or what should we thank for this geographical yuletide? The neocons? Pro democracy protesters? George W. Bush and Tony Blair?

No. Thank instead American shale producers. The shale-gas and hydraulic-fracking revolution is lighting a figurative bonfire under the work's petrocracies. Dictatorships that for years blackmailed the West in the knowledge that we would come crawling back for the black stuff are now catching a glimpse of a bleak future.

As the American people and companies shift more of their consumption to cheaply produced domestic energy, the geopolitical leverage of oil-rich autocrats diminishes. A barrel of crude on Monday sold for less that $60, down nearly 50% since June when it went for $115. Take that, ayatollah.

This is a price drop made in the shale-rich heartlands of the U.S. Between 2007 and 2012, shale production in America jumped by more than 50% a year. In that time the shale share of total U.S. gas production rose to 39% from 5%. Last year the U.S. overtook Russia as the world's leading energy producer; next year America is projected to overtake Saudi Arabia as the world's biggest producer of crude oil.

One consequence is a massive fall in the price of oil just a few years after the words "peak oil" were being bandied around as gospel by environmentalists. Peak oil now looks like one of the most outlandish theories of our era. Rather than contract, the global supply of energy continues to diversify and expand, in no small part because of the boom in American shale.

This ought to put a smile not only on the faces of free-market economists, but liberals and progressives, too. As America becomes a net exporter of energy, shale could help topple some of the world's worst regimes.

The relationship between oil wealth and autocracy is well-established, with a number of studies showing that democracy is less likely in oil-rich nations. Oil wealth helps keep dictators in their palaces by allowing vast military expenditure to repress dissent and providing a ready pool of money with which to coopt their populations through generous welfare stipends.

Sitting atop large and valuable energy reserves also gives autocrats the luxury of keeping a tight lid on economic entrepreneurship. Winning the geographical tottery ensures that the oil money comes in regardless of how little revenue the rest of the economy generates.

Consider Russia and Venezuela. At least some voters in both countries have tolerated the emaciation of civil society while the Putinist and Chavista regimes have learned to use oil money to fend off unrest and buy off loyal cronies. Meanwhile, the armed forces in both nations have been placated with high-tech toys and rising salaries.

Despite legitimate environmental concerns about fracking and horizontal drilling, the long-term impact of shale on the global oil price means that regimes that have long relied on a single export for their survival are facing a potentially ruinous economic future.

Russia's economic woes are well-documented, largely due to the fact that oil revenues make up 45% of the government budget. But elites in Iran and Venezuela also have the jitters and have been pleading with OPEC, the world's largest oil cartel, to cut production to prevent the price of oil from falling any lower. Venezuela needs a price of $151 a barrel next year to balance its budget while Iran requires around $131.

So far Sunni Saudi Arabia has been willing to tolerate low prices in order to hurt its Shiite rival in Tehran. Yet Riyadh is no less worried about the long-term consequences. If oil stays at $60 per barrel in 2015, Riyadh will run a deficit equal to 14% of gross domestic product.

Some of the most vociferous opponents of fracking are liberals, yet the shale revolution has the potential to undermine some of the world's most illiberal regimes, in the process freeing the U.S. from its bondage to Saudi Arabia, as demanded by progressives for decades. Thuggish governments in Caracas, Moscow and Tehran don't much like shale either, which ought to endear it still further to democrats.

This is not to dismiss the environmental concerns regarding shale extraction in urban areas, nor to call for the abandonment of a long-term strategy in the West for the development of green renewables. Yet it is to recognize that American shale producers are engaged in a price war with some of the world's vilest regimes. In that respect, the left should get on board the fracking revolution.

I can also strongly recommend a book, *The Fracking Truth: America's Energy Revolution—the Inside, Untold Story* by Chris Faulkner. This book is a primer on America's ongoing energy revolution published in 2014. The best book I've seen on the subject.

Today is January 5, 2015, coming up on seventy-three years for me and fifty years of wedded bliss this July 10, and likely, the end of my memoirs for now. As I laid out the scope of this, my story, in the introduction, I've covered pretty much my whole life. Breaking it down in chapters about each phase as it unfolded in real time (my time).

I can be happy today finishing this phase of my story, knowing that good things are still coming:

My barrel of 2013 wine, a cabernet/merlot blend, is aging well in its fifty-five-degree cellar on Silverado trail. Jeff Roberts, the renowned vineyard manager and winemaker (Remridg) assisted me every step along the way. One wine aficionado offered an evaluation of my 2013 vintage dirt farmer's cabernet sauvignon this way: "It has a strong, nutty body. It's intense, straightforward and worthy. It will enhance the flavor of red meat and venison. It has character, dirt farmer's character."

My eagle on number 12 (352-yard) par four at the JFK course in Napa, California, witnessed by my playing partner, Ed Murphy, on November 3, 2014, proves my golf game is still improving; so when you—I'm talking about you, my reader—come to San Francisco, be sure to wear some flowers in your hair. Expect to get friendly greetings when you come north to St. Helena and meet some of the folks there:

Ali at Union 76
Francisco at the post office
Max at Mechanics Bank
Janice at the library
JP at Adams Copy Shop
Xochtil at Gilwoods

Dario at Castello di Amorosa
Gary at Steve's Hardware
Laura at Vintage Home
Bailey at Vintage Home
Christine at Lolo's
Father Mac at Grace Church
Linda at Napa Valley Vintners
Zach at Gutenberg Press
Cathy at Cameo Cinema
Judy at St. Helena Antiques
Helen at Grace Episcopal Church
Patty at Penny Weight
Marvin at St. Clement Winery
John at Vineyard Valley
Israel at the Bistro
Daniel at Villa Corona
Rhonda at Safeway
Scott at Stags Leap Winery
John at Bruschetteria
KR at Rombauer Winery
Eddy at Market
Liza at Main Street Books
Alan at Mayor's Office
Pastor Amy at Grace Church
Phyllis at Adams Shipping
Kathleen Tong, MD (Adventist Heart)
Peggy Thomas at St. Helena Medicine
Father Manuel Chavez at St. Helena Catholic Church

And happily we did have three visitors from Grayling, Michigan, this year: Bill and Dee Davis; Kay and Bob Dunn; Tom and Lynn Ruden, Kirtland College promoters; and Lori Hartman, from Indianapolis. Jill Damon and Tony and Madeleine Maurer came in 2014.

My candidate, Mitt Romney, is about to announce his intentions of running for president in 2016. Mitt is leading by a wide margin in the early polls over a large field likely to include viable candidates like Ted Cruz from Texas, Scott Walker from Wisconsin, Marco Rubio from Florida, and the famous Donald Trump from New York, and now Governor Pataki.

My Avita Artesian Spring Water company, which Mary Ann and I founded in 1987, is well on its way to becoming a national brand. This highly alkaline water (pH 7.9) discovered in 1942, my birth year, by Bernard Maurer himself and Dr. Bernard Godfroy, is now managed by professional marketers. Avita Water from Northern Michigan is now the official water for the Detroit Pistons, the Golden State's Warriors, and the Los Angeles Dodgers.

Avita Water ultimately failed when the west coast managers filed bankruptcy taking Avita with them.

I conclude my memoirs today, on January 17, 2015, and realize that today would be the old dirt farmer's birthday, Bernard L. Maurer, my dad's one-hundredth birthday. Happy Birthday, Dad, and thanks for everything!

I look forward to the great-grandchildren who will make their mark when their little feet hit the planet, as Father Mac would say. Welcome to the first great-grandchild for John and Odell Shelton and Mary Ann and me, Dylan Riggs, born to Matt and Jessica in 2015. Our second great grandson Riggs and his name is Elliot and he was born late in 2019. Now I must say that Jessica is married to Matt Riggs, Bryan is married to Sarah, Jonathan Shelton is not married, Michael Schisler is dating Analise Spacucello, Kim Schisler is dating Nick Gripp, Alec Schisler's steady girl friend is Machenzie Maly, Brianna Maurer and Alison Maurer both attend Aquinas College in Grand Rapids, Michigan and Colette is still in High School in South Lyon, Michigan. Trevor Mansfield is a single professional photographer living in Barcelona, Spain. Camille (CAMi) Shelton is attending the University of Oregon (The Mighty Ducks). Now the famous poet Lucian Mattison and his girl friend Blair Nakamoto have joined our group.

My group of like-minded friends from Grace Church in St. Helena (John, Lex, Manfred, Mike L, Mike M, Rodney, Bill, Sam, Mark, Don, Chris, Jurg, and Steve) provide confidential and spiritual support going forward.

Now, on August 18, 2015, I am still tweaking the book, so I have time for one more thing, as they say on *The Five*. Here it is: Today, my Avita attorney, Don Darnell, came to Grayling to gather data and dates as to the Deerfield Estates development. I met Don and his eleven-year-old son, Ben, at Spikes for a burger.

From there, we went to the Crawford County building to see the records.

My cousin Bonnie Cherven, the county clerk, helped us find the deeds we were searching for. Bonnie informed me that our aunt Margaret was failing. Aunt Margaret owns the old Godfroy farm where Avita Water flows. Not good news. Following our research at the county building, Don, a retired guard captain wanted to swing by Camp Grayling, the 147,000-acre Michigan National Guard Camp and introduce his son Ben to his old legal friend and now Brigadier General Mike Stone.

We drove the four miles to the camp and toured the grounds and the old club (a.k.a. the officers' club) before getting a call from General Stone to stop by headquarters. Passing the parade field where Blackhawk helicopters were taking off and landing with contingents from the Ohio Guard getting training rides, we arrived at the main office.

General Mike Stone, the top general of all Michigan National Guard camps, was happy to see Don Darnell and recognized me from a previous economic development meeting. Mike Stone was familiar with Avita Water as he himself had spent four years at Absopure Water in Plymouth, Michigan. It was an honor to listen to the general discuss in very general terms the role the Michigan Guard is playing in the US dustup with Putin and the Russians in the former Soviet Bloc countries as well as the Michigan Guard's presence in Somalia, assisting with the Ebola outbreak. The guard through General Stone's leadership is very interested in the economic growth of Crawford County.

In the summer of 2015, the only thing hotter than the California wildfires, the Tiger Woods come back at the Masters and Jordan Spieth's putter is the presidential campaign of Donald Trump.

Today, August 23, 2015, I have one final chance before the printing of my book to bring everyone up-to-date on the state of affairs in the US. We are about to elect a real competent leader in the person of Donald J. Trump. This is desperately needed after the US has endured fifty-two—yes, fifty-two years of often misguided and outright dishonest, aimless leadership since Johnson became president in 1963. I would call those years the "lost years" in the history of the United States.

The "lost years" began with Johnson and his failed Great Society social experiment, which sucked 10 to 15 trillion dollars out of the economy, combined with the Vietnam War. Gross incompetence was just getting started as the country elected a crook in Nixon. Ford and Carter meant well but were in over their heads. Reagan tried, but the real bad stuff got started with the first Bush when he followed the advice of the "military industrial complex" folks and invaded Iraq in 1991 for oil, which we could have obtained within our borders.

Clinton was immoral, and he was the president who rescinded the Glass Steagall Act, setting the country up the economic collapse of 2008. The second Bush, without any track record of accomplishment, was elected president. We know what happened under his watch: the 9/11 attacks on the towers, which he could have prevented, had he headed the warnings; this was only followed by a more stupid, self-serving second war against Iraq, bringing our country close to the brink with the loss of five thousand brave soldiers and hundreds of thousands of Iraqis, not to mention the Americans maimed and Iraqis displaced. How can anyone call that leadership?

Yet there is more. The "lost years" are just getting into high gear with the election of Obama, a man with no real leadership experience and zero business acumen. He has directed the country with mindless economic policies, premature exit from Iraq, and total lack of judgment on domestic energy production which could be God's life saving jacket for the US.

Now, finally, in 2015, here comes a proven businessman, who has been sober his entire life, reads and learns, and with his own money (no need to be sullied by special interest donations), is about to lead the United States of America out of the swamp with intelligent, straightforward, and brutally honest programs. The country is crying for Mr. Trump.

Donald Trump in my opinion will seal the Southern border, come to the aid of US veterans, deal strongly with ISIS, get domestic energy pumped up, fix our roads and bridges, look after women's health, streamline our tax system, and bring jobs back to the US, which in turn will give hope to the inner cities.

How do we know Trump can do these things? Because we only need to look at his record of personal achievements. You judge a man by his record. Trump is a man of action. Get ready to see Donald J. Trump be elected by a popular landslide of Republicans, Democrats, and independents who are ready to bring the past fifty-two "lost years" to an end. Trump will make America great again!

One more final thing: Donald J. Trump just won seven more states on the super Tuesday election held on March 1, 2016. I predict that Mr. Trump will be the next president because he will win the votes from the 60 to 70 percent of the folks in the middle. The 15 to 20 percent far-left-leaning liberals and the 15 to 20 percent far-right-leaning conservatives don't know what to do about Mr. Trump. These two groups have been manipulating the American public for the last fifty-two years, and that is about to end.

I think my "Dirt Father" father was right. He always told me that the pendulum is always swinging. When it goes too far to the left, it starts to swing back to the right and then starts back to the left again. It's now swinging back to the right.

Regrets? I have a few, but like Yogi Berra said, "When you come to a fork in the road, take it!"

I say, "You'll never know what was down the other path. That is one of life's mysteries."

I like this anonymous saying:
"Never dwell on what you have lost, only on what you
have left. Count your blessings. You'll always find plenty.
Your most prized possessions are your unexpired years."

When it's all over: Play, Hallelujah/Leonard Cohen/Shrek.
Then play, Amazing Grace. Then drink CAMi Wine.
Finish with this Edith Piaf song, 'Je ne regrett rien.'

Now play, 'I Did It My Way' by Frank Sinatra,
'our song'. Now drink more CAMi Wine!!

Terry and Mary Ann celebrate fifty-year
anniversary on July 10, 2015.

Our three children, Laurie, Stephen, and Karin.

Family on Monterey Beach in 2014.

Matt and Jessica Riggs with John Shelton.

Trevor Maurer Scott Mansfield and Laurie in Paris in 2013.

My daughter Laurie with her painting.

My good friend, artist and writer, Zaza
Fetterly, with her paintings.

Photograph by my grandson, Trevor Mansfield.

A pair of blue herons, painted by Mary Ann Maurer

Laurie, Mary Ann, and Karin in the wine country.

vintner press

The Board of Directors and team at the NVV
would like to congratulate our very own
Linda Reiff, who was announced last
Thursday as *Wine Enthusiast's* Person of

CHAPTER XIV

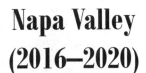

Napa Valley (2016–2020)

Donald J. Trump
(2016–2020)

When you come to wine country, Napa Valley, you can fly into San Francisco, Oakland, Sacramento, or even Santa Rosa. Napa Valley, thirty-five miles long and ten miles wide in parts, is seventy miles north of San Francisco.

As you drive north, out of the city of Napa, on Highway 29, passed the small beautiful city of Yountville—with its French Laundry restaurant and a VA retirement home and golf course—you'll come upon the Oakville grocery. That's a good place to pick up a bottle of CAMi wine. The wine can be enjoyed at the Rutherford Grill, one of Valley's most popular restaurants. No corkage here. The Rutherford Grill is the favorite restaurant in Napa Valley of my friend, Tom Quinn, president of Kirtland College, in Grayling, Michigan.

Going north from the Rutherford Grill, you'll pass Brix and Mustard's two great restaurants.

Continuing north, you'll see the famous Robert Mondavi winery on the left, the Inglenook (owned by Francis Ford Coppola), Whitehall Lane, and the Hall Winery with its graceful stainless steel Rabbit (thirty feet) leaping in the air.

Now you're passing through the heart of Napa Valley, into the city of St. Helena (my hometown). There, you'll find many fine dining and excellent restaurants, including The Market, Cooks,

Archetype, Gotts, Villa Corona, Tra Vigne, The Press, Bistro, The Goose and The Gander, Acadia House, The Farmstead, and others.

The oldest single screen movie theater in the west, The Cameo Cinema, is also in St. Helena. The Cameo has the best sound and screen experience anywhere. The Cameo always shows the latest films while seating a comfortable 140 or so patrons.

Be sure not to miss Nimbus Arts, the community based non-profit which promotes the arts in Napa Valley.

On your way north to Calistoga, out of St. Helena, you'll pass Beringer winery and the Culinary Institute of America (CIA), formerly the Christian Brothers, Brass Wood, and schedule a winery tour at Castello Di Amorosa, Sterling, and the Charles Krug wineries.

About ten miles north of St. Helena, you'll come to Calistoga, where you'll find the new CAMi tasting room and art gallery, with Laurie Shelton's painted 'cows' and Trevor Mansfield's photographs now on display. The gallery will feature different artists from time to time.

If you travel north, out of the city of Napa, on the east side on the winding Silverado trail, you'll pass the Black Stallion winery, Stags Leap Area, Joseph Phelps, Duckhorn, Rombauer, and CAMi vineyards. A good place for lunch is either at the Auberge Du Soleil on Rutherford Hill or at Meadow Wood.

As you enter Calistoga from the east, you'll see the expansive new and pricy Four Seasons Resort on the right, the equally exclusive Solage Resort with its public restaurant on the left.

Now you'll turn left onto Lincoln Street (Calistoga's Main Street), passing Sam's and the Calistoga spa, and hot springs going directly to CAMi's tasting room. CAMi's tasting room and gallery is at 1333B Lincoln Avenue, directly across from the Copperfield's bookstore. You have now arrived.

Dirt Farmer's Son essentially ended in 2016 before the presidential election of Donald J. Trump. Now I know who won. I know about the wall, the impeachment, the rallies, the Syrians and the Kurds, Turkey, Giuliani, the Trump family members, Pelosi, Schiff, Climate Change, Trudeau, Korea, China, Russia, Iran, and the great economy.

The news media should have to discuss the real US issues like:

a. Homelessness
b. Crime
c. Drug overdose
d. Proper diet
e. Climate issues
f. Space force
g. Trade
h. Border security
i. Immigration
j. Other country issues
k. Infrastructurer
l. Health insurance
m. Voter ID and Election transparency.
n. Energy Independence.
o. Domestic Manufacturing.
p. National Security.
q. Covid Vaccines.
r. Race Relations.
s. Education.
t. Term Limits.
u. Balancing the State's and Federal Budgets.

And now the terrible Coronavirus (covid-19)

And not everyday '**who**' is running for president

For the record I think we should make the following changes to the US Constitution:

1. The US President should be elected for one (1) term of 6 (six) years
2. All congressmen or women must be born in the U.S.A
3. All senators must be born in the U.S.A
4. No one can be elected US President if he or she is not 73 or less years of age on election day

That being said. Here is a picture of our President Donald J. Trump and the First Lady, Melania

Here are the 2020 democratic contenders
as they line up for a CNN debate

politics

How to watch the CNN/New York Times Democratic presidential debate tonight

Kate Sullivan, CNN

Trump and Pence
Vs
Democratic Nominee and The Running Mate

And finally, be brave. Brave in your decisions as you go through life. Follow your gut, follow your conscience, follow your convictions. The decisions I made in life and later regretted were those I made out of fear: fear of stock market losses, fear of losing business due to a declining economy, and fear of being tough when toughness was required.

Remember the advice repeated through the ages: Peter could walk on water as long as he had no fear; Roosevelt said, "The only thing we have to fear is fear itself." There is a song which says, "Be brave, young lovers, wherever you are." Others have said that the only things they regretted were the things they didn't do, not the things they did. So consider buying some Beyond Meat stock (BYND).

Be brave, and be happy!

And finally some history of CAMi Wines
please go to:

info@camivineyards.com

Cow painting by Laurie Maurer Shelton. Paintings are available for sale at the art gallery and CAMi wines tasting studio at 1333B Lincoln Avenue, Calistoga, California. USA

These photos of Napa Valley & CAMi wines
and friends were taken by the author. This to
show sites around Napa Valley, a bonus.

CAMi Wine

Laurie M Shelton
with CAMi wine

St. Helena
Mayor, Geoff
Ellsworth & St.
Helena historian,
Mariam Hansen

MaryAnn with Fr. Mac

World Famous CAMi
Winemaker, John Giannini,
opens a bottle of CAMi wine

Oliver Caldwell and
Sandra L. Jones

Polly Keegan
and her
parrot Rosie

Laurie M Shelton
in her
CAMi Vineyards

Chef Michelle Mutrux,
former owner of the Wappo
Grill in Calistoga

Trevor Mansfield and
Gustavo or Jose at
Gillwoods Restaurant

Famous
artist Marvin
Humphrey
with his self
portrait

Camille E. Shelton

Linda Reiff and
Karin Maurer

Barbara Morf and
St. Helena Attorney

323

Kelleen Sullivan with her Art Work

Dave Stoneberg, St.
Helen Star Editor
and Mary Ann

Laurie M. Shelton and
Stephen A. Maurer
At Lake Tahoe

Jewels Drury in great form

Karin Maurer
and
Lisa Brooks

Mary Ann with
K.R. Rombauer
and Fritz Hatton

Camille
jumping
with her
horse
Pete

My family in 1990

May 2020

Sunday	Monday	Tuesday	Wednesday	Thursday	Friday	Saturday
May Day is a public holiday usually celebrated on 1 May. It is an ancient festival of Spring and a current traditional spring holiday in many European cultures. Dances, singing, and cake are usually part of the festivities. May Day was also celebrated by some early European settlers of the American continent. In some parts of the United States, May baskets are made. These are small baskets usually filled with flowers or treats and left at someone's doorstep. The giver rings the bell and runs away. ~Wikipedia					May Day! 1	BROTHER'S & SISTER'S DAY 2
3	STAR WARS DAY 4	CINCO DE MAYO 5	Happy Nurses Day 6	7	NO SOCKS' DAY 8	9
Happy Mother's Day 10	TWILIGHT ZONE DAY 11	INTER-NATIONAL NURSES DAY 12	13	DANCE LIKE A CHICKEN DAY 14	15	LOVE A TREE DAY 16
PACK RAT DAY 17	18	19	BOARD MEETING VIA ZOOM.COM 3 PM 20	NATIONAL MEMO DAY 21	22	LUCKY PENNY DAY 23
NATIONAL ESCARGOT DAY 24	MEMORIAL DAY 25	26	27	NATIONAL HAMBURGER DAY 28	29	WATER A FLOWER DAY 30
31						

The Prez Sez ...by Janeen di Rienzo

This has been the longest month ever and it looks like we have at least another month to go that we will be sheltered in place. I, for one, am not going to rush right out and take up where I left off in March. My life has changed and I suppose that yours has as well. One day the stores and businesses will open again, but what is it going to be like?

With our shelter in place came our own personal protection gear. Most of us still have N95 masks from the fires over the recent years. They are not ones that can be given to medical personnel because most have them have been used by us. We are just fortunate to have them already.

I got a call one day from the office letting me know that Beth Lincoln and the St. Helena Quilters Club, calling themselves **Maisy the Mask Makers,** were making masks and they wanted to do that for Vineyard Valley. One hundred

I've **learned lots** of new things in the kitchen during this SIP, mostly out of necessity. I made my own brown sugar because I wanted to make chocolate chip cookies and didn't have any. I make hand sanitizer, mosquito repellent and now I can open a bottle of Prosecco with one hand. I wonder what size I will be when the quarantine is lifted. I have the big clothes out now.

I have read more interesting articles in the last few months during the stay at home. I have seen pictures of Los Angeles without smog, the canals of Venice clear as can be, but more so, **I have witnessed the flowers in Vineyard Valley** and even my own flowers blooming in some vibrant colors that I haven't seen in recent years. It is amazing what has happened during this big pause. Who would have thought the world would completely stop long enough to heal some of the damage that is done by everyday life?

ABOUT TONY'S

Tony's has been there since 1948, when a hardy Croatian fisherman named...Tony, what else, founded it. The family ran it all the years until Hog Island, a neighbor up the road purchased it in 2017. The building is pretty much the same as it always was, just a bit cleaner and nicer. The menu is greatly increased from the way it started when it was just BBQ'D oysters, clam chowder and sour dough bread. The new menu changes almost daily, here is the one that we had on our New Year's Eve day lunch...

OYSTERS

The number of oysters in the order is in (parenthesis)

Hog Island Sweetwater (Pacific) Tomales Bay, CA $19 (6), $36 (12), $66 (24)

Grays Harbor (Pacific)Grays Harbor, WA $19 (6), $36 (12), $66 (24)

Moon Shoal (Atlantic)Barnstable, MA $21 (6), $40 (12), $72 (24)

SPECIALS

GRILLED OYSTERS

Tony's BBQ'd House-made BBQ sauce, garlic, butter $17 (4)

SMALL PLATES AND SALADS

Warm Olives Garlic, Calabrian chili, grapefruit $6 Steamed Manila Clams or Cove Mussels Garlic, parsley, wine, olive oil $16 Peel & Eat Gulf Shrimp (1/2 lb) Old Bay Court Boullion $18 Market Greens Local baby greens, Sherry-Dijon vinaigrette $8 Little Gem Wedge Watermelon radish, bacon, Pt. Reyes Bay Blue-buttermilk dressing Octopus Salad Arugula, oregano, black olive tapenade, CA seaweed vinaigrette CA Albacore Niçoise Olive oil-poached tuna, little gems, carrot, green beans, sieved egg, olives, radish, garlic-champagne vinaigrette $17

ENTREES

HIOC Clam Chowder Manila clams, aromatic vegetables, bacon, potatoes, cream $16 Tony's Burger Stemple Creek beef, Pt. Reyes Toma, house-made tartar sauce, lettuce, tomato, pickles, red onion $19 Fried Oyster Po' Boy Lettuce, tomato, house-made tartar sauce $19 Fish & Chips & Slaw AK "True" Cod, house-made tartar sauce, hogwash slaw $24 Linguine and Clams Bagna Cauda Pasta Mancini, rapini, anchovy, garlic, shallot, parsley, capers, white wine, olive oil $23 Seafood Stew Market fish and shellfish, shellfish-saffron broth $28

AFTERWORD

Ten Secrets to Success

by
Investor's Business Daily

1. **How you think is everything:** Always be positive. Think success, not failure. Beware of a negative environment.
2. **Decide upon your true dreams and goals:** Write down your specific goals and develop a plan to reach them.
3. **Take action:** Goals are nothing without action. Don't be afraid to get started. Just do it.
4. **Never stop learning:** Go back to school or read books. Get training and acquire skills.
5. **Be persistent and work hard.** Success is a marathon, not a sprint. Never give up.
6. **Learn to analyze details:** Get all the facts, all the input. Learn from your mistakes.
7. **Focus your time and money:** Don't let other people or things distract you.
8. **Don't be afraid to innovate;** be different: Following the herd is a sure way to mediocrity.
9. **Deal and communicate with people effectively:** No person is an island. Learn to understand and motivate others.
10. **Be honest and dependable;** take responsibility: Otherwise, Nos. 1–9 won't matter.

DINING OUT IN
AT LEAST, FOR NOW...

GREAT OPTIONS for Local Restaurants & Grocery Stores

BOOKS

Terry's Recommendations

1. The Bible
2. *Think and Grow Rich* by Napoleon Hill
3. *An Embarrassment of Riches* by Alexander Green
4. *The Fracking Truth* by Chris Faulkner
5. *Secrets of the Ages* by Robert Collier
6. *A Big History* by Cynthia Brown
7. *Essential Philosophy* by James Mannion
8. *I Declare* by Joel Olsteen
9. *The Power of Having Desire* by Bruce Garrabrandt
10. *The Art of the Deal* by Donald Trump
11. *The Power of Positive Thinking* by Norman V. Peale
12. *Killing Kennedy* by Bill O' Reilly
13. *The Seven Storey Mountain* by Thomas Merton
14. *John Adams* by David McCullough
15. *Tale of Two Cities* by Charles Dickens
16. *Dirt Farmer's Son* by Terry A. Maurer
17. *The Winning Spirt* by Joe Montana and Tom Mitchell, PhD
18. *Winning* by Tom Brady JR.
19. BACK by Eldrick Tont 'Tiger' Woods

APPENDIX

Family History

Now finally, just to add some of the real old history about my dad's family, I've included a brief write-up put together by one of my many Maurer cousins, Julie Maurer, daughter of my dad's youngest of twelve siblings, my uncle Pat Maurer, born on St. Patrick's Day in Nashville, Michigan, in 1938.

And also, now a short old history about my mother's family, written by one of my many Cherven cousins, Che-Che (Cherven) Flewelling, daughter of my mother's oldest brother of ten siblings, my uncle Frank Cherven, born in Chicago in 1908.

Two Maurer Family Legends

According to legend, the Maurers originally lived in France in the 1300s or 1400s, three brothers moved to Switzerland due to a food shortage or famine in France. Later in the 1600s several members of the family, again three brothers, moved to Kleinbundenbach in Germany.

One legend has the family related to or of nobility in France. Another legend has them related to the king of Bavaria. Enjoy the legends, none of them probably could be proven to be true or false.

Of the three brothers,
Johann Jacob, Philip Jacob, and Johann Peter,

our side of the family branches from Johann Jacob,
Peter, Peter A, and Laurence:

It's also told that three cousins (all named Peter) came to the
USA. To distinguish the three, they were called Smoky Pete, Crippled
Pete, and Pretty Pete. Our lineage obviously stems from Pretty Pete.

Of Debold Maurer and his wife, Maria Elisabeth Stuppi, there
are no records except that they lived and died in Kleinbundenbach,
Germany. All their children died young except for the three sons
recorded here. Johann Jacob was the only son to cross the ocean and
settle in America. The house these three boys, Johann Jacob, Philip
Jacob, and Johann Peter were born in was built in 1721. It was chis-
eled in the capstone above the front door.

Johann Jacob Maurer and his wife Elizabeth and five children
came to Seneca County, Ohio, in the spring of 1857. In the fall of
that year they migrated to maple Grove Township, Barry County,
Michigan. They made the trip across the Atlantic in a sailboat, being
forty-two days on the water. Their son, Peter, came two years earlier in 1855 with Theobald Maurer, son of Philip Jacob Maurer and
Anna Maria Schweikofer. Theobald did not stay in the US.

Philip Jacob Maurer and his wife lived and died on the old
homestead in Germany. Of their six children that lived to adulthood,
four emigrated to America. They were Peter, Katherine, Philip, and
Maria.

Johann Peter Maurer was twice married and spent all his life
in the village he was born, Kleinbundenbach. He had one child by
his first marriage and eight by his second marriage. Of these, Anna
died young. Maria married Johann Koenig of Hettenhausen, a
nearby village, and had four children. Eva married Johann Bosslet
of Overhausen, also nearby and had seven children. Johann married
Maria Hemmer and inherited the homestead always their home. They
had four children that emigrated to America; they were Katherine,
Magdalena, Peter S., and Amalia, known as Aunt Emma.

Philip and Magdalena Maurer

Philip is the son of Philip Jacob Maurer, and Magdalena is the daughter of Johann Peter Maurer. Philip came to America in 1872; Magdalena came in 1871. They both returned to Germany in 1875 and were married on December 27, 1875, returning to America in 1876 to live in Maple Grove Township, Barry County, Michigan, living on a farm and raising their six children.

Their daughter Minnie Mary was Sister M. Liguori, a member of the Sisters of St. Joseph for forty years. This was located at a small community north of Kalamazoo, known as Nazareth. The Sisters established a school for girls called Nazareth Academy and one for the boys. Sister Liguori was buried at the cemetery near Nazareth Academy. Clara Maurer Coe was buried in Ringling Cemetery, Sarasota, Florida. The rest of the children are buried in Mt. Calvary Cemetery in Hastings, Michigan.

Email from Julie Maurer to Don Maurer

Monday, November 29, 1999
Subject: Mission Accomplished!

Don-

Yesterday I met our relatives in Kleinbundenbach. It was quite a day. Driving there took even longer than I anticipated and I knew that it would be slow. To take break up the trip, I stopped in a city along the way to do some shopping—I'd been there before, and for some reason it's easier for me to shop in Germany than in France. Anyway, I reached the town in mid-afternoon. The main drag is torn apart for construction. It looks like they're getting a new sewer system, but right now all they have is mud! In some ways Kleinbundenbach is in the middle of nowhere: once off the main road I was constantly looking at the map, and missed the correct turn several times. Many of the roads would be suicide sledding hills with snow on the ground. On the other hand, a larger town about twenty minutes away has a McDonald. That's how I judge the extent to which the local culture in Europe has been corrupted by greedy multinational attitudes: Look for McDonalds!

Since the road was closed, I walked through the center of town looking for the bakery. Couldn't find that, but I did find Maurer's pub. Unfortunately the front door was locked. I took a picture. There's not a proper church in the village, but the cemetery on one end has a modern chapel. There are quite a few Maurer markers, including several who have died during this decade. Many of them lived into their 80s or 90s, so I concluded that the German branch of the family has ornery old cusses like Grandpa and your Dad that time just couldn't kill! From the cemetery I walked up the hill and outside the village. I'd only seen a handful of people on the street and no one said anything to me. Well, the higher elevation inspired me or something, because I told myself that if Mom were in the same situation, she would knock on the door of the Pub. It was either that or go home empty-handed, so I practiced what to say in German as I walked back into the center.

The guy who answered the door is named Albert, and he's in his 60s. I asked if he was Mr. Maurer, apologized for disturbing him, and said that in the middle of the 1800's my relatives had left Kleinbundenbach and emigrated to Michigan in the U.S.A. He looked shocked and said that he never expected anyone from the family to return. We went into the pub and he poured me a beer. Turns out that it's not much of a business anymore: His wife died about the time that Mom did, and her cooking was quite a crowd pleaser. Albert lives upstairs above the business. We talked for about 45 minutes until I finished the beer, and he showed me some pictures of his wife and kids when they were young.

Then we walked down the street to meet the Alfons Maurer. He used to run the bakery, but has emphysema or something and doesn't work anymore. He DEFINITELY remembered Steve, although maybe not in the way Steve would like to be remembered! The story I heard was that this big, confident, intimidating officer from the American Air Force (remember, in German that's Luftwaffe) visited them once in 1978. Alfons had never seen a Maurer with red hair, and Steve never came back! They thought that whoever came with Steve to interpret must have messed up the joke and Steve was insulted. I assured them that Steve told us that all the Maurers in Kleinbundenbach were very kind and hospitable to him. Alfons' son, Thomas, lives at home, and it happens that his daughter and granddaughter were visiting yesterday. The daughter speaks English fairly well—definitely much better than I can speak French! She worked in retail shops in a nearby city, where she dealt with a lot of American military people. A couple of times, I asked her to translate some things for me, rather than spending half an hour looking for the right words in German. What really surprised me was when I would say something in "proper German" and she would translate into the local dialect for her father! All the rest of the adults understood me fairly well, or I could get a complex. They are in fairly close contact with a Philip Maurer who lives in Dearborn. He's near your Dad's age, and grew up in Nashville. Dad remembers his parents, and Alfons has pictures of a farm in Nashville that Dad thinks was Philip's parents' place. The old whispered to the English-speaking lady that all of my Dad's brothers had big ears like Philip. Much to my embarrassment, she translated that into German! I KNEW the words in German, just didn't want to announce the comment to the entire room!

They talked about others in the family who they would invite when I visit again, and are quite anxious to meet anyone who visits me from home. It was a bit awkward when they wanted to know when I would come again—I was thinking, "When you invite me!" but could hardly say that! I'd been invited to a party last night, so I only stopped at home to feed Aggie and change my clothes. This afternoon I learned that Albert called me at 10 to make sure I returned safely, when he called again. The answering machine in English must have been enough for him not to leave a message last night, or maybe he just hates those "d...machines" like my Dad. As you can tell, it was a good beginning. I'm looking forward to seeing them again-partly for the family history aspect, and also because it's very interesting to get to know the locals, from the "inside out" so to speak. I'll keep you posted.

Julie Maurer

A Small Cherven History Lesson by Che-Che (Cherven) Flewelling

In the early 1900s, three young men, Matthew, Joseph, and Andrew, traveled from Czechoslovakia/Hungary to find a better life in America. Matthew, the oldest, was already married to his wife, Rozalia, and they had a daughter, Ann. He changed his name to Michael after he arrived in America, as he didn't like the name Matthew. We don't know for sure if the younger brothers, Joseph and Andrew, came at the same time as Matthew/Michael, or if they came over a bit later. Another brother, Michat Cserwien, stayed in the "old country." His last known address was Chyzne Nol, Nowy Targ, Krakow, Poland. My dad, Frank, used to correspond with him. There may still be relatives living at that address, as property usually passes down in the families.

The three brothers originally settled in Chicago. For unknown reasons—possibly immigration officers who spelled it like it sounded to them, Joseph and Andrew's last name was Americanized to *Cherven* while Michael's was spelled *Cerven*. Joseph and Andrew met young women and married. Our grandfather, Andrew, married Justine Glusak in 1907. She had come over from the old country along with her brother Emil and a younger twelve-year-old brother, who, according to stories Grandma used to tell us, died from an infection caused by an unsterile smallpox vaccination.

Lured by tales of fertile farmland in Northern Michigan, the three Cherven brothers bought land in the Roscommon area. Joe bought the property we all remember as Grandpa and Grandma's home—while Michael and Andrew purchased land in Crawford County, just north of where Uncle Andy and Aunt Margaret live now. Neighboring property was owned by the Sopscak family. Grandpa and Grandma moved to their property in 1910 when Frank was two years old, and they raised ten children. Michael and Joseph stayed in Chicago where they raised their families. Michael had seven children who survived to adulthood (there were supposedly eleven children, but we can only account for seven; supposedly the youngest, Anthony, died of pneumonia at an early age). Joe had nine children, most of whom were born in Chicago, although he decided at some

343

point to move his family to Buffalo, New York. He traveled quite a bit to Argentina and Brazil in his job (according to his youngest daughter, Kay). His oldest son, Louis, eventually owned a mink/chinchilla farm and a dog-food factory. I remember going to visit the relatives in Buffalo when I was a little girl, and we would bring home cases of dog food for our beagles. I even took a can to school for show-and-tell because I was so impressed by the Cherven name on the label.

Grandma, Grandpa, and the family lived on their property in Crawford County until 1923 when Frank entered high school. Since it was such a long walk from their property to town, Uncle Joe let them move to his house. They eventually bought it, according to Aunt Pauline's diary (Terry's mother). Grandpa used to go to Buffalo in the winters to work for Uncle Joe, and that is where the family grew up. Just imagine how strong a woman Grandma was to run the household and take care of ten children by herself when Grandpa was away. (Grandma's brother, Emil, a bachelor, lived in the little house that was eventually owned by Uncle John and Aunt Marnie. It was nice that he was close by to help out his sister.)

The family endured many joys and hardships (including losing her husband in 1934 and having five of the boys go off to the service in WWII, but all returned safely) over the years and built a strong, well-known family in the area. This was the foundation on which our family was built. The six boys and Aunt Fran all stayed in Roscommon and raised their families, while Aunt Pauline lived in Grayling, and Aunt Ann lived in Cheboygan, before they moved to Chelsea in later years, and Aunt Teen lived in Saginaw and Bay City. We all used to get together every August to celebrate Grandma's birthday, the forerunner to family reunions. And how could we forget the Christmas Eve celebrations (Vigilia) at her house. Remember how she would pinch our cheeks and give us kisses? Our kids (who were born before her death in 1970) called her the kissing Grandma!

Note for Lawrence Henry Maurer:
Rumor is that there were three first cousins that came over at the same time:
Crippled Pete, Pretty Pete, and Smokey Pete.

GENEALOGY

1794–2016

Genealogy prepared for Stephen A. Maurer
by Matt McCormack

Ancestors of Stephen Andrew Maurer

Generation 1

1. Stephen Andrew Maurer, son of Terry Andrew Maurer and Mary Ann Maurer, was born on September 8, 1967, in Ann Arbor, Washtenaw County, Michigan. He married Nicole Mario Bolcom on August 5, 1995, in Denver Washtenaw County, Michigan. She was born on March 10, 1972, in Allen Park, Wayne County, Michigan.

Generation 2

2. Terry Andrew Maurer, son of Bernard Lee Maurer and Pauleen Elizabeth Cherven, was born on October 1, 1942, in Crawford County, Michigan. He married Mary Ann Horning on July 10, 1965, in Saint Mary's Church, Ann Arbor, Washtenaw County, Michigan.
3. Mary Ann Horning, daughter of Edwin Horning and Amanda Mane Buss, was born on March 13, 1941, in Chelsea, Washtenaw County, Michigan.

Mary Ann Horning and Terry Andrew Maurer had the following children:

i.   Laurie Lynn Maurer was born on January 25, 1966, in Ann Arbor, Washtenaw County, Michigan. She married Scott David Mansfield on August 8, 1987, in Dexter Washtenaw County, Michigan. He was born on December 13, 1958, in Michigan. She married Thomas Howell Shelton on January 25, 1997, in Saint Helena, Napa County, California. He was born on January 24, 1953, in Washington District of Columba. He died on July 26, 2008, in Napa Valley, California. She married George Schisler on November 11, 2011 (11,11,11), in Carmel, California. He was born, date unknown, in Atlanta, Fulton County, Georgia.

ii. Stephen Andrew Maurer was born on September 9, 1967, in Ann Arbor, Washtenaw County, Michigan. He married Nicole Balcom on August 5, 1995, in Dexter, Washtenaw County, Michigan. She was born on March 10, 1972, in Allen Park, Wayne County, Michigan.

iii. Karin Mee-Lyn Maurer was born on March 15, 1976, in Seoul, South Korea. Karin Mee-Lyn Maurer was naturalized as an American citizen on November 3, 1981 in Ann Arbor, Michigan. Karin declared "I got American."

Generation 3

4.   Bernard Lee Maurer, son of Lawrence Henry Maurer and Gertrude Bernice Lennon, was born on January 17, 1915, in Nashville Barry County, Michigan. He died on April 24, 1985, in Grayling, Crawford County, Michigan. He married Pauline on October 29, 1939, in Roscommon. Roscommon County, Michigan.

5.   Pauline Elizabeth Cherven, daughter of Andrew Cherven, was born on December 26, 1917, in Roscommon.

Roscommon County, Michigan. She died on October 23, 1990, in Grayling, Crawford County, Michigan.

Pauline Elizabeth Cherven and Leo Maurer had the following children:

i.   Anthony Leo Maurer was born on May 26, 1941, in Grayling, Crawford County, Michigan. He married Marilyn Juanita Elberts on December 21, 1968. She was born on July 29, 1933, in Sheburn, Minnesota.

ii. Terry Andrew Maurer was born on October 1, 1942, in Grayling Crawford County, Michigan. He married Mary Ann Horning on July 10, 1965, in Saint Mary's Church, Ann Arbor, Washtenaw County, Michigan. She was born on May 13, 1941, in Chelsea, Washtenaw County, Michigan.

iii. Louis G Maurer was born on October 14, 1951, in Crawford County, Michigan. He married Elsie Mae Smith in Crawford County, Michigan. She was born, date unknown. She died on May 27, 2014.

6. Edwin Gottfried Horning, son of Christian Horning and Amelia C. Eiseman, was born on August 14, 1911, in Washtenaw County, Michigan. He died on February 1, 1992, in Chelsea, Washtenaw County, Michigan. He married Amanda Marie Buss on June 4, 1939, in Chelsea, Washtenaw County, Michigan.

7. Amanda Mario Buss, daughter of William H. Buss and Emma A. Schichz, was born on May 1, 1911, on Manchester, Washtenaw County, Michigan. She died on January 2, 2000, in possibly Washtenaw County, Michigan.

Amanda Mario Buss and Edwin Gottfried Horning had the following children:

i.   Mary Ann Horning was born on March 13, 1941, in Chelsea, Washtenaw County, Michigan. She married Terry Andrew Maurer on July 10, 1965, in Saint Mary's Church, Ann Arbor, Washtenaw County,

Michigan. He was born on October 1, 1942, in Grayling, Crawford County, Michigan.

ii. Dale Edwin Horning was born on May 10, 1944, in Ann Arbor, Washtenaw County, Michigan. He married Gaelene Wurster on August 27, 1366, in Manchester, Washtenaw County, Michigan. She was about September 1947 in Manchester, Washtenaw County, Michigan.

Generation 4

8. Lawrence Henry Maurer, son of Peter A. Maurer and Rosella, was born on July 6, 1891, in Maple Grove, Barry County, Michigan. He died on December 24, 1981, in Battle Creek, Calhoun County, Michigan. He married Gertrude Bernice Lennon on October 15, 1913, in Barry County, Michigan.

9. Gertrude Bernice Lennon, daughter of William H. Lennon and Mary, was born on December 6, 1891, in possibly Barry County, Michigan. She died on September 3, 1953, in Hastings, Barry County, Michigan.

Gertrude Bernice Lennon and Lawrence Henry Maurer had the following children:

i. ★Bernard Leo Maurer (the Dirt Farmer) was born on January 17, 1915, in Nashville, Barry County, Michigan. He died on April 24, 1985, in Grayling, Crawford County, Michigan. He married Pauline Elizabeth Cherven on October 28, 1939, in Roscommon. Roscommon County, Michigan. She was born on December 26, 1917, in Roscommon County, Michigan. She died on October 23, 1990, in Grayling, Crawford County, Michigan.

ii. Mary Rose Maurer was born on September 3, 1916, in Michigan, and Edwin Lawrence Maurer was born on April 28, 1916, in Michigan. He died on August 28, 1993, in possibly Sacramento County, California.

iii. Francs William Maurer was born on July 31, 1919, in Michigan.

iv. Edward Maurer was born on July 4, 1921, in Barry County, Michigan. He died in San Francisco.

v. Dale Henry Maurer was born on February 3, 1923, in Michigan. He died on November 16, 1977, in possibly Barry County, Michigan.

vi. Hugh Lennon Maurer was born on September 19, 1924, in Michigan. He died on September 24, 1967, in possibly Blount County, Tennessee.

vii. Ruth Luella Maurer was born on April 19, 1927, in Michigan.

viii. Annette Barbara Maurer was born on June 23, 1926, in Michigan.

ix. Louise A. Maurer was born on August 5, 1931, in Michigan.

x. Clarence Joseph Maurer was born on December 19, 1932, in Michigan.

xi. Bernice Bertha Maurer was born on June 29, 1934, in Michigan.

xii. James Patrick Maurer was born on March 17, 1936, in Michigan.

10. Andrew Cherven was born in about 1865 in Czechoslovakia. She died in 1940 in Roscommon County, Michigan. He married Justine Glusak before 1908 in Cook County, Illinois.

11. Justine Glusak was born on August 28, 1889, in Czechoslovakia. She died in June 1970 in Roscommon County, Michigan.

Justine Glusak and Andrew Cherven had the following children:

i. Frank Cherven was born in about 1908 in Illinois. He died on October 13, 1959, in possibly Roscommon, Roscommon County, Michigan. He married Cecelia M. Balwinski on November 23, 1935, in Bay City,

Bay County, Michigan. She was born on November 21, 1914, in Bay City, Bay County, Michigan. She died on August 20, 2004, in possibly Roscommon, Roscommon County, Michigan.

ii. Anna Cherven was born in about 1910 in possibly Roscommon, Roscommon County, Michigan. She died, date unknown. She married (?) on a Friday, date unknown. He was born, date unknown.

iii. Paulina Elizabeth Cherven was born on December 26, 1917, in Roscommon, Roscommon County, Michigan. She died on October 23, 1990, in Grayling, Crawford County, Michigan. She married Bernard Lee Maurer on October 28, 1939, in Roscommon, Roscommon County, Michigan. He was born on January 17, 1915, in Nashville, Barry County, Michigan. He died on April 24, 1985, in Grayling, Crawford County, Michigan.

iv. John E. Cherven was born on January 16, 1914, in possibly Roscommon, Roscommon County, Michigan. He died on August 2, in possibly Mountain Home, Baxter County, Arkansas. He married Margaret A. Lake on July 23, 1949, in Flint, Genesee County, Michigan. She was born on October 17, 1929, in Flint, Genesee County, Michigan. She died on April 10, 2005, in Mountain Home, Baxter County, Arkansas.

v. Alcise B. Cherven was born on November 3, 1915, in possibly Roscommon, Roscommon County, Michigan. He died date on unknown. He married Kathleen, date unknown. She was born in about 1924.

vi. Edward J. Cherven was born on February 20, 1918, in Beaver Creek Township, Roscommon County, Michigan. He died on August 25, 2004, in Roscommon, Roscommon County, Michigan.

vii. Justine Monica Cherven was born on May 4, 1920, in Roscommon, Roscommon County, Michigan. She died on May 8, 2005, in possibly McKinney, Collin

County, Texas. She married Albert Leo Leonard in August 1941 in possibly Michigan. He was born on March 12, 1918, in possibly Michigan. He died on February 2, 1975, in Bay City, Bay County, Michigan.

viii. Andrew Cherven was born in about 1923 in possibly Roscommon, Roscommon County, Michigan. He died, date unknown. He married Margaret, date unknown. She was born, date unknown.

ix. Michael A. Cherven was born on March 31, 1925, in possibly Roscommon, Roscommon County, Michigan. He died on December 23, 2001, in possibly Roscommon, Roscommon County, Michigan. He married Gertrude, date unknown. She was born, date unknown.

x. Frances Cherven was born in January 1928 in Roscommon, Roscommon County, Michigan. She married Dorian R. Diss, date unknown, in possibly Michigan. He was born on January 10, 1927, in possibly Illinois. He died on April 26, 1999, in possibly Roscommon, Roscommon County, Michigan.

12. Christian F. Horning was born on March 11, 1872, in Wurttemburg, Germany. He died in 1958 in Washtenaw County, Michigan. He married Amelia C. Eiseman, about 1906, in Washtenaw County, Michigan.

13. Amelia C. Eiseman, daughter of Gottfried Eiseman and Mary 7, was born on August 29, 1672, in Washtenaw County, Michigan. She died on July 21, 1957, in Washtenaw County, Michigan.

Amelia C. Eiseman and Christian F. Horning had the following children:

i. Bertha C. Horning was born in about 1908 in Washtenaw County, Michigan. She died, date unknown, in possibly Washtenaw County, Michigan.

ii.   Ernest G. Horning was born on September 6, 1909, in Washtenaw County, Michigan. He died on September 4, 1985, in Chelsea, Washtenaw County, Michigan.

iii. Edwin Gottfried Horning was born on August 14, 1911, in Washtenaw County, Michigan. He died on February 1, 1992, in Chelsea, Washtenaw County, Michigan. He married Amanda Marie Buss on June 4, 1939, in Chelsea, Washtenaw County, Michigan. She was born on May 1, 1911, in Manchester, Washtenaw County, Michigan. She died on January 2, 2000, in possibly Washtenaw County, Michigan.

iv.   Waldo C. Horning was born on November 14, 1913, in Washtenaw County, Michigan. He died on September 19, 1992, in Chelsea, Washtenaw County, Michigan.

14. William H. Busa, son of John P. Buss and Emma, was born in May 1870 in Michigan. He died in 1941 in Manchester, Washtenaw County, Michigan. He married Emma in about 1898 in Manchester, Washtenaw County, Michigan.

15. Emma A. was born in May 1874 in Michigan. She died in 1942 in Manchester, Washtenaw County, Michigan.

Emma A. and William H. Buss had the following children:

i.   Anna Buss was born in about 1901 in Manchester, Washtenaw County, Michigan. She died, date unknown.

ii.   John W. Buss was born on November 2, 1902, in Manchester, Washtenaw County, Michigan. He died on March 26, 1982, in Tecumseh, Lenawee County, Michigan.

iii. Frederick W. Buss was born on September 11, 1904, in Manchester, Washtenaw County, Michigan. He died on June 26, 1978, in Saline, Washtenaw County, Michigan

iv. Martha Buss was born in about 1907 in Manchester, Washtenaw County, Michigan. She died, date unknown

v. Lillian Buss was born in about 1908 in Manchester, Washtenaw County, Michigan. She died, date unknown.

vi. George Buss was born on September 5, 1909, in Manchester, Washtenaw County, Michigan. He died in August 1967 in possibly Washtenaw County, Michigan.

vii. Amanda Marie Buss was born on May 1, 1911, in Manchester, Washtenaw County, Michigan. She died on January 2, 2000, in possibly Washtenaw County, Michigan. She married Edwin Gottfried Horning on June 4, 1939, in Chelsea, Washtenaw County, Michigan. He was born on August 14, 1911, in Washtenaw County, Michigan. He died on February 1, 1992, in Chelsea, Washtenaw County, Michigan.

viii. Ella Buss was born in about 1918 in Manchester, Washtenaw County, Michigan. She died, date unknown.

ix. Erwin Buss was born in about 1922 in Manchester, Washtenaw County, Michigan. He died, date unknown.

Generation 5

16. Peter A. Maurer, son of Peter Maurer and Rosina Cook, was born on March 3, 1865, in Maple Grove, Barry County, Michigan. He died on July 31, 1936, in Maple Grove. Barry County, Michigan. He married Rosolla Blatt on August 26, 1890, in possibly Michigan.

17. Rosalia Blatt was born on May 28, 1865, in possibly Michigan. She died on June 24, 1909, in possibly Maple Grove, Barry County, Michigan.

Rosalia Blatt and Peter A. Maurer had the following children:

i. Lawrence Henry Maurer was born on July 6, 1891, in Maple Grove, Barry County, Michigan. He died on December 24, 1961, in Battle Creek, Calhoun County, Michigan. He married Gertrude Bernice Lennon on October 15, 1913, in Barry County, Michigan. She was born on December 6, 1891, in possibly Barry County, Michigan. She died on September 3, 1953, in Hastings, Barry County, Michigan.

ii. He married Carrie Scott in 1955 in possibly Michigan. She was born, date unknown. She died, date unknown, in possibly Michigan. Bertha Rose Maurer was born on March 9, 1893, in Barry County, Michigan. She died in January 1969 in possibly Hastings, Barry County, Michigan. She married Henry Smith on June 25, 1913, in possibly Michigan. He was born, date unknown. He died, date unknown.

iii. Hilda Mary Maurer was born on July 27, 1895, in Barry County, Michigan. She died in February 1987 in possibly Milwaukee, Milwaukee County, Wisconsin.

18. William H. Lennon, son of Hugh Lennon and Elizabeth, was born in February 1664 in Michigan. He died, date unknown, in possibly Eaton County, Michigan. He married Mary in about 1890 in possibly Michigan.

19. Mary was born in March 1869 in Michigan. She died, date unknown, in possibly Eaton County, Michigan.

Mary and William H. Lennon had the following children:

i. Gertrude Bernice Lennon was born on December 6, 1891, in possibly Barry County, Michigan. She died on September 3, 1953, in Hastings, Barry County, Michigan. She married Lawrence Henry Maurer on October 15, 1913, in Barry County, Michigan. He was born on July 6, 1891, in Battle Creek, Calhoun County, Michigan.

ii.   Bernard Lennon was born on December 20, 1894, in Bellevue Township, Eaton County, Michigan. He died date unknown in possible Eaton County, Michigan.

iii. Bernice Lennon was born on December 20, 1894, in Bellavue Township, Eaton County, Michigan. She died, date unknown, in possibly Eaton County, Michigan.

26. Gottfried Elseman was born in May 1835 in Wurttemberg, Germany. He died unknown in possibly Washtenaw County, Michigan. He married Mary in about 1862 in possibly Michigan.

27. Mary was born in December 1836 in Wurttemberg, Germany. She died date unknown in possibly Washtenaw County, Michigan.

Mary and Gottfried Elseman had the following children.

i.   Frederick Elseman was born in about 1862 in Washtenaw County, Michigan. He died, date unknown, in possibly Washtenaw County, Michigan.

ii.   Barbara Elseman was born in about 1863 in Washtenaw County, Michigan. She died, date unknown, in possibly Washtenaw County, Michigan.

iii. Christine Elseman was born in about 1866 in Washtenaw County, Michigan. She died, date unknown, in possibly Washtenaw County, Michigan.

iv.   Mary Elseman was born in about March 1869 in Washtenaw County, Michigan. She died, date unknown, in possibly Washtenaw County, Michigan.

v.   Gottfried Elseman was born in about October 1862 in Washtenaw County, Michigan. He died, date unknown, in possibly Washtenaw County, Michigan. He married Bertha in about 1903 in possibly Washtenaw County, Michigan. She died, date unknown, in possibly Washtenaw County, Michigan.

vi. Amelia C. Elseman was born on August 29, 1872, in Washtenaw County, Michigan. She died on July 21, 1957, in Washtenaw County, Michigan. She married Christian F. Horning in about 1906 in Washtenaw County, Michigan. He was born on March 11, 1872, in Wurttemberg, Germany. He died in 1958 in Washtenaw County, Michigan.

vii. Louise Elseman was born in about 1874 in Washtenaw County, Michigan. He died, date unknown, in possibly Washtenaw County, Michigan.

viii. Emmanuel Michael Elseman was born on July 2, 1877, in Washtenaw County, Michigan. He died, date unknown, in possibly Washtenaw County, Michigan. He married Christina before 1917 in possibly Washtenaw County, Michigan. She was born, date unknown. She died, date unknown.

28. John P. Buss, son of George Buss and Adelaide, was born in about 1839 in Michigan. He died in 1897 in possibly Washtenaw County, Michigan. He married Emma, date unknown, in possible Washtenaw County, Michigan.

29. Emma was born in May 1837 in Russia. She died after 1910 in possibly Washtenaw County, Michigan.

Emma and John P. Buss had the following children:

i. Sarah Buss was born in about 1868 in Michigan. She died before 1880 in possibly Freedom Township, Washtenaw County, Michigan.

ii. William H. Buss was born in May 1870 in Michigan. He died in 1941 in Manchester Washtenaw County, Michigan. She was born in May 1874 in Michigan. She died in 1942 in Manchester Washtenaw County, Michigan.

iii. Charles H. Buss was born in March 1872 in Michigan. He died date unknown in possibly Manchester,

Washtenaw County, Michigan. He married Emma in April 1990 in possibly Manchester Washtenaw County, Michigan. She was born in May 1874 in Michigan.

iv. Aaron H. Buss was born in about 1878 in Michigan. He died date unknown in possibly Manchester Washtenaw County, Michigan.

Generation 6

32. Peter Maurer, son of Johann Jacob Maurer and Elizabeth Huther, was born on May 20, 1834, in Kleinbundenbach, Rhineland Palatinate, Germany. He died on June 3, 1910, in possibly Maple Grove, Barry County, Michigan. He married Rosina Cook, date unknown.

33. Rosina Cook was born in 1845 in Maple Grove, Barry County, Michigan. She died in 1867 in Barry County, Michigan.

Rosina Cook and Peter Maurer had the following children:

i. Peter A. Maurer was born on March 3, 1865, in Maple Grove, Barry County, Michigan. He died on July 31, 1936, in Maple Grove, Barry County, Michigan. He married Rosetta Blatt on August 26, 1890, in possibly Michigan. She was born on May 28, 1865, in possibly Michigan. She died on June 24, 1809, in possibly Maple Grove, Barry County, Michigan.

ii. Johann Jacob Maurer was born on March 23, 1667, in Maple Grove, Barry County, Michigan. He died on January 4, 1937. He married Margaret Tobin on February 12, 1997. She was born, date unknown. She died, date unknown.

36. Hugh Lennon was born in September 1828 in Scotland. He died, date unknown, in possibly Eaton County, Michigan. He married Elizabeth in about 1853 in possibly Michigan.

37. Elizabeth was born in April 1833 in Canada. She died, date unknown, in possibly Eaton County, Michigan.

Elizabeth and Hugh Lennon had the following children:

i.　Mary E. Lennon was born in about 1859 in Michigan. She died, date unknown.

ii.　William H. Lennon was born in February 1864 in Michigan. He died, date unknown, in possibly Eaton County, Michigan. He married Mary in about 1890 in possibly Michigan. She was born in March 1669 in Michigan. She died, date unknown, in possibly Eaton County, Michigan.

56.　George Buss was born in about 1800 in Germany. He died, date unknown. He married Adelaide, date unknown.

57.　Adelaide was born in about 1811 in Germany. She died, date unknown.

Adelaide and George Buss had the following children:

i.　John P. Buss was born about 1839 in Michigan. He died in 1897 in possibly Washtenaw County, Michigan. He married Emma, date unknown, in possibly Washtenaw County, Michigan. She was born in May 1837 in Russia. She died after 1910 in possibly Washtenaw County, Michigan.

ii.　Allen M. Buss was born in 1837. He died in 1916.

iii.　Mary A. Buss was born in 1642. She died in 1917. She married Kuhl. He was born, date unknown. He died, date unknown.

Generation 7

64.　Johann Jacob Maurer, son of Debold Maurer and Marla Elizabeth Sluppi, was born on May 26, 1806, in Kleinbundenbach, Rhineland Palatinate, Germany. He died on May 29, 1881, in Maple Grove, Barry County, Michigan. He married Elizabeth Huther in 1830 in possibly Germany.

65. Elizabeth Huther was born in 1809 in Kleinbundenbach, Rhineland Palatinate, Germany. She died on January 17, 1886, in Barry County, Michigan.

Elizabeth Huther and Johann Jacob Maurer had the following children:

   i.   Mary Kathonne Maurer was born on November 2, 1831, in Germany. She died on December 18, 1860, in possibly Michigan. She married George Jacob Kunz in 1857. He was born, date unknown. He died, date unknown.

   ii.   Peter Maurer was born on May 20, 1834, in Kleinbundenbach, Rhineland Palatinate, Germany. He died on June 3, 1910, in possibly Maple Grove. Barry County, Michigan. He married Rosina Cook, date unknown. She was born in 1845 in Maple Grove, Barry County, Michigan. She died in 1867 in Barry County, Michigan.

   iii.   Henry Maurer was born on December 20, 1835, in Germany. He died in 1924 in possibly Michigan.

   iv.   Katherine Elizabeth Maurer was born on March 19, 1837, in Germany. She died on November 12, 1932, in possibly Michigan.

   v.   Johann Jacob Maurer was born in 1840 in Germany. He died on December 6, 1886, in possibly Michigan.

   vi.   Phillip Maurer was born on March 24, 1846, in Germany. He died on January 24, 1922, in possibly Michigan.

Generation 8

128. Debold Maurer was born in 1794 in Kleinbundenbach, Rhineland Palatinate, Germany. He died, date unknown, in Kleinbundenbach, Rhineland Palatinate, Germany. He married Maria Elizabeth Sluppa in 1805 in possibly Germany.

129. Maria Elizabeth Stuppi was born, date unknown, in Kleinbundenbach, Rhineland Palatinate, Germany. He died, date unknown, in Kleinbundenbach, Rhineland Palatinate, Germany.

Maria Elizabeth Stuppi and Debold Maurer had the following children:

i.   Johann Jacob Maurer was born on May 28, 1806, in Kleinbundenbach, Rhineland Palatinate, Germany. He died on May 29, 1881, in Maple Grove, Barry County, Michigan. He married Elizabeth Huther in 1830 in possibly Germany. She was born in 1809, in Kleinbundenbach, Rhineland Palatinate, Germany. She died on January 17, 1886, in Barry County, Michigan.

ii. Philipp Jacob Maurer was born on November 16, 1810, in Germany. He died on January 4, 1891. He married Anna Marie Schweikofer, date unknown. She was born, date unknown. She died, date unknown.

iii. Johann Peter Maurer was born on November 16, 1816, in Germany. He died on June 9, 1900. He married Katherine Brock, date unknown. She was born, date unknown. She died, date unknown. He married Elizabeth Strazer in 1846. She was born, date unknown. She died, date unknown.

TERRY'S FIRST COUSINS

54 Maurers and 50 Chervens

Maurer First Cousins

Bernard Maurer/Pauline Cherven
  Anthony Maurer
    Terry Maurer
      Louis Maurer

Dale Maurer/Lilian Smith
  Debbie Maurer
    Judy Maurer
      Sandy Maurer

Clarence (Joe) Maurer/Nina Peterson
  Kim Maurer
    Lynn Maurer

Leon Frith/Bernice Maurer
  Cynthia Frith
    LuAnn Frith
      Rose Frith
        Michelle Frith

Patrick Maurer/Julie Jackson
  Julie Maurer
    Joanna Maurer
      Jeff Maurer
        Jeanne Maurer
          John Maurer
            Jamie Maurer

Harold Figg/Ann Maurer
  Kathleen Figg
    Marilyn Figg
      Diane Figg
        Frances Figg
          Janice Figg
            Karl Figg
              Jeffery Figg
                John Figg
                  Jill Figg

Robert Stockham/Louise Maurer
  Stanley Stockham
    Renee Stockham
      Susanne Stockham

Francis Maurer/Marge Tellas
  Gerald Maurer
    Donald Maurer
      Carol Ann Maurer
        David Maurer
          Robert Maurer
            Michael Maurer
              Darlene Maurer

Lenny Maurer/Lois Ann Fuen
  Linda Ann Maurer

Virginia Carol
Kathleen Rose

Lawrence O'Mara/Ruth Maurer
Patricia O'Mara
Dennis O'Mara
Teresa O'Mara
Michael O'Mara
Edward O'Mara
Shawn O'Mara
Melissa O'Mara

Edwin Maurer/Edith Beison
Stephen Maurer
Theron Maurer
Rebecca Maurer

Mary Rose Maurer/Arlo Bishop
Alan Bishop
Ronald Bishop
Ted Bishop
John Bishop

Cherven First Cousins

Cherven Second Generation—First Cousins 1-22-2021
Frank Cherven and Ceil (Balwinski)
Joy Granlund
Thom Cherven (deceased 6-21-2014)
Patty French
Cecelia "Che-Che" Flewelling
Mary Ann Brown
Chris Cherven (deceased 6-30-1974)

Ann Cherven Friday (Hank)
Johnny Friday (deceased 6-13-1794)

Jerry Friday (deceased 11-7-2018)
Ginny Wheaton
Richard Friday

Pauline Cherven Maurer (Bernie)
Anthony Maurer
Terry Maurer
Eileen Maurer(deceased 4-12-1945)
Josesph Maurer (deceased 4-24-1946)
Louis Maurer

John Cherven and Marnie (Lake)
Andrea Hanel (deceased 3-15-2002)
Dale Cherven
Jacqui Bickel
Yvonne Bedford
Margaret "Midge" Hellebuyck (deceased 3-13-1992)
March Cherven

Aloise Cherven and Kathleen (Krause)
Philip Cherven
Connie Bucklew
Patrice Lockwood
John Cherven

Edward Cherven

Justine "Teen" Leonard (Albert "Mose")
Susie Mitas
Sally Baker
Leo "Beezer" Leonard (deceased 5-29-1997)
Mary Margaret Cagel (deceased 6-2014)
Tom Leonard
Joe Leonard
Jimmy Leonard (1-22-2017)

Andrew Cherven and Margaret (Charron)
  Larry Cherven
    Kathy Hall
      Drew Cherven
        Jim Cherven
          Paul Cherven
            Nancy Goodrich (deceased 1-5-1985)
            Charlie Cherven

Michael Cherven and Tudy "Murie" (Trombley)
  Dianne Boyer
    Lynda Stark
      Mike Cherven
      Dave Cherven

Fran Cherven Diss (Dorian "Skip")
  Steve Diss
    Ann "Peachy" Legg
      Jane Varcoe
        Jim Diss
          Lauara Diss Queener
          Jerry Diss

CPSIA information can be obtained
at www.ICGtesting.com
Printed in the USA
FSHW021626250421
80740FS